The Glory of Kings

Developing Godly Character

Collegium Books

Mark David Shaw

Foundation Series

The Glory of Kings
by Mark David Shaw

ISBN 978-0-9801865-1-2

Published by Collegium Books
PO Box 6885
Rochester, MN 55903

To reach us on the Internet:

www.collegiumbooks.com
www.collegiumbibleinstitute.com

The Glory of Kings
Developing Godly Character

"To learn of Christ is to know Him. To know Him is to be transformed by Him. To be transformed by Him is to be made into His image. To be made into His image is to walk as He would walk."

To the Students of Collegium Bible Institute

Acknowledgements

To my wife Kathryn, I love you. Thank you for hours upon hours of work that you put into this project. Thank you for believing in me. Thank you for making this much easier by your wise counsel. Thank you for being a fellow soldier and mate in pursuit of our King, Jesus.

To Jennifer Zempel, once again thank you for your proofing, suggestions, and all of your hard work. Your help was much appreciated.

To John and Judy Kolb of Clarion Call Ministries in Post Falls, Idaho, thank you for your unceasing encouragement; the confidence that you placed in this ministry and the prayers that have found the ear of Providence on our behalf.

To Dr. Michael Lake of Biblical Life College & Seminary in Marshfield, Missouri, thank you for your wise advice, it has never fallen on deaf ears. Thank you for your friendship, it is cherished as a valued possession and thank you for your encouragement in the ministry of the Word of God. Thank you for gracing us with your visits to the school.

Table of Contents

Introduction

> **Proverbs 25:2** It is the glory of God to conceal a matter, But the glory of kings is to search out a matter.

In the discourse of human events nothing stands out as a greater influence of human decision and history like the impact that the Word of God has had upon mankind. This resource is sorely undervalued and underused. The Word of God not only has the power to influence history and human events, it has the unmitigated energy to develop godly character.

In developing godly character there is not the enforcement of the power of the will but a kingly search for the Creator. We are brought to godly living through the exercise of our faith. God has planted His word but it is up to us to nourish and grow it in our lives. When we do this it has the wonderful effect of developing your character and through God's Word you will find yourself being transformed into the image of His Son.

Make no mistake, if you are a Christian, you are invited to enter the training that will develop you into a king. Not all Christians will engage in this process though. Many are not even aware of it. I wrote this book to assist you in developing the king in you in the hope that you would help others. By giving understanding to biblical foundation subjects, you are released to interpret the deeper things of those hidden treasures found in the Bible.

This is not about your ego. If you are excited about being a king because of power, you have missed the point. The excitement of becoming a king is found in the proximity that you find yourself as a king to the King of kings. This is about finding, understanding, and learning of Jesus. The Prophet Jeremiah invites you by prophetic revelation to enter into that process.

> **Jeremiah 6:16** Thus says the LORD, "Stand by the ways and see and ask for the ancient paths, Where the good way is, and walk in it; **And you will find rest for your souls.** But they said, 'We will not walk in it.'

The glory of kings is found in looking, seeking, and understanding that ancient path. God has endowed man with the ability to discover the beauty of His ways. The end product is rest for your souls. In a world of such confusion and turmoil, rest for your soul could be a very welcomed repose. What is interesting about Jeremiah 6:16 is the revelation Jesus brings to this passage.

> **Matthew 11:28-30** "Come to Me, all who are weary and heavy-laden, and I will give you rest. "Take My yoke upon you and **learn from Me**, for I am gentle and humble in heart, and YOU WILL FIND REST FOR YOUR SOULS. "For My yoke is easy and My burden is light."

Jesus gives a name for that ancient path. It is He. What does it mean to take His yoke upon yourself? We know that it is defined as easy. Some say that the yoke represents what Jesus requires of you and it is easy and light because it isn't much. We can learn of this by finding the true meaning of the words used elsewhere in Jeremiah.

***Jeremiah 18:15** 'For My people have forgotten Me, They burn incense to worthless gods And they have stumbled from their ways, From the ancient paths, To walk in bypaths, Not on a highway,*

Whereas Jesus invites us to learn of Him, the prophet reveals that His people have forgotten Him. It is in knowing Him that we find rest for our souls. Take special note of the word *"bypath."* This Hebrew word means *"trodden of foot."* It is the picture of a well worn path because of the human traffic. The path becomes a reminder of what is the popular way to travel.

Note that the ancient path is not this way. It is not a well worn path of human activity. It is not the popular way to go. The ancient path is a highway. Now we need to resist the temptation to think in terms of western culture regarding this word. This word (highway) means to *"lift up or cast up into a heap."* It is literally a "high way". A *"bypath"* paints the picture of a rut worn into the ground whereas a highway paints the picture of being lifted up to walk upon a prepared path.

The yoke represents making the decision to walk this ancient path, this high way. It represents thinking in a new way. Thinking in a way that is not subjected to the elementary principles of this world. The yoke fits upon the shoulder of the oxen. Now consider the following.

***Isaiah 9:6** For a child will be born to us, a son will be given to us; And the government will rest on His shoulders; And His name will be called Wonderful Counselor, Mighty God, Eternal Father, Prince of Peace.*

Could the government be the yoke that Jesus asks us to take upon ourselves? Think about the invitation. Seek, understand, ask, learn, and walk. If we are talking about the government, then we are talking about the government of the King. The government of the King is also the way of the King. That means that in the King's kingdom, things work the way the King says for them to work.

That means that the government of King Jesus, is composed of the governing principles of the King. Learning of those government principles and walking in them is how we find rest for our souls. Learning the governing principles of the King is akin to walking on the "high way."

Learning of Him is how we find "the way." Becoming a disciple of Jesus is how we access the "high way." There is no doubt, we are learning to be kings by learning the King's ways. Taking His yoke, His government, and His ways upon us moves us into the environment of rest.

Before you begin to think that this may be too hard for you, consider what Jesus said. He said, *"Take My yoke upon you."* A yoke takes two oxen, not one. That means that Jesus is inviting you to put that yoke of destiny upon your shoulders and He will do most of the pulling. Consider the words of the Apostle Paul.

> ***Colossians 1:9-10*** *For this reason also, since the day we heard of it, we have not ceased to pray for you and to ask that you may be filled with the knowledge of His will in all spiritual wisdom and understanding,* **so that you will walk in a manner worthy of the Lord,** *to please Him in all respects, bearing fruit in every good work and increasing in the knowledge of God;*

Developing godly character is manifest through seeking, finding, walking, and believing those things God has revealed about Himself. Keep that in mind as you traverse the pages of this book knowing that you are being transformed as you believe. Now, develop the king you are called to be!

The Knowledge of God

> PURPOSE: *In this chapter the reader will learn the importance of the "Knowledge of God." They will learn an accurate definition of the phrase and that it is the key that opens the Christian up to experience the divine nature of God. When properly applied, this chapter has the power to alter any Christian's life and behavior.*

I t is not uncommon when reading your Bible that there will be a certain phrase or word that seems to all of a sudden stand out from the rest of the text. Such is the case when I was reading the Word one day. The title of this study bears the phrase that stood out to me. Before we explore the Word concerning this fascinating phrase, let us look at what it is really saying.

The term *"knowledge"* will bring to your mind a certain understanding of that word. Whether accurate or not, we do have these concepts based upon what we have learned and heard in our everyday life. Often times a word will take on an overabundance of meanings that really do not promote the original intent of the word.

I have had many folks tell me that knowledge is information. This is incorrect. Information is only bits of data that we hear, taste, see, feel, or smell. These packets of data are only data; they have not been processed to determine if they are accurate data or false data. Therefore, information is not known until it is processed and believed. **At the point of belief** and only at this point does it become knowledge. To know something is to have inherent within it the belief of what you know.

Definition

According to American Heritage Dictionary, *"know"* is, *1. To perceive directly; grasp in the mind with clarity or certainty. 2. **To regard as true beyond doubt: To know something is to believe it.***

Knowledge is those packets of information that we consider to be true. The knowledge of God is those things that we know about God to be true. The **knowledge of God** therefore could also be synonymous with *"faith"* in God.

It is one thing to say, *"I believe in God;"* it is another thing entirely to say, *"I believe all things about God's nature and all of what He says and is."* It is also one thing to say, *"I know God,"* and another thing to say, *"I know who God is because He dwells in me."* The one is shallow, and the other is intimate. According to the Book of James, even the devils believe in God and tremble. They obviously do not have salvation. They know that He exists and that is apparently all that they believe. If they would believe in Who God is, that He is love, justice, and mercy, they would certainly change what they do!

Many in Christendom think that if they believe in God, that is all they need for eternal life. Many think that a simple belief in God is all there is and refuse to grow from there. God indeed invites humanity to believe in Him, but if they really do believe in Him and Who He is, this should produce a desire to know Him. Our foundation text for this study, II Peter 1:1-9, will show us that there is so much more that we are to comprehend and know in order to have access to the kind of life that we were promised by God.

The Change of Behavior

*II Peter 1:1-9 Simon Peter, a bond-servant and apostle of Jesus Christ, to those **who have received a faith of the same kind as ours**, by the righteousness of our God and Savior, Jesus Christ: Grace and peace be **multiplied** to you in **the knowledge of God** and of Jesus our Lord; seeing that His divine power has granted to us everything pertaining to life and godliness, **through the true knowledge of Him** who called us by His own glory and excellence.*

*For by these He has granted to us His precious and magnificent promises, so that **by them you may become partakers of the divine nature**, having escaped the corruption that is in the world by lust. Now for this very reason also, applying all diligence, in your faith supply moral excellence, and in your moral excellence, knowledge, and in your knowledge, self-control, and in your self-control, perseverance, and in your perseverance, godliness, and in your godliness, brotherly kindness, and in your brotherly kindness, love. For if these qualities are yours and are increasing, they render you neither **useless nor unfruitful in the true***

knowledge of our Lord Jesus Christ. *For he who lacks these qualities is blind or short-sighted, having forgotten his purification from his former sins.*

Let us start by keying in on verse one. When Peter uses the term *"same faith as ours,"* he reveals to us that there are faiths that are not like ours. That means some will have faith in false knowledge or false truths.

> ***1 Timothy 6:20-21*** *O Timothy, guard what has been entrusted to you, avoiding worldly and empty chatter and the opposing arguments of what is **falsely called "knowledge"**— which some have professed and thus gone astray from the faith.* ***G****race be with you.*

This false knowledge caused some to go astray from the faith. There is much import in understanding this principle. There are many philosophies in the world that claim to be *"a way"* to the kingdom of God. As intolerant as Christians have been accused of being, we must acknowledge by the Words of our God, that our faith is one faith and it is the only faith capable of saving humanity. If there is a different faith, it will result in being lost forever.

It seems that in today's climate of political correctness and multiculturalism, even Christians are embracing the idea that other faiths can access eternal life. Yet their own Bibles tell them that Jesus is the only way; that there is no other name under heaven whereby men may be saved; that there is one Lord, one faith, one baptism. Only those who do not understand who God is, how salvation was accomplished, and the need of a sacrifice, would believe that other religions lead to the same God. They literally have *"another faith."*

Verse two tells us that grace and peace are multiplied to us in the knowledge of God. This is saying then, that in order to acquire more grace and more peace, it can be done by gaining more of the knowledge of God. This is something that is going to become more evident as we proceed. When you understand that grace and peace are actually inside of the knowledge of God, you are motivated to find more.

> *Philippians 4:7 And the peace of God, which surpasses all comprehension, will guard your hearts and your minds in Christ Jesus.*

It is important to connect the dots here. First, peace comes to us in the knowledge of God, and this peace will then be a guard over our hearts and minds. That means that as you believe the things God has revealed about Himself, it will produce grace and peace in you. Remember this as we continue and it will make increasingly greater sense to you.

The problem we have lies in that we are trying to treat the symptom rather than affecting a cure in trying to change behavior. **Behavior is the outward expression and manifestation of an inward belief.** This is why Jesus said, *"By their fruit (behavior) you shall know them."*

> *Mark 7:21-23 "For from within, out of the heart of men, proceed the evil thoughts, fornications, thefts, murders, adulteries, deeds of coveting and wickedness, as well as deceit, sensuality, envy, slander, pride and foolishness." All these evil things proceed from within and defile the man."*

Can you see from this Scripture that behavior is a result of what you believe in your heart? All of the bad things we do proceed from the heart and all of the good things we do also proceed from the heart. Therefore, the only sure way to change an outward behavior is to change the inward belief associated with it.

Before I go any further, I want you to understand a psychological aspect of yourself. I want you to get a thorough understanding between the relationship of believing something and doing something. I have often heard the statement, *"That person needs to change their behavior."* How does one change their behavior? Do they just start acting different?

If that were the case, then each of us would just start acting differently. That is not going to work. One might succeed for a while through sheer willpower, but that behavior inevitably returns because the belief associated with it was not changed. In order to understand this, let us look at an example.

EXAMPLE

A man named Alan worked at a tire manufacturing plant. He had worked there for 17 years. One day his co-worker and friend, Carl, told him that the supervisor did not like Alan and was looking for a way to dismiss him. As Alan believed his friend, anger began to surface. While Alan pondered this revelation he began to show expressions and manifestations of anger which began to demonstrate itself at home and in the workplace. He was slamming the equipment around; he was being short to his fellow workers; he was treating his wife and kids poorly; he had become intolerable to those that loved him.

Alan's behavior was based upon a belief. Since the information was hearsay, there is the possibility that Carl was lying to him. Therefore, Alan's behavior could have been based upon a lie or deception. If this information were a lie, can you see the damage it could do to Alan and those around him as well as to his job and his relationship with his boss? **The reality of the information has nothing to do with the behavior, but it has everything to do with whether or not you are acting upon truth or deception.** Do you see that just changing his behavior could only have temporary results?

For the sake of understanding let us consider that Carl lied to Alan. Carl began to feel bad for Alan and told him that he just made the story up. Alan's behavior would now make a change. He changes from being angry with his boss to being angry with his friend. Why? It is **because the knowledge has now changed.** The information once accepted as true is now rejected. That which Alan used to consider as true, is now found to be false. The information that used to be believed, is no longer believed, and **it is this belief that has the effect of changing Alan's behavior.**

Kindness and Severity

The same process works in our spiritual lives. When we learn and believe something about God, it has the power to change our behavior. The flip side is also true, if we believe a lie about God that too will change our behavior. If our view of God is one in which we paint an image of an old man with a scowl on his face and a big stick in his hand in which to smack us when we do something wrong, it will cause us to avoid God and to run away from God, not to Him. We must understand both the kindness of God and the severity of God to form a correct representation of God. Either idea without the other is out of balance.

There is also the problem of ignorance. When we do not know something about God, we lack faith in that area and our behavior will show it. If we are to access all that God has for us, then we need to apply ourselves to learn all that He has revealed to us.

> **Romans 11:22** Behold then the kindness and severity of God...

Kindness

The child who has been well trained in safety who then suddenly bolts into the road will experience the severity of his father. Yet the father does not only show displeasure but also grabs the child and holds him close, and in this *kindness* is shown.

Let us consider one without the other for a moment. If God were only kind, then the image that we would have is that we could do **anything** wrong without experiencing His discipline and the consequences. Many already have this view of God; they are the ones who declare that, *"God is a loving God so I will go to heaven and so will others in the other religions. God will forgive the Muslims, the Buddhists, the Hindus, the New Agers, the Satanists, the Wiccans, etc. because He is a loving God."*

These are people who know **NOT** the severity of God, nor do they know the consequences of what they are saying, nor the eternal consequences of spending eternity without God. God did not overlook sin! We forget that the Creator is not only love, but

He is justice. We don't realize that God cannot lie or violate His own Words. God declared at the beginning of the creation that, *"the soul that sins shall die."*

Could God say, *"Oh that was a long time ago, I've changed, I just love everyone."* If He could say that, He could not be God. One of the qualities of our Lord is that, *"He changes not."* God judges your sin along with mine. He did not ignore, He did not wink at it, and He did not forget it. He judged it in the most horrible way. He allowed His Son to take your sin upon His body and then God judged His own Son with your sin.

Severity

Those that only know the severity of God are also controlled by what they believe. Their thoughts are such that they think God is mean and domineering. The consequence of having this image of God, is that they will not come close to God.

Unlike the child who has done wrong and received a bit of discipline but knows that he can still come to his father to receive love, those that only know the severity of God are so fearful of God that they never try. They are like the children of Israel who, when God spoke to them, they were terrified of Him. God was too terrible, so they asked that Moses be their go-between. They were terrified to have a relationship with God. They only knew His severity and were not aware of His kindness.

To understand this is to know that we have to know God in His **complete** nature so that we do not come short in our relationship with Him. We must know both His kindness and His severity. As the Word says:

Proverbs 1:7 *The fear of the Lord is the beginning of knowledge; fools despise wisdom and instruction.*

The Key to Change

Now what if the information our character Alan heard was verified? Alan overheard his supervisor saying the same thing that Carl had told him. Now the information is irrefutable since Alan has heard it for himself. Alan's behavior does not change because the information believed has not changed.

Now we have a problem, if the information is true, how can Alan overcome his outbursts of anger and quit being so short with his co-workers? How can he stop treating his family poorly? After all, the information is true, and he is livid. He cannot suppress what he is feeling; it just keeps surfacing. In fact, with time it is getting worse. Is he locked into this behavior?

No, he is not. Alan can still change his belief, and it will have the effect of changing his behavior. What can Alan do**? Alan can apply a biblical principle that will alleviate his anger.** He can believe that God is the One that he relies on and that God directs his paths. Then he can forgive his supervisor. By forgiving his supervisor, Alan has given up all rights to vengeance. This has the effect of bringing God into the picture to apply His revenge based upon true justice. By believing the biblical principle that states:

Romans 12:19-21 (NCV) *"My friends, do not try to punish others when they wrong you, **but wait for God to punish them with His anger.** It is written: "I will punish those who do wrong; I will repay them,"* *says the Lord. But you should do this: "If your enemy is hungry, feed him; if he is thirsty, give him a drink. Doing this will be like pouring burning coals on his head." Do not let evil defeat you, but defeat evil by doing good".*

__I Peter 5:7 (AMP)__ "Casting the whole of your care [all your anxieties, all your worries, all your concerns, once and for all] on Him, for He cares for you affectionately and cares about you watchfully." [Ps. 55:22.]

Alan is placing his situation in God's hands. He believes that God is better at taking care of him and his situation than he is. In essence, God will now fight Alan's battle, and Alan can now stop his destructive behavior. Alan is secure and peaceful in the knowledge that God has counted even the hairs of his head and takes notice when one falls to the ground.

However, if Alan remains unforgiving and unbelieving, he is doomed to experience the feelings and behavior associated with his belief. **This is the type of thing that can lock him into anger for the rest of his life.** Even long after the event is gone, the anger is still there because of the lack of forgiveness. Every time we have dealt with a person who has anger problems, we have always been able to trace it back to events of unforgiveness. Once the person makes the willful choice to forgive, it has the effect of eliminating the anger problem. If they truly forgive, they will find that all of a sudden they are not experiencing those angry feelings anymore.

With this in mind I want you to remember the following statement; it is very important. Dr. Wilfred Kent, the founder of Today's World Ministry said, *"The concept that you accept as true is the concept that will control you."* Those things that you have accepted as true will control your behavior. It matters not if they are true as we seen in the story of Alan; **if you believe they are true, they will control you.**

When we are behaving based upon false information, we have what the Bible calls a **stronghold** in our lives. First, we gather information through our five senses, and then we process this data by weighing and comparing it to what we already consider to be true. After this, we do one of three things with this data.

1. *We reject it,* because we have verified it as false by comparing it with what we know already, either by external data or our internal core beliefs (it is then **tagged** as false) or:
2. *We accept it* as true because we have external data that proves it, or it is something that is in our internal core beliefs (it is then **anchored** as true) or:
3. *We put this data in a holding cell* in order to gather more data to determine its value. This means that there is not enough external knowledge to either support or deny this information, and/or our core beliefs do not have a reference by which to determine its validity. (This last category is important and we will deal with it in greater depth later.)

If we accept the information that came to us through one or more of our senses as true, then it will produce feelings or **emotions** according to the content of the information. This could be joy, for instance, if one has just found out he was promoted at his job. On the other hand, it could be deep sadness if one finds out his or her spouse has been unfaithful.

Feelings or emotions are an extension of believing something to be true, and behavior is an extension of these feelings or emotions. Remember, what we accept as truth will from that day forward control us. It is therefore very important to consider what you hear and what you do with data. You should also be able at this point to see how damaging a lie can be.

DEFINITION

The word "emotion" comes from the Latin, "exmovere." This is a compound word that means "ex=to" and "movere=move." Thus the origin of the word emotion means "to move."

Satan is constantly trying to get us to believe a lie. His lies will always produce negative emotions. He tries to destroy relationships by getting a person to think something is true without a shred of evidence to back it up. Speculation, rumor, gossip, conjecture, hearsay, and assumption are very real enemies to your evaluation of information!

If you cannot verify the information, then you either have to reject it out-right, or do enough research to validate the truth. It is the rumors and the gossip that destroy so many relationships. It starts with a lie or a misunderstanding and that lie or misunderstanding, if believed, weaves its web of destruction upon your life and the lives of others.

Since God defines reality, He not only is truth, but He defines truth. When we live in truth, **the knowledge of God**, we are not locked into those negative emotions that are an extension of our beliefs. This is why forgiveness and believing in the promises of God are such powerful elements in changing our behavior. By forgiving, we no longer hold that person accountable, and our feelings of ill will toward that person will subside, causing a change in behavior that can literally save a relationship.

When the disciple Peter asked Jesus how many times he should forgive a single person who sins against him in a single day, the response was not seven times as the apostle had thought, but seventy times seven.

The Treasure

Now let's revisit verse three of our foundation text. *"...seeing that His divine power has granted to us everything pertaining to **life** and **godliness**, through the true knowledge of Him who called us by His own glory and excellence."* Everything that we need for life and godliness has already been granted to us by His divine power. Nevertheless, in order to access it we have to gain the knowledge of God. All life and all godliness comes **through** the knowledge of God. Every time I learn something new about God and I accept that as true, that knowledge has the power to control me. It can literally cause godliness in my life!

DEFINITION

***Life-...**The life given by Christ is an abundant life, a life of the very highest quality, a life that overflows with all the good things of life: love, joy, peace, goodness, satisfaction, and security.*

Godliness-Is living like God and being a godly person. It is living life like it should be lived. God gave man life; therefore, God knows what life should be, and above all things life should be godly just like God. The word "godliness" (eusebeian) actually means to live in the reverence and awe of God; to be so conscious of God's presence that one lives just as God would live if He were walking upon earth. It means to live seeking to be like God; to seek to possess the very character, nature, and behavior of God. The man of God follows and runs after godliness. He seeks to gain a consciousness of God's presence-a consciousness so intense that he actually lives as God would live if He were on earth. Note: godliness means to be **Christlike.** *Godliness is* **Christlikeness***: it is living upon earth just as Christ lived.* —Preacher's Outline and Sermon Bible - Commentary

Notice that these two qualities are gained in increasing measure according to the knowledge of God. In order to access what God has granted me, I have to search for the knowledge of God and believe it. Now the question arises, *"Where do I search?"*

Before I answer that, I want to explore something. Here is another statement for you to remember. ***"The value I place on the item I am looking for will determine how diligently I search for it."*** With that in mind, let us explore some Scripture so as to associate value to the item for which we are searching.

Proverbs 8:9-11 "They are all straightforward to him who understands, and right to those who find knowledge. Take my instruction and not silver, and knowledge rather than choicest gold. For wisdom is

better than jewels, and all desirable things cannot compare with her."

Proverbs 20:15 *There is gold, and an abundance of jewels; but the lips of knowledge are a more precious thing.*

II Corinthians 4:6-7 *For God, Who said, "Light shall shine out of darkness," is the One who has shone in our hearts to give the Light of the knowledge of the glory of God in the face of Christ. But we have this treasure in earthen vessels, so that the surpassing greatness of the power will be of God and not from ourselves;*

If this is not enough evidence for you, consider the parables of Jesus concerning the kingdom of God to show you the immense value of the knowledge of God. He compares the kingdom of God to a treasure found in a field, a pearl of great price, lost money being found, etc.

The promises of God are synonymous to the knowledge of God, and this is the flow of thought in II Peter. If we now look at verse four we see it clearly. *"For by these He has granted to us His precious and magnificent **promises**, so that **by them** you may **become partakers** of the **divine nature,** having escaped the corruption that is in the world by lust."*

It is clear then that it is by the promises of God that we become partakers of His divine nature. This is where we get abundant *life* and the ability to walk in *godliness*. First, you must search for them, find them, and then believe them. If you think about it, God's knowledge is what His nature is based upon. Therefore, if God makes this knowledge available to us and we believe it, it will have the effect upon our lives of transforming us into the image of His Son.

Entering His Rest For Your Soul

> *Matthew 11:29-30 (KJV) Take my yoke upon you, and **learn of me**; for I am meek and lowly in heart: and **ye shall find rest unto your souls**. For my yoke is easy, and my burden is light.*

We can learn an important principle from this Scripture. Jesus actually quoted the last part of that verse from the Old Testament. If we look at it, we find an interesting point.

> *Jeremiah 6:16 Thus says the Lord, "Stand by the ways and see and ask for the ancient paths, Where the good way is, and walk in it; And you will find rest for your souls. But they said, 'We will not walk in it.'*

Reading this leaves us no doubt that Jesus was revealing that He is *"the good way, the ancient path."* Elsewhere Jesus said, *"I am the way…, I am the door…"* Many of us see the way, and we ask for the way but many of us fail by not walking in it. What does it mean to walk in it?

As we learn about God, we will find that our lives are gaining an ease that they did not previously know. It is because we are finding rest through the knowledge of God. By believing things about God, and things that God says, we are causing our feelings to change which causes our emotions to change which causes our behavior to change. Walking in it then is acknowledging the Word of God as truth. That knowledge will produce if we would believe.

It is a wonderful thing to know that my will power is not what changes my behavior; it is what I believe that produces change! If you want to change your behavior, change your mind first! Just think of how you behave when you are experiencing joy, peace, love, contentment, and security. God has provided us a way to live godly. It is His divine power that empowers us to do so. It is, therefore, only my duty to study, to believe, and to act. The disciples asked the Lord, *"What must we do to do the work of God?"*

> **John 6:28-29** *Therefore they said to Him, "What shall we do, so that we may work the works of God?" Jesus answered and said to them, **"This is the work of God, that you believe in Him whom He has sent."***

The author of the book of Hebrews also supports this.

> **Hebrews 4:9-12** *So there remains a Sabbath rest for the people of God. For the one who has entered His rest has himself also rested from his works, as God did from His. **Therefore let us be diligent to enter that rest,** so that no one will fall, through following the same example of disobedience. For the word of God is living and active and sharper than any two-edged sword, and piercing as far as the division of soul and spirit, of both joints and marrow, and able to judge the thoughts and intentions of the heart.*

Jesus said that we will find rest for our souls if we learn of Him. The author of Hebrews tells us to be diligent (steady effort in the pursuance of something) to enter that rest. He even goes on to say that if we do not, we are in disobedience.

That means that we have a duty to be diligent in learning of Jesus that we might have rest for our souls. It will not come naturally by conversion. It will not come by osmosis. It will not come by transference. It is something over which we have complete control. If we apply ourselves to pursue the truth, we will be rewarded with rest.

Notice then that verse twelve speaks of the power of the Word of God. What a wonderful gift we have been given. In light of this, let us look at the consequences of not having the knowledge of God.

Lack of Knowledge

Now I want to get back to the question: *"Where can we find the knowledge of God?"* Well, the answer is obvious. The Word of God is our great source of the knowledge of God. There is also the indwelling Spirit who the Bible tells us will lead us and guide us in truth and will teach us. Since we now know what the knowledge of God consists of and we know where to find it, we are now going to look at the consequence of rejecting the knowledge of God.

> *Isaiah 5:13 Therefore My people **go into exile for their lack of knowledge**; and their honorable men are famished, and their multitude is parched with thirst.*

It is important to contrast the Scripture in II Peter with this. If I do not have all things pertaining to life and godliness, it is because I lack the knowledge of Him. It is because people lack the knowledge of God that they go into **bondage** and are **famished** and they **thirst**; all of this is because they lack knowledge. Now let's look at some more. We can also contrast this with the idea of strongholds. Strongholds are bits of information that exalt themselves against the knowledge of God that we believe to be true. The result is bondage.

> **Hosea 4:1-3** Listen to the word of the Lord, O sons of Israel, For the Lord has a case against the inhabitants of the land, **Because there is no faithfulness or kindness Or knowledge of God in the land.** There is swearing, deception, murder, stealing and adultery. They employ violence, so that bloodshed follows bloodshed. Therefore the land mourns, And everyone who lives in it languishes Along with the beasts of the field and the birds of the sky, And also the fish of the sea disappear.

Notice the words *"faithfulness"* and *"kindness."* Faithfulness is believing and trusting in God. It means that one is accepting what God is saying about Himself and that would produce kindness. Because there is no faithfulness there is no kindness because there is no knowledge of God.

> **Hosea 4:6 My people are destroyed for lack of knowledge.** Because you have rejected knowledge, I also will reject you from being My priest. Since you have forgotten the law of your God, I also will forget your children.

How many Christians actually see that they are destroying themselves by not acquiring the knowledge of God? Look at the wording. Since you have rejected knowledge, I also will reject you from being my priest. Remember that Jesus said to learn of Him. He wants us to know Him in intimacy.

People think that they can get intimate with God through worship. I ask my people to try to build a human relationship on worship alone. In other words, don't get to know them, don't learn of them, just worship them. It does not take long until the light bulb goes off and they realize that worship is a result of knowing the person. It is the same with God, knowing Him is the progenitor of worship.

> *Romans 1:28-32 And just as **they did not see fit to acknowledge God any longer,** God gave them over to a depraved mind, to do those things which are not proper, being filled with all unrighteousness, wickedness, greed, evil; full of envy, murder, strife, deceit, malice; they are gossips, slanderers, haters of God, insolent, arrogant, boastful, inventors of evil, disobedient to parents, without understanding, untrustworthy, unloving, unmerciful; and although they know the ordinance of God, that those who practice such things are worthy of death, they not only do the same, but also give hearty approval to those who practice them.*

If you look at the etymology of the word *"acknowledge"* you will find that it means *"to know."* With that information look at how it would read. *"They did not see fit to know God any longer."* Remember the previous Scripture? *"Because you have rejected knowledge I will also reject you…"* Once a person decides that they do not want to know God, they are given over to the imaginations of their minds.

It amazes me that with this list of Scriptures, folks are not more interested to learn of the Lord. My goodness, look at the consequences of rejecting the knowledge of God! It is vital to our lives that we seek to know of God and to know God. We do not know all there is to know concerning God. What are we doing to ourselves?!

We are dooming our own lives to lives of un-holiness, depression, bondage, etc. There are so many examples of people searching for their solutions to life in many different ways, and all the while their Bible, if they own one, is gathering dust. They have not gone off by themselves to have a talk with God for a long time. Friend, God is the only solution to your problems.

Food For Thought

Think about what we are missing by not applying ourselves to learn of the Lord. Our society is being hammered with numerous stresses that have been brought about by various causes. The speed at which information now travels has had the effect of speeding up our lives and this has had the effect of creating an environment of greater stress. The ways in which we cope from day to day have very little semblance to the way instructed to us by our Lord. We have a need for the knowledge of God in a way that is unprecedented.

What about our pastors? Are they part of the equation of gathering the knowledge of God? Yes, indeed! When Jesus asked Peter if he loved Him, He countered with, *"Feed My sheep."* It is then an incumbent duty for all ministers of the gospel to feed God's flock. The question then is, *"What are they to feed God's flock with?"*

> *Jeremiah 3:15 "Then I will give you shepherds after My own heart, who will **feed you on knowledge and understanding.***

The Bible identifies the food with which God's shepherds are to feed His flock. It is **knowledge and understanding**. It is a given that God desires the shepherd to feed His flock with truth, the truth about Him and about ourselves. Imagine the discouragement when God's ministers teach false doctrine and place God's people into bondage!

> *Jeremiah 50:6 "My people have become **lost sheep**; Their shepherds have led them astray. They have made them turn aside on the mountains; They have gone along from mountain to hill And **have forgotten their resting place.***

Because the shepherds led the people astray, *they have forgotten their resting place!* Compare that with what Jesus said in Matthew about finding rest for your souls and Hebrews about being diligent to enter His rest. When false information is believed, it causes real feelings that cause real behaviors. Yet, that false information will only produce anxiety rather than rest. It is up to us to guard our minds so that we do not fall into the bondage of deception.

The Good News

It is irrefutable that shepherds feed the flock knowledge and understanding. It is also irrefutable that it is by the knowledge of God that we enter His rest. There only remains the engaging of our wills to search for the Lord and the promise that if we search for Him, we will find Him. When we find Him, there will be the products of peace, joy, and contentment in our lives no matter the circumstances. Let us look some more at the benefits that are afforded us just by learning of Jesus.

*II Corinthians 2:14-16 But thanks be to God, who always leads us in triumph in Christ, and manifests through us the **sweet aroma** of the **knowledge of Him** in every place. For we are a fragrance of Christ to God among those who are being saved and among those who are perishing; to the one an aroma from death to death, to the other an aroma from life to life. And who is adequate for these things?*

This fragrance is discerned differently by the believer and the unbeliever. To the believer, you will smell like a sweet perfume, something that will cause other believers to want to be around you. However, to the unbeliever, your fragrance will be the fearful smell of death and doom. This is why there are often extremes in the reactions we get when we share the gospel of God.

*Ephesians 1:17-21 that the God of our Lord Jesus Christ, the Father of glory, may give to you **a spirit of wisdom and of revelation in the knowledge of Him.** ~~I pray that~~ the eyes of your heart may be enlightened, so that you will know what is the hope of His calling, what are the riches of the glory of His inheritance in the saints, and what is the surpassing greatness of His power toward us who believe. ~~These are~~ in accordance with the working of the strength of His might which He brought about in Christ, when He raised Him from the dead and seated Him at His right hand in the heavenly ~~places~~, far above all rule and authority and power and dominion, and every name that is named, not only in this age but also in the one to come.*

You will notice the three places that I struck out the text in this passage. If you look this up in your own Bible, you should see that the struck out text here is italicized in your Bible. This is how the translators show that it was added to show clarity. However, it is possible that sometimes they give us the wrong idea. I think this may be the case here. If you take out the phrase *"I pray that"* in verse 18, you will find a melding of verses 17 and 18. This is important because now it would appear that being enlightened with the knowledge of God has the effect of opening the eyes of our hearts! This will have the effect of the following:

- that we may know the hope of His calling,
- that we may know what are the riches of the glory of His inheritance,
- that we may know what is the surpassing greatness of His power toward us.

Now, if we are rejecting the knowledge of God, we will not be experiencing these wonderful benefits of knowing Him.

> ***Colossians 1:9-12*** *For this reason also, since the day we heard of it, we have not ceased to pray for you and to ask that **you may be filled with the knowledge of His will in all spiritual wisdom and understanding**, so that you will walk in a manner worthy of the Lord, to please Him in all respects, bearing fruit in every good work and increasing in the knowledge of God; strengthened with all power, according to His glorious might, for the attaining of all steadfastness and patience; joyously giving thanks to the Father, who has qualified us to share in the inheritance of the saints in Light.*

If you add this to the previous passage it is a powerful one-two punch! Verse nine sets up the rest of the text. Paul again is praying that they be filled with the knowledge of His will in all spiritual wisdom and understanding, SO THAT....

- You will walk in a manner worthy of the Lord.
- You will please Him in all respects.
- You will bear fruit in every good work
- You will increase in the knowledge of God.
- You will be strengthened with all power according to His glorious might.
- You will attain all steadfastness and patience.

Remember our foundation text? *"By His divine power, He has granted to us all things pertaining to life and godliness through the knowledge of Him."* Number one on the list is *"so that you will walk in a manner worthy of the Lord."* If you desire to live a godly life, then your access to the objective reality of that desire is through attaining the knowledge of Him. He will literally grant you godliness just by learning of Him.

You cannot produce godliness from your own will power. Your will can produce works that have the appearance of good, but as the Scriptures say:

> ***Isaiah 64:6*** *For all of us have become like one who is unclean,* ***And all our righteous deeds are like a filthy garment;*** *And all of us wither like a leaf, And our iniquities, like the wind, take us away.*

You cannot do good because you are not good; however, good can be granted to you by the only One that is good. Even Jesus said to the rich young ruler, *"Why do you call me good, there is no one good but God."* Since these good works are granted to us by the knowledge of God, we cannot boast in them for they did not proceed from us but came from the Holy One!

In I Corinthians 4:7 Paul asks some important questions. The first question asks, *"What do you have that you did not receive?"* This shows us that anything we do that can be claimed as good was given to us, and this sets up the next question he asks. *"And if you did receive it, why do you boast as if you had not received it?"* Very important to understand here is the idea that you have received all the good things that you do, and you do not have the right of boasting because they did not emanate from you, meaning you received them. God is the One that has granted to you all things pertaining to godliness!

The Other Side and the Battle

Satan understands the power of belief. It is his desire to get you to believe him **so that his thoughts may direct your paths.** *"The concept that you accept as true is the concept that controls you"* (Dr. Wilfred Kent),

If I believe it is going to rain, my behavior reacts to this *"knowledge,"* and I take an umbrella. Whether or not it rains is not the issue but rather whether or not I believe it is going to rain. If it does not rain that day, then I have carried my umbrella with me all day regardless. My behavior was directed by my belief. Can you see how you can change your behavior by changing your belief? Let's consider the battle that we are in. This battle is for the supremacy of your heart.

> *II Corinthians 10:3-5 For though we walk in the flesh, we do not war according to the flesh, for the weapons of our warfare are not of the flesh, but*

divinely powerful for the destruction of fortresses.
We are destroying speculations and every lofty
thing raised up against the knowledge of God, *and*
we are taking every thought captive to the
obedience of Christ,

The battle is between truth and untruth, between reality and deception, between accuracy and inaccuracy, between light that reveals and darkness that hides, between that which is authentic and that which is feigned, and between the Father of lights and the father of lies. In order to dispel darkness I must have a light. It is not enough to know about the battle, nor where the battle is, nor who the battle is between, but it is necessary to know what weapons we need to win the battle.

II Corinthians 11:3 But I am afraid that, as the
serpent deceived Eve by his craftiness, your minds
will be led astray from the simplicity and purity of
devotion to Christ.

This statement by Apostle Paul is directed towards his fellow Christians. It is important to understand that Satan does indeed try to deceive Christians. The Word of God is likened to a two-edged sword. It is the weapon that Jesus used in the wilderness when He was being tempted by the devil. Jesus quoted the Word to destroy the enemy's speculations. This same weapon is for you, too. However, there are three things necessary before you can use it.

First, you must pick up the weapon. The way that you pick up the truth is to read and study those things that are true. Since the Bible is truth, we must access it. This leads us to the second necessary aspect. Before you are able to use a weapon that you have picked up, you must learn how to use that weapon. There are correct ways to use a weapon and there are incorrect ways to use a weapon. If a weapon is used incorrectly, it can cause harm to the wielder or to fellow soldiers.

> *II **Timothy 3:16-17** All Scripture is inspired by God and profitable for teaching, for reproof, for correction, for training in righteousness;   so that the man of God may be adequate, equipped for every good work.*

> *Hebrews 5:14 But solid food is for the mature, who because of practice have their senses trained to discern good and evil.*

You must be skilled in the use of this weapon. Once truth gets into your heart, you are then skilled in using that weapon as far as understanding goes. In addition, you must believe in your weapon. No one would want to go into battle if they thought that their weapon would fail.

By believing the truth and that it can be used to destroy lies, you will be bold to enter the battle. That battleground is your mind and the minds of those with whom you come in contact. There is another element to the use of this weapon that we have not discussed yet.

The Missing Ingredient

The weapon of the Word of God can often be used like any manmade weapon. It can be used against the enemy or against an ally. The determining factor in using your weapon is the attitude behind your use of it. Satan even quotes the Word accurately at times, but he always has a twisted attitude behind it. If you quote the Word to condemn a fellow Christian, you have just wielded your weapon unlawfully. Without love, all of the knowledge of God is useless. We are nothing without love.

> *Galatians 5:6 (KJV) For in Jesus Christ neither circumcision availeth any thing, nor uncircumcision; but faith which worketh by love.*

Imagine the soldier that does not love his fellow soldiers. He will endanger them not only to the enemy but also they are endangered by his very presence. One of the things that we often see that comes out of a war is that the participants on the same side love one another like brothers. In a physical war on this earth, relationships are formed that last a lifetime. Each soldier is careful to fight **for** his fellow soldier. Why then do we see so much infighting among Christians? It is a disgrace to our Superior that we cannot even fight FOR one another because we are too busy fighting AGAINST one another.

If I see my brother falling, I am supposed to run to his aid that I might restore him. Instead, we see the wounded being harmed further by their own brothers and sisters. I don't care what the infraction is, if you are not willing to fight for that person, then you keep your mouth shut and you stay out of the picture!

It is necessary to use the knowledge of God in love. To do otherwise is to only do harm to others and to the name of our Lord. Love never fails. It is the power to restore. The love of Jesus restored us to the family of God. Your love for others, no matter how much they irritate you, has the power to restore them to their true heritage.

Conclusion

The knowledge of God has the ability to change you completely. Your maturity as a Christian is directly tied to it. Your provision in life is tied to it. Your spiritual warfare is tied to it. It is the greatest treasure for which you can ever search. The knowledge of God will give you access to the divine nature of God! If this is so and you believe it, what are you waiting for? Go find the knowledge of God and be transformed by it!

The Garden and the Cross

> *PURPOSE: This chapter was developed to raise the reader's knowledge of the completed redemption that Jesus accomplished. It stresses the three parts of the atonement: the mind, the spirit, and the body. The reader will come away with a full understanding of the word "salvation."*

I n talking about what Jesus accomplished on the cross, it is often overlooked what He accomplished in the garden. The scene in the garden has often been presented as a time of fighting off the fear of the cross. It has been proffered that when Jesus prayed to His Father to let this cup pass from Him, that He was referring to the cross. I have always felt like this undermined the character and nature of Jesus; that there was something missing or not making sense. It just seemed so out of character for Jesus to all of a sudden fear going to the cross after telling His disciples that He must do this and for their hearts not to be troubled. Are we then to believe that after telling His disciples to not let their hearts be troubled, that His heart was troubled?

It was always as if Jesus suddenly changed in His character. He was always so matter of fact when He talked about dying on the cross. I always accepted what I was told, but in my spirit it just did not seem to set right. I want to take a closer look at this passage and determine what did happen and why Jesus prayed for the cup to pass from Him.

Atonement Part 1

*Isaiah 53:3-4 He was **despised** and **forsaken** of men, a man of **sorrows** and acquainted with **grief**; and like one from whom men hide their face He was **despised**, and we did not esteem Him. Surely our **griefs** He Himself bore, and our **sorrows** He carried; yet we ourselves esteemed Him stricken, smitten of God, and afflicted.*

Notice all the emotions that were prophesied that the Christ would go through; they were not only emotions, but events that cause emotional responses.

DEFINITION

__Despised__-- (Baw-zaw) "To trample under foot." To be considered worthless.

__Forsaken__-(Khaw-dale) Rejected, Ceasing to be something is the Hebrew meaning of the original word.

__Sorrows__-(Mak-obe) The Hebrew here refers to "pain in the heart or inner man" Depression.

__Grief__-(Khol-ee) This is an interesting Hebrew word that means "to be rubbed or polished." It has the idea that one is worn down through constant

*rubbing. If applied to the inner man, one can see
the picture of grief.*

In that passage, Jesus experienced grief, sorrow, rejection and devaluation. He was despised. He was forsaken. All of these are emotional elements. If emotions are based in what a person believes, what would Jesus have believed that would cause Him to experience these emotions? Would these emotions then, if based in belief, actually be the indicator that there was a lapse of faith? Let us go to the garden to take a look at this event spoken of in Isaiah.

> **Matthew 26:38** *Then He said to them, "My soul is
> deeply grieved, to the point of death; remain here
> and keep watch with Me."*

This was the night before Jesus went to the cross. He was in the garden of Gethsemane. Notice Jesus said that His soul (inner man i.e. mind, spirit) was *"grieved to the point of death."* These are the words of Jesus not the exaggerations or idiom of a mere human. He said that He was about to die from the sorrow, depression, and grief He was experiencing. He even began to sweat great drops of blood. Jesus then prayed to the Father and said....

> **Matthew 26:39** *And He went a little beyond them,
> and fell on His face and prayed, saying, "My Father,
> if it is possible, let this cup pass from Me; yet not as
> I will, but as You will."*

> **Luke 22:44** *And being in **agony** He was praying very
> fervently; and His sweat became like drops of
> blood, falling down upon the ground.*

ALTHOUGH THIS MEDICAL CONDITION IS RELATIVELY RARE, ACCORDING TO DR. FREDERICK ZUGIBE, CHIEF MEDICAL EXAMINER OF ROCKLAND COUNTY, NEW YORK, IT IS WELL-KNOWN, AND THERE HAVE BEEN MANY CASES OF IT. THE CLINICAL TERM IS "HEMATOHIDROSIS." AROUND THE SWEAT GLANDS, THERE ARE MULTIPLE BLOOD VESSELS IN A NET-LIKE FORM. UNDER THE PRESSURE OF GREAT STRESS THE VESSELS CONSTRICT. THEN AS THE ANXIETY PASSES THE BLOOD VESSELS DILATE TO THE POINT OF RUPTURE. THE BLOOD GOES INTO THE SWEAT GLANDS. AS THE SWEAT GLANDS ARE PRODUCING MUCH SWEAT, IT PUSHES THE BLOOD TO THE SURFACE, COMING OUT AS DROPLETS OF BLOOD. IT IS CAUSED BY GREAT STRESS, AND IN THIS CASE, IT IS THE POINT BEFORE THE STRESS LITERALLY KILLS THE PERSON.

Now if Hebrews states, *"for the joy set before Him, He endured the cross,"* how could Jesus be praying to miss the cross if to Him it was worth it for the joy?

Hebrews 12:2 *fixing our eyes on Jesus, the author and perfecter of faith, Who for the joy set before Him endured the cross, despising the shame, and has sat down at the right hand of the throne of God.*

This means that when Jesus prayed to the Father for this cup to pass, He was not talking about the cross. That cup could not have been a code word for the cross. It is a much more likely explanation that since Jesus said Himself that He was about to die in the garden from the great stress, it is this death in the garden that He was speaking of when He prayed. He knew He had to go to the cross; this means His prayer was for His life to be spared for now so He could finish the job that the Father had given Him. This idea is supported in Luke. Notice that after Jesus prayed for the cup to be taken from Him, an angel was sent to minister to Him.

> *Luke 22:43 Now an angel from heaven appeared to Him, strengthening Him.*

This revelation shows us the actual answer to the prayer that He just prayed. If this angel strengthened Him physically, then we know that He was about to die physically which agrees with Jesus' statement about being near death. Another point that I would like to interject here is that the Jewish day started at sundown. That means that the garden experience took place on the same day as the trial, beating, and crucifixion did.

God the Father was the One pouring all of this on His Son, Jesus. *Isaiah 53:10 But the LORD was pleased To crush Him, putting Him to grief; If He would render Himself as a guilt offering, He will see His offspring, He will prolong His days, And the good pleasure of the LORD will prosper in His hand.* Jesus knew that He had to get to the cross, but submitted His will to the Father. In other words He was saying, *"Father if you want me to die now, so be it......but I really want to get to the cross!"* In light of that statement, it makes sense with Hebrews that for the joy set before Him, He endured the cross. Since Jesus wanted to go to the cross, He wasn't praying to miss it!

Now I want to revisit why Jesus would be feeling these emotions in the first place. Remember, emotions are an extension of believing something. Jesus was rejected and despised during His earthly ministry and yet He did not have this outburst of emotion at that time. So why now? I would contend that it was not His emotion but yours and mine. Jesus took our grief, our sorrow, our rejection, our depression, and all the emotional baggage that we are inflicted with, and nailed it to the cross. This is the part one of the atonement. Now if you keep reading in Isaiah, you will see that *"by His stripes we are healed."* That was part two of the atonement, and blood was also shed here as he was beaten He took all of our disease and infirmity. Finally, on the cross, the sins of the world were placed upon Him, and blood was also shed. That was part three.

Jesus redeemed your spirit (on the cross), your body (at the whipping post), and your mind (in the garden). Blood was shed at all three events. Jesus drank of the three cups of suffering that were given to Him. The garden was only one of those cups. It is interesting, that there are four cups at the Passover celebrated in Jewish households. Remember, Jesus died on Passover. These four cups are filled with wine and water. When Jesus sweats in the garden, it was mixed with blood. When He was being whipped, again His sweat and blood was mixed. When He was pierced in the side on the cross, both blood and water flowed.

Atonement Part 2

Isaiah states in verse five that, *"by His stripes we are healed."* This is the second part, and blood was also shed.

> ***Isaiah 53:5 (NKJV)*** *But He was wounded for our transgressions, He was bruised for our iniquities; the chastisement for our peace was upon Him, **and by His stripes we are healed.***

*The Hebrew word for **"healed"** (Raw-faw) literally means to sew or mend. It carries the idea of fixing a tear in a piece of clothing.*

*The Hebrew word for **"scourging"** (khab-boo-raw) literally means "the mark of strokes on the skin."*

The completed idea is this: Jesus allowed His skin to be ripped so that our bodies could be sewn or mended. Our salvation is much more than attaining eternal life. Our salvation includes healing for the spirit, the soul, and the body.

The Curse

***Galatians 3:13** Christ redeemed us from the curse of the Law, having become a curse for us—for it is written, "Cursed is everyone who hangs on a tree"—*

All we need to do is to look up what the curse of the Law is so that we can get an understanding of from what we have been saved. This information can be found in the twenty-eighth chapter of Deuteronomy. We will only list those verses that make our point, but it would be a good idea to read them all.

__Deuteronomy 28:15, 21- 22, 27-28, 35, 45__

15"But it shall come about, if you do not obey the Lord your God, to observe to do all His commandments and His statutes with which I charge you today, that all these curses will come upon you and overtake you:..."

21-22"The Lord will make the pestilence cling to you until He has consumed you from the land where you are entering to possess it. The Lord will smite you with consumption and with fever and with inflammation and with fiery heat and with the sword and with blight and with mildew, and they will pursue you until you perish."

27-28"The Lord will smite you with the boils of Egypt and with tumors and with the scab and with the itch, from which you cannot be healed. The Lord will smite you with madness and with blindness and with bewilderment of heart;"

35"The Lord will strike you on the knees and legs with sore boils, from which you cannot be healed, from the sole of your foot to the crown of your head."

45"So all these curses shall come on you and pursue you and overtake you until you are destroyed, because you would not obey the Lord your God by keeping His commandments and His statutes which He commanded you."

If we also note the blessing in this section of Scripture, we will find that there are no sicknesses or plagues mentioned. Therefore, it should be assumed that physical and mental health was a promise. Other Scriptures support this as well.

Exodus 15:26 And He said, "If you will give earnest heed to the voice of the Lord your God, and do what is right in His sight, and give ear to His commandments, and keep all His statutes, I will put none of the diseases on you which I have put on the Egyptians; for I, the Lord, am your healer."

Psalm 103:2-3 Bless the Lord, O my soul, And forget none of His benefits; Who pardons all your iniquities, Who heals all your diseases;

If physical health was a benefit in the Old Testament, and if we have a New Testament that is enacted on better promises, would it not make sense that we who are participants in the New Covenant have physical healing too?

Atonement Part 3

Isaiah 53:5 But He was pierced through for our transgressions, He was crushed for our iniquities; the chastening for our well-being fell upon Him, and by His scourging we are healed.

When Jesus was pierced on the cross, it was for the salvation of your spirit, or inner man. Blood and water flowed from His side. It was now complete. As Jesus' final drop of blood oozed from His body, the sacrifice was completed, and those for whom He came are now able to partake of His divine nature.

Salvation

The word *"salvation"* means much more than eternal life. Let's take a look at this Greek word and see if it supports the three-fold atonement of Christ.

DEFINITION

*The **Hebrew** is Yaw-shah, and it literally means "to be spacious." The idea of this word is that of liberty. That is, one is free from danger from without. There is a lot of space between me and my enemy. It is the opposite of being incarcerated. Contrast this with narrowness of space in the Hebrew. This word is used to describe danger or distress.*

Yaw-shoo-ah is the name given to our Lord which means God is salvation.

*The **Greek** word is [soteria /so-tay-ree-ah]*

1 deliverance, preservation, safety, salvation. 1A deliverance from the molestation of enemies. 1B in an ethical sense, that which concludes to the souls safety or salvation. 1C of Messianic salvation. 2 salvation as the present possession of all true Christians. 3 future salvation, the sum of benefits and blessings which the Christians, redeemed from all earthly ills, will enjoy after the visible return of Christ from heaven in the consummated and eternal kingdom of God.

Strong, J. (1996).

*Saving. These terms first refer to salvation (human or divine) from serious peril. **Curing from illness** is another sense... At times protection may be the meaning, and soteria can have the sense of a "safe return."*

*Keeping. The meaning at times may be that of **keeping alive**, e.g., pardoning, protecting, keeping from want, keeping a fire going.*

*Benefiting. The idea of rescuing from peril disappears when the idea is that of **keeping in good health**, or benefiting, or when the noun means "well-being."*

Preserving the Inner Being. A special nuance is when the terms refer to preserving the inner being or nature. In philosophy inner health may be the point or the preservation of one's humanity. [1]

In the definition of this one word, we have the idea of the three parts of the atonement. We have the spiritual, emotional, and physical elements represented.

---

[1] *Kittel, G., Friedrich, G., & Bromiley, G. W. (1995, c1985). Theological dictionary of the New Testament. Translation of: Theologisches Worterbuch zum Neuen Testament. (Page 1132). Grand Rapids, Mich.: W.B. Eerdmans.*

The Cups

Now we need to look closer at those four cups I mentioned earlier. Again, these four cups are used in the celebration of Passover in Jewish household. These four cups are filled with wine and water.

- The Passover meal starts with drinking the first cup.
- Then during the meal, the second cup is drunk.
- Then right after the meal, the third cup is drunk.
- After the blessing, the fourth cup is drunk.

> **Luke 22:20** *And in the same way He took the cup after they had eaten, saying, "This cup which is poured out for you is the new covenant in My blood."*

It is because the Bible records that *"after they had eaten"* we know that it represents the third cup. Jesus made a **promise** to His disciples and to all that would become believers in Him. He said that He would not drink again of the fruit of the vine until He does so with us in heaven. That means that Jesus partook of three cups and is waiting to partake of the fourth cup. This corresponds to the fact that Jesus drank the first three cups of suffering in the garden, at the whipping post, and on the cross. That leaves one cup left to drink to finish the work of Passover.

The Names of the Cups

Now let's look at the names of these cups. They are based upon the following Scripture.

Exodus 6:6-7 "Say, therefore, to the sons of Israel, 'I am the LORD, and I will bring you out from under the burdens of the Egyptians, and I will deliver you from their bondage. I will also redeem you with an outstretched arm and with great judgments. 'Then I will take you for My people, and I will be your God; and you shall know that I am the LORD your God, who brought you out from under the burdens of the Egyptians.'"

Cup #1

The Cup of Sanctification - This corresponds to *"I will bring you out from under the burdens of the Egyptians."*

It is meant to cause remembrance of the anguish of slavery. Here we find a connection with sorrow and grief. This cup corresponds to the garden experience and the healing of our minds.

Cup #2

The Cup of Judgments or Plagues - This corresponds to *"I will deliver you from their bondage."*

During the consumption of this cup, the ten plagues of Egypt are recited. This corresponds to the whipping post experience where Jesus allowed His skin to be torn so that ours could be mended or sewn.

Cup #3

The Cup of Redemption - This corresponds to *"I will redeem you with an outstretched arm."*

This cup corresponds to Jesus hanging on the cross and being pierced through for our transgressions, thus representing the healing of our spirits.

Cup #4

The Cup of Consummation or **The Cup of the Kingdom** - This corresponds to *"I will take you for my people."*

After Jesus drank the three cups of suffering (the garden, the whipping post, and the cross), there is the fourth cup waiting to be consumed.

When Jesus was sweating in the garden, it was mixed with blood. When He was being whipped, again His sweat and blood were mixed. When He was pierced in the side on the cross, both blood and water flowed. Nevertheless, that fourth cup – that cup represents the joy that was set before Him. It was taking us as a people unto Himself. What a glorious picture of the love that God has for you!

The fourth cup is the Cup of Consummation. We shall share that cup at the marriage supper of the Lamb. Marriage, that is what that fourth cup is all about. Since each cup represents the shedding of blood, what about that last cup? In the wedding ceremony in the Hebrew culture, the purity of the bride must be proven by the shedding of blood. It was a sign that the bride was a virgin. However, we have a problem.

We, the bride of Christ are certainly not virgins. We have failed our Lord at many junctures and turns. This is where Jesus helps us again. I believe that the blood of Jesus that was shed on Calvary will again be used to prove the purity and virginity of the bride. That means that Jesus shed His own blood to make us, His bride, pure. That is why it is the called the Cup of Consummation. It is a beautiful picture of our total redemption: mind, body, and spirit culminating in our being joined to Him in marriage.

If we would believe that Jesus did provide all of these things through His sacrifice, then it is time for us to take what is ours by faith. Hope in God, hope in His plan for you, believe in His provision, and forget none of His benefits. We cannot be saved without faith in Christ's blood. We cannot be healed unless we have faith in the provision of the cross.

That is how we access what God has provided us. It is by faith that we are saved. Okay, using that same logic, we must apply our faith to the other aspects of our redemption as well. That is, we cannot have soundness of mind, unless we realize what He did for us in the garden and access it by faith. We cannot walk in divine health without realizing what He did for us at the whipping post and access it by faith. I want you to know, Jesus paid the price for the pain of emotional difficulties, but you must access it by faith. He also paid for your physical difficulties and your spiritual difficulties, but you can only access them by faith.

The Fear of God

Chapter Three

> *PURPOSE: This chapter is designed to teach a biblical description of "The Fear of God." The reader can expect to learn the biblical definition, and how to acquire the benefits the fear of God promises.*

A young lad named Randy was playing in the front yard of his modest dwelling. Randy had just arrived at the age of eight and was thoroughly enjoying his new, red racing bicycle. Suddenly, Randy darted out into the street that ran in front of his family's home. Randy's father, Richard, was strolling to the mailbox to get the afternoon delivery left by the mailman. Just as he was opening the mailbox, Richard saw out of the corner of his eye two moving objects.

One object was the size and shape of his son, Randy; the other object was the size and shape of an automobile. The angle that both objects were traveling was bringing them on a course of collision. In a split second, Richard's mind engaged his body, and he ran to save his son. All of the adrenalin running through Richards's body was assisting him in reaching his son before the automobile did. At the very moment Richard reached his son, so did the automobile.

Page | 47

Before I tell you the end of this story, let me give you some background information on Richard and his son, Randy. Richard was a good father. He did everything he knew to provide for and protect his family. Richard worked hard to make sure that his family had a respectable house in which to live. Yet Richard knew the importance of being there for his family as well, so he balanced his work and his family life so that neither would be neglected.

Richard wanted his son to be able to grow up and have the things that he was not able to have as a child. He wanted his son to do better than he had. Richard took the time to instruct his son about all the things that were dangerous in life. He had instructed his son to always stay close to him when they would walk downtown. Richard would show Randy how to fasten his seat belt when they would go for a ride in the car. There was also instruction on how to safely ride a bicycle on the neighborhood streets.

Yes, the automobile beat Richard to his son, and Randy did not survive. Just as this story has a tragic ending, millions of people are rushing out into the street of eternal consequences, and they are about to be struck by death. Needlessly, millions will forfeit their eternal life with their Father because they too, have ignored or forgotten their Father's instruction.

If Randy truly feared his father's discipline concerning the safety instructions about riding a bicycle, he would not have rushed into that street without first searching for cars as his father, Richard, had warned him. I tell this story in order to put in proper perspective and what is meant by *"the fear of God."*

What do We Mean by "The Fear of God?"

I have heard many people water down concept of the fear of God by saying that it only means to be awestruck. I think this is so because they **do not understand the difference relationship makes to the concept.** Indeed being awestruck is indicated, but it does not take away from the fact that being afraid is also implied. People reject the notion that they should be afraid of God. They think that it would be impossible to love someone of whom you were also afraid.

If you look at the relationship between yourself as a child and your father, you find that there is a healthy fear. You probably were not afraid in the sense that at any moment your father would harm you or that he was an evil man. You knew that you could run to your father if you were worried about your safety, so you were not literally afraid of your father at every moment. You were only afraid when you did not follow your father's instruction. You were only afraid when you were disobedient. This is what is meant by *"the fear of God."* There is a moral element to your fear. If your father was a moral man, then you realized that you did not need to fear as long as you lived your life within the boundaries of your father's moral compass.

When we do not heed the instruction of our Father God, it places us, his children, in real life danger. What if Richard had gotten to Randy in time to save him from is disobedient action? Do you think Richard would have disciplined his son? Now think this through for a moment.

Do you think that we could say Richard really loved Randy if, after saving him from death, he patted him on the head and sent him off to play? Does not love require and even demand that Richard discipline his son? Would we not question Richard's ability to be a good father to Randy if he did not discipline his son? If our heavenly Father just ignored our running out into the street of sin and just picked us up and patted us on our head and sent us off, we would question whether He really loved us!

> **Hebrews 12:7-11 (NCV)** *So hold on through your sufferings, because they are like a father's discipline. God is treating you as children. All children are disciplined by their fathers. If you are never disciplined (and every child must be disciplined), you are not true children. We have all had fathers here on earth who disciplined us, and we respected them. So it is even more important that we accept discipline from the Father of our spirits so we will have life. Our fathers on earth disciplined us for a short time in the way they thought was best. But God disciplines us to help us, so we can become holy as He is. We do not enjoy being disciplined. It is painful, but later, after we have learned from it, we have peace, because we start living in the right way.*

God is not opposed to discipline. Discipline is what we actually fear. We know that God loves us for we run to Him for safety. It does not make sense to be afraid of Him indiscriminately. Yet when we walk away from Him morally, then we have a reason to fear His discipline in our lives, and that is a good, healthy fear of God.

CASE IN POINT

> *We can watch a thunderstorm from a distance and gaze in wonderment at the lightning. We can*

remark at how beautiful it is as it dances across the sky. We can be in awe of that kind of power being displayed at a distance. However, when that storm is in our proximity, we should be too fearful to grab hold of a flagpole. You see, our fear depends on our proximity to that power. Lightning is amoral and indiscriminate in who or where it strikes. It may strike either saint or sinner if the law of safe proximity is broken. We do not fear lightning at a far enough distance from us, but we do if we are in the storm.

How does all of this relate to God? God is **not** amoral. When He disciplines, it is righteous. In other words, it is deserved. We are not afraid of God as long as we are walking in submission to God. In this state we are rightly related to Him. He is a tower of safety; He is a very present help in a time of trouble (Psalm 46:1).

At this position, like the storm that is off in the distance, you can ooh and aah over His magnificent power. However, if we get on the wrong side of God through disobedience, unlike lightning, God is very discriminate in His dealings. God is just, and justice must be done. Just as the storm is now in your proximity, you are fearful of its power. God's justice is first applied to His own family before it extends to those beyond.

I Peter 4:17 For it is time for judgment to begin with the household of God; and if it begins with us first, what will be the outcome for those who do not obey the gospel of God?

How you relate to God determines if you are coming from a position of submission or rebellion. When we are walking in the instruction of our heavenly Father, we walk in awe of His presence in our lives; we feel safe because we are rightly related to His absolute power. However, when we walk away from the instruction of our heavenly Father, we walk in fear of His presence.

In fact, if we thought it were possible, we would try to hide from Him as well. If Adam and Eve did not have a fear of God, they would not have hid themselves when they had sinned against God. The fear of God actually has many wonderful benefits that we are going to take a look at now.

Restraining Evil

> **Genesis 20:11** Abraham said, "Because I thought, surely there is no **fear of God** in this place, and they will kill me because of my wife.

The first place in the Bible the phrase *"fear of God"* is used tells us much about the concept. Abraham feared Abimelech, the king of Gerar, because he thought the king did **not** fear God.

The fear of God is what restrains evil behavior just as a fear of your earthly father caused you to be obedient to his instructions. **If we know that God will deal with us according to our actions as they relate to His morality**, then we know that certain actions cause God to be displeased. God will then discipline those who are His children, and He will also judge those who are not. If we fear God, we will live our lives in a manner that is congruent to the instructions that He delivered to us.

People who do not fear God will live lives that are marked by being unrestrained. They will take what they want, they will lie in order to deceive, and they think nothing of harming others. They do not believe there is a God who will bring justice. They think that they can do anything they want without consequence. Hence, the first time we see this phrase being used it is done so in a way that shows us that the fear of God restrains evil behaviors.

> **Exodus 20:20** *Moses said to the people, "**Do not be afraid;** for God has come in order to test you, and in order that **the fear of Him may remain with you,** so that you may not sin."*

This is a very impressive verse with regard to understanding the fear of God. God told Moses to summon the people of Israel to the mountain so that He could talk to the people of Israel. God wanted to have a relationship with all of the people like a father would have with his children. Nonetheless, when the people heard God from the mountain, they were frightened. Verse twenty is Moses' response to the people because of the reaction they had to God when He spoke to them.

(1) God did not want them to be afraid of Him in the sense that they would hide from Him, (2) but rather God wanted them to fear Him so that they would not sin. The first idea would cause one to hide from God. The second idea would cause one to hide from sin. The first idea would be destructive to a relationship with God. The second idea would build a relationship with God.

There are dangers in life, and God's children need basic instructions that would cause them to navigate life in such a way that they would walk in safety. Like Richard sitting his son, Randy, in his lap and lovingly instructing him in how to safely ride his bicycle in the street, God was trying to be a Father to His children. No genuine father wants his children to be so afraid of him that they avoid all contact. Rather, a true father would want his children to be afraid to reject his instruction for fear of the consequences and the discipline that would follow disobedience.

Other Effects

There are tangible effects that the fear of God has upon our lives, but first I would like to establish that the fear of God is not something you can just put on momentarily. The fear of something is based in what you believe that something can do to harm your life. You may be afraid of heights. If so, that fear is based in falling and the result that would have on your person. If you had no fear of falling, you would have no fear of heights. So fear is based in belief. If your father told you to do your chores, your fear would be a result of not doing those chores and the resulting discipline.

I say all of this so that it would be clear to you that if you do not believe that God disciplines His children, then you will not have a fear of God. There are those who have this sense of a hyper-grace where they think that they can sin all they want without any consequences. That is not the witness of Scripture as we will see. The foundation of having a fear of God is that we believe what He has said and that He will indeed discipline us. If we do not believe these things, then we will not have a fear of God.

POWER THOUGHT

WHATEVER IT IS YOU FEAR, AT ITS ROOT, IS A BELIEF OF WHAT THE THING FEARED CAN DO TO HARM YOUR LIFE.

Proverbs 16:6 (NKJV) *In mercy and truth atonement is provided for iniquity; and by the fear of the Lord **one departs from evil.***

Even though we have already mentioned this, it bears repeating. The first benefit that the fear of God has upon our lives is that it restrains our temptation to engage in any behavior that would be seen by God as hostile toward His instruction for us. Thus, we could say that **the fear of God has the effect of perfecting holiness in each of us.**

> *II Corinthians 7:1 (NKJV) Therefore, having these promises, beloved, let us cleanse ourselves from all filthiness of the flesh and spirit, **perfecting holiness in the fear of God.***

The fear of God should have the effect of bringing holiness into our lives. For those who do not think that the fear of God is a New Testament principle, look up the phrase *"fear of God"* in your Bibles, and you will see that indeed it is. The Bible is full of examples of those who did fear God and those who did not. The consequences of both positions are also clear. Listen to this next Scripture and see what effect there is in not having a fear of God.

> *Psalm 36:1-4 (NKJV) An oracle within my heart concerning the transgression of the wicked: **there is no fear of God** before his eyes. For he flatters himself in his own eyes, when he finds out his iniquity and when he hates. The words of his mouth are wickedness and deceit; he has ceased to be wise and to do good. He devises wickedness on his bed; he sets himself in a way that is not good; he does not abhor evil.*

You may know people who flatter themselves with their sin or their hate for others. You may hear them brag about getting away with this or that; you may hear them speak of how they told this or that person off, and how they hate them. If you do, then you have met someone who does not have a fear of God. Like Abraham, we must be careful in our dealings with those that do not fear Him because they have no moral restraint in their dealings with you. The next benefit of having a fear of God is life!

Life

> *Deuteronomy 6:24 (NKJV) And the Lord commanded us to observe all these statutes, to **fear the Lord our God**, for our good always, **that He might preserve us alive,** as it is this day.*

> *Psalm 33:18-19 (NKJV) Behold, the eye of the Lord is on those **who fear Him**, on those who hope in His mercy, **To deliver their soul from death**, and **to keep them alive** in famine.*

> *Proverbs 10:27 (NKJV) The **fear of the Lord prolongs days,** but the years of the wicked will be shortened.*

> *Proverbs 19:23 (NKJV) The **fear of the Lord leads to life,** and he who has it will abide in satisfaction; He will not be visited with evil.*

> *Proverbs 14:26-27 (NKJV) In **the fear of the Lord** there is strong confidence, and His children will have a place of refuge. **The fear of the Lord is a fountain of life,** to turn one away from the snares of death.*

*GOD DID NOT JUST THROW HIS LAWS AT US SO THAT HE COULD CONDEMN OR CONTROL US. FAR FROM THE MIND OF GOD IS THE IDEA OF CONTROLLING HUMANITY. NO, OUR GOD, OUR HEAVENLY FATHER LOVES US SO MUCH THAT HE GIVES US, HIS CHILDREN, INSTRUCTION TO KEEP US FROM HARM. **JUST AS RANDY DID NOT SEE THE AUTOMOBILE THAT CAUSED HIS DEATH, WE DO NOT SEE THOSE INVISIBLE POWERS THAT OPERATE UPON OUR DISOBEDIENCE TO TAKE ADVANTAGE OF US AND OUR LIVES.***

Prosperity

The next benefit of fearing God is prosperity. When you finish reading these next verses, there should be no question that God's desire is that His children be prosperous. There are those that think living in poverty is actually a sign of holiness. Poverty does not bring God glory any more than it would for an earthly father to bestow poverty upon his children. Poverty is not a virtue. We need to understand that when a man or woman of God really fears the Lord, they will be blessed.

> *Psalm 112:1-3 (NKJV) Praise the Lord! Blessed is the man who **fears the Lord**, who delights greatly in His commandments. **His descendants will be mighty on earth**; the generation of the upright will be blessed. **Wealth and riches will be in his house**, and his righteousness endures forever.*

*Proverbs 22:4 (NKJV) By humility and the **fear of the Lord** are **riches** and honor and life.*

It does not mean that every Christian will be a millionaire but that God wants His children to live in satisfaction. Satisfaction can take many forms. As the apostle Paul said, he had learned to be content in whatever state he was in, whether abased or exalted. It also does not mean that you won't suffer persecution. There are many stories of folks that have precious memories even when they did not have much because they lived in contentment and satisfaction. They were rich because of the relationships they had. When we are in relationship with the King of Kings, we are rich!

Wisdom, Understanding, and Knowledge

The next benefit really excites me! Having a fear of God causes one to live under the promise of revelation. Left to our own thinking, we are wholly inadequate in running the affairs of our lives and the lives of those in our charge. Yet when armed with the wisdom, understanding, and knowledge that God gives, we are able to make proper decisions.

*Psalm 111:10 (NKJV) The **fear of the Lord** is the beginning of **wisdom**; a good **understanding** have all those who do His commandments. His praise endures forever.*

*Proverbs 1:7 (NKJV) The **fear of the Lord** is the beginning of **knowledge**, but fools despise wisdom and instruction.*

*Proverbs 2:5 (NKJV) Then you will understand the **fear of the Lord**, and find the **knowledge** of God.*

*Psalm 25:12-15 (NKJV) Who is the man that **fears the Lord**? Him shall He **teach** in the way He chooses. He himself shall dwell in **prosperity**, and his descendants shall inherit the earth. The **secret of the Lord is with those who fear Him**, and He will show them His covenant. My eyes are ever toward the Lord, for He shall pluck my feet out of the net.*

"The secret of the Lord is with those who fear Him" (Psalm 25:15). That is an exciting statement. God has given us all we need in which to order our lives in such a way that brings holiness, life, prosperity, wisdom, knowledge, and understanding. We are not done yet; there is more.

Family

The fear of the Lord blesses not only you but your family as well. What would you say if you were told that if you fear the Lord, your wife and your children will be blessed? With all of the dangers facing women and children, wouldn't it be great to know that God will bless your wife and your children because of your life being walked out in the fear of God?

In this world today so many parents feel so helpless in raising their children. They see the claws of societal amorality begin to take hold of their children. What a great promise to have that if I order my life according to the instruction of my Father in heaven, I will bring blessing to my children and my wife.

*Psalm 128:1-4 (NKJV) Blessed is every one who **fears the Lord**, who walks in His ways. When you eat the labor of your hands, **you shall be happy**,* *and it shall be well with you. **Your wife shall be like a fruitful vine** in the very heart of your house, **your children like olive plants** all around your table. Behold, thus shall the man be blessed who fears the Lord.*

Safety

How would you like to know that no matter where you go, whether you find yourself in safety or you find yourself in danger, that there is an encampment of angels around you? Would that not bring great comfort to you?

> ***Psalm 34:7-14 (NKJV) The angel of the Lord encamps all around those who fear Him** and delivers them. Oh, taste and see that the Lord is good; blessed is the man who trusts in Him! Oh, fear the Lord, you His saints! There is **no want to those who fear Him.** The young lions lack and suffer hunger; but those who seek the Lord shall not lack any good thing. Come, you children, listen to me; I will teach you the fear of the Lord. Who is the man who desires life, and loves many days, that he may see good? Keep your tongue from evil, and your lips from speaking deceit. Depart from evil and do good; seek peace and pursue it.*

By now you might be thinking, *"This fear of God stuff sounds pretty good!"* But wait! It is not something that Christians choose to do or not do. The fear of God is something that is inherent in the Christian's life. If you do not fear God, then you do not really know and believe Him. To know Him is to fear Him. These are not just my words.

> **Proverbs 14:2 (NKJV)** *He who walks in His uprightness fears the Lord, but he who is perverse in his ways despises Him.*

That was what God was trying to accomplish with the children of Israel when He talked to them from the mountain. He was trying to show His children that He was powerful and His children had nothing to fear from others, for God would fight their battles. However, the people became afraid of God. Rather than see Him as their Father, they saw Him as a terrible powerful figure that was disconnected from their needs. They had a wrong knowledge about who God is.

> **Psalm 103:13** *Just as a father has compassion on his children, so the Lord has compassion on those who fear Him.*

Just as Richard wanted his son, Randy, to prosper, to be blessed in life, to live in safety, to be in good health and contentment, God wants the same for His children. Yet if we do not heed His instruction then we can expect to bear the consequence of our actions. Moreover, if the consequences of our actions do not take our physical life as it did Randy's, we can and should expect our loving Father to discipline us.

When we have been trained by it, it will produce the peaceful fruit of righteousness in our lives. If you endeavor to get to know God in a greater capacity, expect to find that you will also begin to fear God in a greater capacity. Doing so will bring life, safety, prosperity, and blessing to your life and the lives of your family members.

True & False Conversions

> *PURPOSE: This chapter teaches a clear method of biblical evangelism that stresses the model that Jesus and the Apostles used. The reader will come away with the confidence and the tools needed to reach out to the world. They can expect to get a strong understanding of what constitutes a true conversion and a false conversion.*

There is much information out there concerning how one gains access into Heaven. Much of it is not biblically based and has caused many to enter into a false hope of being saved. It is my desire that in this lesson we will be able to gain a simple understanding of what it means to be a Christian, how we get to be a Christian, and how to stay a Christian. It is not my intention to go against any person, church, or denomination. All that I am seeking to do is to put into simple terms what it means to be saved from a biblical perspective.

What must we do to be saved?

First we need to understand how we CANNOT be saved.

- We cannot be saved by being good.

- We cannot be saved because we belong to a church or denomination.
- We cannot be saved by going to church regularly.
- We cannot be saved by following church traditions such as, confirmation, catechism, etc.
- We cannot be saved by other religions like Buddhism, Hinduism, New Ageism, etc.
- We cannot be saved by proxy or association (i.e. country, parents, etc.).
- We cannot be saved by baptism, whether as a baby or otherwise.

The Bible tells us how we are saved.

A. **The first thing we must understand in our steps to becoming saved is how costly our sin is.**

> *Romans 3:20 (JNT) For in His sight no one alive will be considered righteous on the ground of legalistic observance of Torah commands, because what Torah really does is show people how sinful they are.*

> *Romans 7:12-13 So then, the Law is holy, and the commandment is holy and righteous and good. Therefore did that which is good become a cause of death for me? May it never be! Rather it was sin, in order that it might be shown to be sin by effecting my death through that which is good, so that through the commandment sin would become utterly sinful.*

We know the depth, the cost, and the depravity of any sin by the measurement of justice handed out to those who commit that sin. For instance, if I break the speed limit by ten miles per hour, I may get a $100.00 fine; however, if I break the speed limit by thirty miles an hour, that fine goes up drastically. This is why a thief may get a fine and some jail time and a murderer may get life or capital punishment.

In God's measurement, we find that even the smallest infraction requires a punishment of death. This is so because God's demand is perfection which is a causation of His perfection. Because God is perfect, He must be a perfect Judge and He must show perfect justice.

When comparing ourselves with other people there are variations put on different crimes because everyone comes short of perfection. But when we compare ourselves with God, there can be no room for failure. Therefore, we can only conclude that our sin is indeed a very serious infraction in the eyes of God.

B. **This should lead you to the conclusion that you are not a good person in the eyes of God.**

> *Mark 10:17-18 As He was setting out on a journey, a man ran up to Him and knelt before Him, and asked Him, "Good Teacher, what shall I do to inherit eternal life?" And Jesus said to him, "Why do you call Me good? No one is good except God alone.*

> *Romans 3:12 (NKJV) They have all turned aside; they have together become unprofitable; there is none who does good, no, not one."*

C. When we are convinced of our sinful condition before God, we need to then come to Him in repentance.

> *II Peter 3:9 (NLT) The Lord isn't really being slow about his promise to return, as some people think. No, He is being patient for your sake. He does not want anyone to perish, so he is giving more time for everyone to repent.*

> *II Corinthians 7:9-10 (ESV) As it is, I rejoice, not because you were grieved, but because you were grieved into repenting. For you felt a godly grief, so that you suffered no loss through us. For godly grief produces a repentance that leads to salvation without regret, whereas worldly grief produces death.*

POWER THOUGHT

A. *If God was to forgive you for your sin just because you asked, He would be an unjust Judge.*

B. *Therefore the only hope we have is if someone will take our penalty for the sins we committed so that God can declare us righteous by the blood of another.*

C. *The problem with this is if a person was to offer their life for my sins, and they had* committed even one sin, then they can only die for their own sin, not mine.

   D. Since every person that has ever lived has sinned, there is no one able to die as an innocent lamb for the rest of us.

A. This brings us to the solution and raises the question, *"Is there a sinless person?"*

How Do You Know You Are Saved?

There are PROOFS that you are saved.

   A. **We have the witness of the Holy Spirit.**

   II Corinthians 1:21-22 (NLT) It is God who gives us, along with you, the ability to stand firm for Christ. He has commissioned us, and he has identified us as his own by placing the Holy Spirit in our hearts as the first installment of everything He will give us.

   Romans 8:16 (NLT) For his Holy Spirit speaks to us deep in our hearts and tells us that we are God's children.

   Ephesians 1:12-14 (NLT) God's purpose was that we who were the first to trust in Christ should praise our glorious God. And now you also have heard the truth, the Good News that God saves you. And when you believed in Christ, he identified you as his

*own by giving you the Holy Spirit, whom he
promised long ago. The Spirit is God's
guarantee that he will give us everything he
promised and that he has purchased us to
be his own people. This is just one more
reason for us to praise our glorious God.*

Just as a man will give the love of his life a ring to signify
his promise to marry her, Jesus gave His bride a deposit, the
security, or the down payment of His Spirit as an earnest payment
that signifies our marriage to Him. A payment in earnest is a
payment that signifies a promise that the whole will be paid in full
as well. It was the first installment paid on an item to guarantee
that the rest would be paid.

We have not received all of our redemption; we have not
received all of our salvation. God's earnest payment of His Spirit
guarantees us, however, that we will receive it all. There will be a
day where payment will be made in full; a day where your spirit,
your mind, and your body will all be spiritual and eternal.

B. There is the proof of a changed life.

*II Corinthians 5:17 (NKJV) Therefore, if
anyone is in Christ, he is a new creation; old
things have passed away; behold, all things
have become new.*

*Romans 6:4 (ESV) We were buried therefore
with him by baptism into death, in order
that, just as Christ was raised from the dead
by the glory of the Father, we too might
walk in newness of life.*

To walk in newness of life, one must be a new person; if one is a new person, then one must exhibit traits that he did not previously possess. These traits become most visible by the one possessing them. New Christians find that they have new desires and drives. They find new love and affection in their hearts.

These are tangible changes that show that there is a change, and that change can only be completed by God. Every true Christian has all the evidence he will ever need that he is saved. God has so changed us, that there is no doubt as to our metamorphosis.

Remember, that first we must understand that we are lost and that we are exceedingly sinful. Secondly, we must hear the good news of Jesus. Thirdly, we must believe on Him and confess Him before men. This produces salvation. This also raises our next question.

What do You Have to do to Keep Your Salvation?

A. First, if we **COULD NOT** gain salvation by doing or being good, then we **CANNOT LOSE** our salvation by doing or being bad.
B. If it is by faith that we are saved, then it is **BY NOT HAVING FAITH** that we are no longer saved. Once you believe in Christ, the only way to lose Him is to stop believing in Christ.
C. There is nothing you could do by your own effort to be saved. Our salvation is not tied to our works, merits or ceremonies; instead it is a sure, confident belief from the heart on the Son of God as Lord.

How Can We Tell if a Person Has Had a False Conversion?

Signs of a False Conversion:

There are many false converts who think they are Christians because of what they have been told.

A. **Many have been told that all they need is to do something, whether it is baptism, communion, self flagellation, good deeds, prayers, proclamations, etc. All of these may be false converts because they may not understand the life of Jesus and what He did for them.**

Baptism

Can baptism of itself save you? First, let us deal with infant baptism. Those groups that believe infant baptism is necessary to save the person have some hurdles to overcome. If baptism saves you, then it can no longer be by faith. The Bible says that we are saved by faith, *"not of works, lest any man should boast"* (Ephesians 2:8-9).

LOGIC BOX

If it was true that infants would go to hell if they die before being baptized, why isn't the minister there at the birth of the child to baptize them?

Since Hell and Heaven are eternal places, in other words once there one cannot change residence,

does that not place the infant in serious peril in
waiting for baptism?

Communion

Missing communion can damn one to Hell according to some groups. If this is so, then where is faith? Do I even need faith? All I need then is to show up and actively participate in the ceremony. This again is suggesting to God that somehow you can be good enough to gain entrance to Heaven.

Self Flagellation

Some groups suggest that one must cause themselves a certain threshold of suffering in order to be saved. Again, where is faith? This idea has the same problem. It is suggesting to God that I can make myself good enough to gain entrance to Heaven.

Good Deeds

There are some groups that believe that all you need to do is to make sure that your good deeds outweigh your bad ones. It carries the idea that God has this scale in Heaven and is weighing your good against your bad. Again, where is faith? Also, God cannot claim to be a just and perfect Being, and then allow sin to go unpunished.

Prayer

Some say that by saying a certain prayer one is saved. This falls short for the same reason the others do. It ignores faith.

Some say that just by proclaiming your belief in God you can be saved. People who rest upon their own achievements to gain entrance into heaven are deceived. Jesus gives us a clear picture of the uselessness of trying to use these things for honor and recognition.

> *Matthew 7:21-23 (NCV)* "Not all those who say that I am their Lord will enter the kingdom of heaven. The only people who will enter the kingdom of heaven are those who do what my Father in heaven wants. On the last day many people will say to me, 'Lord, Lord, we spoke for you, and through you we forced out demons and did many miracles.' Then I will tell them clearly, 'Get away from me, you who do evil. I never knew you.'

So the key phrase is, "I never knew you." To be known of God means that we are intimately familiar with God. When we believe on His Son, we are adopted into God's household and we literally become sons and daughters of God. A father knows his children, and he is unfamiliar with those who are not his children.

To be familiar with God, then, means we must become part of His household, and we do this through the new birth experience of salvation when we are adopted into His family.

B. Many have been told to just accept Christ and He will give you joy and peace.

What happens to the soul who believes that he is accepting Jesus because Jesus will make his life better?

When people try Jesus as a life improvement experiment and then experience persecution, they are dismayed that this Jesus did not make their life better, and so they do not continue to believe. **THEN, THEY BECOME INOCULATED TO EVER HEARING THE GOSPEL AGAIN!**

C. **Another sign of false converts is that they create a god in their own image.**

People create a god in their mind that suits them and their lifestyle. This is a condition that is actually a result of secular humanism conditioning. People will have their own moral code based on their own lifestyle. If they believe in living with someone before marrying them, they will fashion a god who allows and understands this behavior. The reality however is that God does not overlook sin based upon the situation. The reality of God does not invade the perception of the sinner.

POWER THOUGHT

Any attempt to explain God using human intellect is the act of creating your own false god to worship.

God can only be defined by what God has said about Himself. We cannot add to that or take away from it without mutilating the reality of who God really is.

When defining God, we must condition our thinking to only accept those attributes that God has attributed to Himself.

D. **Another sign of a false conversion is that they will fall away when hard times come.**

> *Matthew 13:20-21 "The one on whom seed was sown on the rocky places, this is the man who hears the word and immediately receives it with joy; yet he has no firm root in himself, but is only temporary, and when affliction or persecution arises because of the word, immediately he falls away.*

POWER THOUGHT

If a person gives up Christ because of hard times, it shows us that the person did not believe in Christ in the first place.

If they had believed in Christ, they would not give up eternal life with Christ in Heaven. Giving up on life shows us that that person has never come to the place of believing with his heart.

E. **Another sign of a false convert is that he will not have a zeal for the lost, a hunger for the Word, or a desire to be in fellowship.**

> *Hebrews 10:24-25 and let us consider how to stimulate one another to love and good deeds, not forsaking our own assembling together, as is the habit of some, but encouraging one another; and all the more as you see the day drawing near.*

> *I John 2:19 They went out from us, but they were not really of us; for if they had been of us, they would have remained with us; but*

they went out, so that it would be shown
that they all are not of us.

I Peter 2:1-3 (NCV) So then, rid yourselves of
all evil, all lying, hypocrisy, jealousy, and evil
speech. As newborn babies want milk, you
should want the pure and simple teaching.
By it you can grow up and be saved,
because you have already examined and
seen how good the Lord is.

F. Another sign of a false convert is that sin is still alive in his heart.

The Christian has had a spiritual change in the inner man. However, his body is still sinful. The Bible talks about a war that is taking place between the flesh and the spirit. Our new inner man is what drives us to do the things that God wants.

Therefore, because the false convert has not experienced this change in their spirit, there is not a war between the spirit and the flesh. They are both in agreement to sin.

Signs of a True Convert:

A. The true convert shows signs of repentance.

These are signs to others as opposed to signs to one's self as we covered earlier

Matthew 3:8 "Therefore bear fruit in
keeping with repentance;

B. The true convert will not fall away and leave the faith.

The reason this is so obvious is that when one understands the depth of his sins, he realizes his only hope of life is Jesus. It would be the same as taking your parachute off on a plane that just lost all its engines. It would be completely suicidal to do so, and no one in his right mind would do that.

C. **A true convert shows that he has a desire to live for God.**

> *I Peter 2:1-3 Therefore, putting aside all malice and all deceit and hypocrisy and envy and all slander, like newborn babies, long for the pure milk of the word, so that by it you may grow in respect to salvation, if you have tasted the kindness of the Lord.*

D. **Another sign of a true convert is that, while sin is still alive in his flesh, he is dead to sin in his heart.**

> *Romans 7:20-21 But if I am doing the very thing I do not want, I am no longer the one doing it, but sin which dwells in me. I find then the principle that evil is present in me, the one who wants to do good......*
> *Wretched man that I am! Who will set me free from the body of this death? Thanks be to God through Jesus Christ our Lord! So then, on the one hand I myself with my mind am serving the law of God, but on the other, with my flesh the law of sin.*

E. **A true convert will never look back**

> *Luke 9:62 But Jesus said to him, "No one, after putting his hand to the plow and looking back, is fit for the kingdom of God."*

What is Born Again?

The term *"born again"* has been maligned by the world to the point that most Christians are ashamed to use the term in public conversation. There has been a consistant and relentless attack against the idea of being born again to have access to our God. People are angry about that term. They are angry with Christians. They see Christians as the most intolerant group in the world and they hate us.

Surprised? You shouldn't be. Jesus said that if the world hated Him it will hate you also. Understand that you will be hated. It is not if but when. With this in mind it should not surprise us that the term *"born again"* brings out such angst in those that belong to the world. Actually, that term is a picture of the most beautiful love ever demonstrated in the world. It really is amazing that people have such a hate for it.

First, this term was coined by Jesus. It is not a term that was invented by man. Looking at what Jesus said and subsequently what the apostles said we get complete understanding of its meaning.

> *John 3:1-8 Now there was a man of the Pharisees, named Nicodemus, a ruler of the Jews; this man came to Jesus by night and said to Him, "Rabbi, we know that You have come from God as a teacher; for no one can do these signs that You do unless*

God is with him." Jesus answered and said to him,
*"Truly, truly, I say to you, **unless one is born again***
***he cannot see the kingdom of God.**" Nicodemus*
said to Him, "How can a man be born when he is
old? He cannot enter a second time into his
mother's womb and be born, can he?" Jesus
answered, "Truly, truly, I say to you, unless one is
born of water and the Spirit he cannot enter into
the kingdom of God. "That which is born of the
flesh is flesh, and that which is born of the Spirit is
spirit. "Do not be amazed that I said to you, 'You
must be born again.' "The wind blows where it
wishes and you hear the sound of it, but do not
know where it comes from and where it is going; so
is everyone who is born of the Spirit."

Being born involves seed. There is no birth without the conception of seed. We know this in the physical realm but it is a truth in spiritual realm also. The new birth is actually a change that is committed by God in the one who believes in the Son of God. If we are talking about a spiritual birth, then we need to understand that we are talking about our human spirits.

That means that there must be the impregnation of seed into our spirits which will cause a regeneration of life. The product that is produced by this seed is completely different then it was before it was impregnated. What is the seed?

I Peter 1:22-25 Since you have in obedience to the
truth purified your souls for a sincere love of the
brethren, fervently love one another from the
*heart, **for you have been born again not of seed***
which is perishable but imperishable, that is,

through the living and enduring word of God. *For,*
"ALL FLESH IS LIKE GRASS, AND ALL ITS GLORY LIKE THE
FLOWER OF GRASS. THE GRASS WITHERS, AND THE FLOWER
FALLS OFF, BUT THE WORD OF THE LORD ENDURES FOREVER."
And this is the word which was preached to you.

Here the seed that produces the born again process is the Word of God. When we hear the message of Jesus and we believe, the seed of the Word of God impregnates our spirit and causes us to be regenerated into a new spirit.

> ***Colossians 3:9-10*** *Do not lie to one another, since you laid aside the old self with its evil practices, and have put on the new self who is being renewed to a true knowledge according to the image of the One who created him—*

> ***II Corinthians 5:17*** *Therefore if anyone is in Christ, he is a new creature; the old things passed away; behold, new things have come.*

So the power of the Word of God when it is believed is that it will cause a regeneration of our spirits. Once our spirits have changed we become a different person. This different person is actually a new creation of God. We also will have a quality that we were never able to have before.

> ***I John 3:9*** *No one who is born of God practices sin, because His seed abides in him; and he cannot sin, because he is born of God.*

This new spirit cannot sin. The reason it cannot sin the seed of God dwells in it. When we believe the Word of God unto salvation it remains in us. The power of the Word of God keeps our spirit in a sinless state. Remember however, your body has not been born again and it still has sin dwelling in it.

> *I John 4:7 Beloved, let us love one another, for love is from God; and everyone who loves is born of God and knows God.*

Being born again gives us an ability to love that we did not have before. We have the ability to love our enemies; to love those who despise us; to love those who strike us; to love those who hate us. God's love is given to us to be used to love others. The same love Jesus demonstrated on the cross is now available to you.

> *I John 5:1 Whoever believes that Jesus is the Christ is born of God, and whoever loves the Father loves the child born of Him.*

Being born of God produces a special love for others who have been born of God.

> *I John 5:4 For whatever is born of God overcomes the world; and this is the victory that has overcome the world—our faith.*

We overcome the world because of our new birth. Your faith is the quality that overcomes the kingdom of this world which is ruled by the god of this world which is the devil.

> *I John 5:18 We know that no one who is born of God sins; but He who was born of God keeps him, and the evil one does not touch him.*

Being born again puts us in a place where the evil one cannot touch you. You would not know this by how many Christians act. I choose to believe the Word of God and His power over what man may say.

God's intent is to use our lives.

Jeremiah 29:11 (NLT) "For I know the plans I have for you," says the LORD. "They are plans for good and not for disaster, to give you a future and a hope."

God has a plan for each person. Often we are taught about a god who is far away and disinterested in the minutia of our lives. But the Bible declares differently. We are told in the Bible that God has numbered every hair upon our heads, and if one hair falls out, He takes note of it. Now that does not sound like God is disinterested in the small things of our lives.

It is clear from Scripture that God wants to have a very intimate relationship with us. The first key issue when standing before Jesus is not *"what have I done"* but *"does He know me and do I know Him."* Jesus tells us that there will be those who seek entrance into Heaven based upon what they have done, and He will tell them, *"depart from Me you workers of lawlessness, **FOR I NEVER KNEW YOU.**"* To be known by God is the greatest honor, and to know Him is the greatest quest we could ever engage in.

How to Know the Will of God

> *PURPOSE: In this chapter the reader will find out how to discern God's will. They will learn that they can create the right atmosphere that will allow them to hear what God is saying to them as well as entering into a rest that God will direct them because they have positioned themselves under the wing of the Almighty God.*

O ne of the most frequent questions that I receive as a pastor is, *"How do I find out what God's will is for my life?"* We can be very excited and committed to doing God's will but if we are not discerning what that will is, we will be making decisions that will result in mistakes. Lost time in the kingdom of God has huge ramifications. Before we discuss how to find God's will, we need to know what is meant by God's will.

If you ask people what *"God's will"* means, you will get many different answers. The word *"will"* has as its first sense *"to purpose."* We could say then that God's will is God's purpose. This raises the question, *"Do we actually see God's will as His purpose?"*

Do we see the great import of doing God's purpose for us? We ask God, should I go here or should I go there? Then we go in the direction that we believe God is taking us and when we find resistance we say, well I must not have heard God's voice. Yet following God's will almost always involves resistance. It is the pressure that produces the deliverer. You were created to be a deliverer. You have a purpose and a mission. You are empowered by God's Holy Spirit.

Do we actually think of God's will in terms of His purpose or do we think of it in terms of what is best for us? How many people actually give up their life to become a song in the heart of God? Your life is a song when you walk out God's will. There is a harmony when we partner with our Creator to walk us down the path that He created for us from the foundation of the world.

Do we really want to accomplish His purpose or do we want to accomplish our purpose with His blessing? Many Christians only want God's blessing on their plans. God is not going to follow you as you walk down your path doing your thing. God will be back there where you left him when you started out on your own. Once you surrender to the reason of your creation, you and God are now walking together.

The next sense of the word *"will"* is *"to do."* It is not enough to find out the will of God if we do not do it. If we do not supply action with the revelation of God's will, then it can no longer be considered God's will. Only when we add *"doing"* to *"purpose"* can we say that we are accomplishing His will. In fact when we add *"doing"* to *"purpose"* we find destiny.

Purpose without doing is no longer purpose and doing without purpose is no longer doing. It is only when purpose is connected to action that it becomes God's will activated. It seems to me that many have downplayed the role of action. They usually connect it to legalism. Yet Jesus put emphasis on doing the Word as well as the believing the Word. His story of the man who built his house on the sand versus the man that built his house on a rock or foundation, gives us a picture of a person who acts upon the

Word and one who does not. The one who built his house on the rock is likened to the man who heard the Word and did it.

If we divorce action from our faith, our faith is no longer faith. You cannot say you believe something that disagrees with your actions. It is what you do that actually proves what you believe.

There are some things that we need to clarify at this point. We must discern between God's individual will, His corporate will, and His general will.

God's **general will** cannot be altered in any way. It is His dealings with the universe. Nothing will stop Jesus from coming back to rule this earth. That is an example of God's general will.

God's **corporate will** can only be affected by the group not any single individual. In this case we can find God's dealing with groups. No example is as strong as the city of Jerusalem. God's dealing with that city is an excellent example of God's corporate will. God's dealing with the corporate is found both in His blessing and in His judgment.

"If you are trying to find out what God's will is so that you can make the decision whether to do it or not, you will not find His will."

God's **individual will** is solely the individual's responsibility and this is the subject of this writing. Just as the corporate will of God is susceptible to the will of the group, God's individual will is susceptible to your will.

There is a concept concerning our God that seems to have been diminished along the way. It is the idea of the faithfulness of God. The faithfulness of God is relative to the subject of God's will.

There are certain conditions that must be met in order to properly discern His will. Those that just want to know for knowing sake will be deceived.

Some people are actually saying in their heart, *"God tell me what your will is and then I will tell you whether I will do it!"* God does not work in that environment. God will share His will but that does not mean you will know it. To know God's will is to understand what God wants you to do.

Do you think that God revealed His will to Judas?

Do you think that Judas understood that will?

The reason Judas did not understand the will of God is found in the fact that His will was competing with God's will. If you allow your will to compete with God's will, your will will win! Judas heard all of Jesus' sermons. He even heard Jesus call him an apostle. Judas had plenty of evidence as to the will of God for him. His inability to understand God's will was revealed in his actions against the Son of God.

We have to have certain conditions met that will open us up to find and know God's will for our lives. If we practice these things, we will only have to ask God what He would have us do and He will reveal His will to us and we will understand it and do it.

> **Romans 12:1-2** *Therefore I urge you, brethren, by the mercies of God, to present your bodies a living and holy sacrifice, acceptable to God, which is your*

spiritual service of worship. And do not be
conformed to this world, but be transformed by the
renewing of your mind, so that you may prove what
the will of God is, that which is good and
acceptable and perfect.

"*THEREFORE…* " Before we can go forward we must go backward to see what *"therefore"* is there for.

Romans 11:32-36 *For God has shut up all in*
disobedience so that He may show mercy to all. Oh,
the depth of the riches both of the wisdom and
knowledge of God! How unsearchable are His
judgments and unfathomable His ways! For who
has known the mind of the Lord, or who became His
counselor? Or who has first given to Him that it
might be paid back to him again? For from Him and
through Him and to Him are all things. To Him be
the glory forever. Amen.

The context of therefore is to know the unknowable! To know His judgments…to know His ways…to know His mind!

Judgments—What does it mean to know His judgments? To judge rightly is to choose the correct direction from two or more selections. Only God knows the correct direction for our lives and is willing and able to communicate it to us.

Ways—The ways of God are demonstrated in the nature of God. When He shows us His nature then we have in a sense God's will on many different things. We know instantly what we are to do because we have become students of His ways and when we know His ways, we know what He would do thereby revealing what we ought to do.

Mind—The mind of God is where the strategy of God is. We can know His mind and find His strategy. God wants to use us strategically. These are the very smallest of details concerning our lives and movements.

I URGE YOU... Paul's emphatic call to what he is about to say, gives the full intention of the importance given it in the mind of this apostle.

BY THE MERCIES OF GOD... This can be taken two ways. First that the mercy of God is an active force in the ability to accomplish what Paul is about to say or second, that Paul's urging is in accompaniment with God's mercy. From here we enter into the three atmospheres that are necessary in order to know God's purpose and doing in your life.

The Atmosphere of Surrender

...to present your bodies a living and holy sacrifice, acceptable to God, which is your spiritual service of worship...

We may not get the full gist of this statement because of the difference of our culture and the culture of that time. That period of time reveals a culture that practiced sacrificing to gods. Rome was a heathen nation and a pagan nation. But the picture that Paul gave presented a stark realization.

> It is true that animal victims were living when they were brought to the altar (a dead animal could not be brought for sacrifice), but as offered they were dead. Paul can speak of believers as dying to sin, but his emphasis is on the glorious life they now live with Christ; they are "alive from the dead". As

offered they are alive. The sacrifice of which Paul writes demands not the destruction but the full energy of life. It is positive and dynamic. This sacrifice is also holy, which we understand as "consecrated" or "dedicated". It is given over entirely to God, the believer is His alone. Further, it is pleasing to God. [2]

I am not sure many have a correct view of this text in Romans. They may read it and understand what it said, but I don't think that they understand the depth of sacrifice that it is actually calling for. This is not a **show-up-on-Sunday-and-do-what-I-want-on-Monday-through-Saturday** attitude.

This is serious submission to a call for a whole lifetime span of a whole person. It is the giving of the *"full energy of life"* toward this endeavor. What would giving my whole life to the purpose of God look like? It would look like you have lost your mind to the world. It would look like you are a fanatic to some. Some will say that you have too much Jesus in your life.

Whatever the form looks like, it will involve persecution from the world, family and even brothers and sisters. It is not easy to give one's full energy to Jesus in a world that has so many things pulling upon their time and energies. Yet this giving is called your spiritual service of worship. Another version says it is your reasonable service. The word service in the Greek is a word that means working for a wage.

Luke 18:29-30 *And He said to them, "Truly I say to you, there is no one who has left house or wife or*

---

[2] –The Pillar New Testament Commentary

brothers or parents or children, for the sake of the
kingdom of God, who will not receive many times
as much at this time and in the age to come,
eternal life."

When we surrender, we put ourselves in a place where we can hear and understand God's will. God will communicate His will to His servants, however those that are waiting to hear in order to decide whether they want to follow that direction for their life, will never understand it nor hear it correctly.

God is inviting you to believe Him **before you hear Him**. In this way you are putting Him in a place of trust and reverence that shows your faith in Him. You are proving by your actions that God is faithful and whatever He asks you to do, He will empower you to do.

Atmosphere of Non-Conformity

"And do not be conformed to this world..." We cannot know the will of God while we are holding on to the vestiges of this world as we try to serve God. This section could be rendered, *"Do not be fashioned into a likeness that represents the pop culture of this age."*

When we conform to the age in which we live we say by our actions that we are not willing to be a part of the will of God for our lives. This will hide the will of God from us. Why is this? It is because friendship with the world is hostility toward God. You are actually asking God to tell you what He wants you to do while you dabble in Satan's system.

I don't think we take this serious enough with regard to the fashion of this world. The world seeks to identify you with it by conforming to its likeness. Can we say then that if we try to look like the world to win the world, we are conforming to the world? To answer that we need to look at the definition of the word *"conform."*

4964 *συσχηματίζω [suschematizo*

/soos·khay·mat·id·zo/] v. From 4862 and a derivative of 4976; GK 5372; Two occurrences; AV translates as "conform to" once, and "fashion (one's) self according to" once. **1** *to conform one's self (i.e. one's mind and character) to another's pattern, (fashion one's self according to). Additional Information: For synonyms see entry 4832,* **summorphos.***See entry 5873 for comparison of synonyms.* [3]

---

v **v**: verb

GK Goodrick-Kohlenberger

AV Authorized Version

[3]Strong, James: *The Exhaustive Concordance of the Bible : Showing Every Word of the Test of the Common English Version of the Canonical Books, and Every Occurence of Each Word in Regular Order.* electronic ed. Ontario : Woodside Bible Fellowship., 1996, S. G4964

It simply means to fashion one's self after another. So we could render it, *"And do not fashion yourself after this world."* Okay so we understand that we should not seek to be like the world but what does world really mean? Does it point to this present time; the globe we call earth; or a specific period of time that is defined by something that separates it from all other periods of time?

aiŐn.

The Nonbiblical Use. Meanings are a. "vital force," b. "lifetime," c. "age" or "generation," d. "time," and e. "eternity." [4]

1. AIŌN (αἰών , (165)), an age, era (to be

connected with aei̯, ever, rather than with aō, to breathe), signifies a period of indefinite duration, or time viewed in relation to what takes place in the period.

The force attaching to the word is not so much that of the actual length of a period, but that of a period marked by spiritual or moral characteristics. This is illustrated in the use of the adjective [see Note (1)

---

[4]Kittel, Gerhard ; Friedrich, Gerhard ; Bromiley, Geoffrey William: *Theological Dictionary of the New Testament*. Grand Rapids, Mich. : W.B. Eerdmans, 1995, c1985, S. 31

below] in the phrase "life eternal," in John 17:3, in respect of the increasing knowledge of God. [5]

The term *"world"* then is a period of time marked by certain characteristics much of which are moral. If you look at our history you can section it according to movements. In fact, we can see changes based upon generations. One generation is marked by this factor and another, that. You have generation X, Y, me generation, etc.

II Corinthians 4:4 *in whose case the **god of this world** has blinded the minds of the unbelieving so that they might not see the light of the gospel of the glory of Christ, who is the image of God.*

Satan is the god of this world. Note that the term *"world"* is the same as our definition earlier. This means that Satan is the one who is defining what is acceptable in this era. Each generation is marked by trying to stand out from previous generations. Satan seeks to degenerate each generation into an immoral spiral of sin. The devil seeks to steal our children and eventually destroy a whole nation.

If we look at other nations in our past we see this same pattern repeated over and over. Each generation is slightly more immoral than the one before it. This degeneration takes its people to destruction. With this information, I am convinced that God's people and especially God's leadership should not try to look like

---

[5]Vine, W.E. ; Bruce, F.F.: *Vine's Expository Dictionary of Old and New Testament Words*. Old Tappan NJ : Revell, 1981; Published in electronic form by Logos Research Systems, 1996, S. 43

the world in order to win the world. That was the message Jezebel was preaching to the church in Revelation.

God is not so impotent that we need to look like the world in order to get the world to listen to the gospel. The world understands power no matter what the latest fashion is. This is why Paul said that he did not come in the wisdom of men, but in the demonstration of the Spirit. The power of God's Word is able to reach the lost no matter what the vessel speaking it looks like. The anointing of God on a man or woman is all that is needed to reach the world. If you seek to look like the world to win the world, what reason would the world have to change if you look like them?

I have met so many people that have that one toe dipped in the world and they are shockingly unable to discern the will of God for their life. God does not accept partial sacrifices nor does He accept defective sacrifices. There is a reason the Old Covenant uses the term *"whole sacrifice."*

Can you imagine what God's response would have been if the priest only took a portion of the animal to sacrifice? God does not want your partiality and He does not want your lack of desire to fulfill His will. He does not want a part of you, He does not want half heartedness, He does not want feigned dedication, He does not want false platitudes, He does not want your lies, and He does not want anything less than all of you, your life, your desires, and your love.

Stand up, separate yourself from the world and allow God to transform you into the image of Christ. An image that does not change with each generation; an image that does not change with every style; an image that is unchangeable across all generations; an image that is attractive in every generation; and an image that will produce a harvest of souls because of the anointing that rest upon it.

Atmosphere of Transfiguration

"...but be transformed by the renewing of your mind..." The word *"transformed"* is the same word used for the transfiguration of Jesus. The renewing of the mind is not an automatic born again response. One has to diligently apply themselves to it.

> **Ephesians 4:20-24** But you did not learn Christ in this way, if indeed you have heard Him and have been taught in Him, just as truth is in Jesus, that, in reference to your former manner of life, you lay aside the old self, which is being corrupted in accordance with the lusts of deceit, and that you **be renewed in the spirit of your mind,** and put on the new self, which in the likeness of God has been **created** in righteousness and holiness of the **truth.**

The renewed spirit of the mind is created in truth. That means as you access and believe in the truth as presented by God in His Word, your mind is renewed. This puts that renewing of the mind in your control. We can have as much or little as we like.

> **Colossians 3:9-10** Do not lie to one another, since you laid aside the old self with its evil practices, and have put on the new self who is **being renewed to a true knowledge** according to the image of the One who created him—

Here again is the same idea. This third atmosphere of renewing the mind will produce in you the ability to know the will of God in your life. Paul also says, *"Let this mind be in you that was also in Christ Jesus"* (Philippians 2:5)

Do you think Jesus gave His complete life energy to the fulfillment of His call? You might say, *"Yeah but His calling was of mega proportions."* Does your call require less dedication?

It must be noted that there are many things that we do not need to seek God's will. The reason for this is that we already have instruction in the Word of God concerning the matter. I have had many requests for prayer to give instruction for something that was clearly revealed in the Word of God. I have had to tell people that God has already addressed this in His Word and when you are ready to come into agreement with His Word then you are going to be walking in His will.

Even the prophetic cannot override God's Word. If a prophet speaks a word that is contrary to God's Word, you are to follow after God's Word. Look at the following example.

> **Deuteronomy 13:1-4** *"If a prophet or a dreamer of dreams arises among you and gives you a sign or a wonder, and the sign or the wonder comes true, concerning which he spoke to you, saying, 'Let us go after other gods (whom you have not known) and let us serve them,' you shall not listen to the words of that prophet or that dreamer of dreams;* **for the Lord your God is testing you to find out if you love the Lord your God with all your heart and with all your soul.**

Too many times people want to believe something that is contrary to God's Word. They will cite this prophetic word or that prophetic word all the while ignoring the clear instruction given in Scripture. The weight of the Word of God is even higher than God's name. God placed His Word above His name.

Psalm 138:2 ~NKJV~ *I will worship toward Your holy temple, And praise Your name For Your lovingkindness and Your truth; For You have magnified Your word above all Your name.*

Abiding in the Vine

> *PURPOSE: Jesus was a master storyteller. He had the ability to take common surroundings and turn them into essential lessons that concern our lives. By doing this, it helps us to remember these lessons as we come in contact with these common surroundings. One of these stories is the story of "Abiding in the Vine." Gardeners especially will remember the lessons that Jesus taught through this story. As you consider the growth of plant life, let this story become a part of your life, and let it inform your life in a way that produces godly character.*

The Christian is promised many things in this life. Some of these things are joy, peace, contentment, love, answers to prayers, etc. As I look around me, I notice that so many Christians are not experiencing the life that the Word of God has promised us. When I asked the Lord why this is, He kept nudging at me in my spirit this Scripture in **John 15:7** which says, *"If you abide in me, and my words abide in you, ye shall ask what ye will, and it shall be done unto you."*

What would you say to the following? **Not everything you read in the Bible may be for you.** You may be reading something and think, *"Wow! That is for me!"* There are many examples of this but I want to zero in on one in particular.

Discipleship in the Context of Persecution

> **Matthew 10:24-25** *"A disciple is not above his teacher, nor a slave above his master. "It is enough for the disciple that he become like his teacher, and the slave like his master. If they have called the head of the house Beelzebul, how much more will they malign the members of his household!*

The context of the above text is obviously discipleship. Jesus is pointing out that those that are disciples will be maligned because Jesus was maligned. This is speaking of disciples. Not everyone who is a Christian is a disciple. There are those who believe in Jesus and repent of their sins and that is all they do. In fact I would argue that if we associate the same meaning to the term *"disciple"* as it was used in that time period, we could say that most Christians are not disciples.

> **Matthew 10:26-33** *"Therefore do not fear them, for there is nothing concealed that will not be revealed, or hidden that will not be known. "What I tell you in the darkness, speak in the light; and what you hear whispered in your ear, proclaim upon the housetops. "Do not fear those who kill the body but are unable to kill the soul; but rather fear Him who is able to destroy both soul and body in hell. "Are not two sparrows sold for a cent? And yet not one of them will fall to the ground apart from your*

Father. *"But the very hairs of your head are all
numbered. "So do not fear; you are more valuable
than many sparrows. "Therefore everyone who
confesses Me before men, I will also confess him
before My Father who is in heaven. "But whoever
denies Me before men, I will also deny him before
My Father who is in heaven.*

Remember that this piece of Scripture is addressed to the
disciple only. The disciple is the one who will suffer persecution.
But they also have a promise that your life is in the control of the
Creator.

*Matthew 10:34-37 "Do not think that I came to
bring peace on the earth; I did not come to bring
peace, but a sword. "For I came to SET A MAN AGAINST
HIS FATHER, AND A DAUGHTER AGAINST HER MOTHER, AND A
DAUGHTER-IN-LAW AGAINST HER MOTHER-IN-LAW; and A
MAN'S ENEMIES WILL BE THE MEMBERS OF HIS HOUSEHOLD.
"He who loves father or mother more than Me is
not worthy of Me; and he who loves son or
daughter more than Me is not worthy of Me.*

I found this portion especially interesting. I have watched
as people have made a commitment to become a disciple of Jesus
only to be persecuted by the members of their own family. It seems
that church attendance if just fine. But cross that border to become
a disciple and you have become a fanatic. It is at this point that
many families feel the need to rescue you. What is it that is so
offensive to people that one would become a disciple of Jesus?

Some have succumbed to the pressure and pulled out of
discipleship. It is to them that the last part of that text is quoted.
Jesus reveals that He is more worthy of our devotion then our own

parents. This does not mean that we mistreat our parents for the sake of Jesus. Jesus is the One who said, *"honor your mother and father."*

> **Matthew 10:38-40** *"And he who does not take his cross and follow after Me is not worthy of Me. "He who has found his life will lose it, and he who has lost his life for My sake will find it. "He who receives you receives Me, and he who receives Me receives Him who sent Me.*

I found it interesting that Jesus mentions picking up our cross before He went to the cross. I think we have misinterpreted this well known piece of Scripture. I've always been told that to pick up my cross was akin to pick up my suffering. I want to explore something else, especially in light of the context of discipleship.

If Jesus came to do the will of the Father and it was the will of the Father for Jesus to endure the cross, could it be the cross represented the destiny Jesus was to accomplish? If this is so, then Jesus was calling for disciples to pick up their destinies and to follow Him.

> **Matthew 10:40-42** *"He who receives you receives Me, and he who receives Me receives Him who sent Me. "He who receives a prophet in the name of a prophet shall receive a prophet's reward; and he who receives a righteous man in the name of a righteous man shall receive a righteous man's reward. "And whoever in the name of a disciple gives to one of these little ones even a cup of cold water to drink, truly I say to you, he shall not lose his reward."*

Many conversations and sermons have used this section of the Bible. Everyone seems to want to know what is a prophet's reward. However there is also mentioned a righteous man's reward. What I want to focus on is something different. What I find striking is that that we are talking about two individuals not one. After Jesus states that those that *"receive you receives me, and he who receives Me receives Him who sent Me."*

Then context is that when we receive a minister we receive those who sent them as well. Thus if we receive a prophet in the name of a prophet shall receive a prophet's reward. There are a couple of things that this could mean.

1. Jesus is a Prophet and those that receive a prophet in the name of Jesus the Prophet will receive a prophets reward.
2. That this actually points to discipleship is found in the revelation that a prophet is sent by another prophet. This points to the equipping ministry of the five-fold.

I think it is clear that we are looking at a prophetic statement by Jesus pointing to the existence and purpose of the five-fold ministry. Now let's shift to the Gospel of John.

Discipleship in the Context of Leadership

We are going to pick up in John where Jesus is about to wash His disciples' feet. It bears looking at because again the context is discipleship.

John 13:5-11 Then He poured water into the basin, and began to wash the disciples' feet and to wipe *them with the towel with which He was girded. So He came to Simon Peter. He said to Him, "Lord, do You wash my feet?" Jesus answered and said to him, **"What I do you do not realize now, but you will understand hereafter."** Peter said to Him, "Never shall You wash my feet!" Jesus answered him, "If I do not wash you, you have no part with Me." Simon Peter said to Him, "Lord, then wash not only my feet, but also my hands and my head." Jesus said to him, "He who has bathed needs only to wash his feet, but is completely clean; and you are clean, but not all of you." For He knew the one who was betraying Him; for this reason He said, "Not all of you are clean."*

This is a touching exchange between Jesus and His disciples. Remember that the context is the Mentor Jesus interacting with His students. When He began to wash Peter's feet, Peter rebelled immediately. Imagine the scene. Peter knows who Jesus is. It was Peter who confessed that Jesus was the Son of the living God. Peter had submitted himself to Jesus to be taught and equipped to be an accurate replica of Him who taught him.

To this reaction Jesus said something quite profound. He told Peter that, *"What I do you do not realize now, but you will understand hereafter."* When that was said Peter was a disciple. Hereafter however points to the time when Peter would be a minister. We can conclude that Jesus was addressing a time when Peter would be one of the leaders in the Church.

John 13:12 So when He had washed their feet, and taken His garments and reclined at the table again,

He said to them, "Do you know what I have done to you?

Jesus always accomplished something by His Words and His actions. The disciples only saw the moment and that Jesus was washing their feet. Jesus saw the future and what this washing of feet would accomplish in time. It wasn't just a demonstration but it was something done to them.

> *John 13:14-15 "If I then, the Lord and the Teacher, washed your feet, you also ought to wash one another's feet. "For I gave you an example that you also should do as I did to you.*

Now Jesus reveals what He did to them. He commanded them to do as He had done to one another. But think this out. Again, Jesus is addressing them for a time when His disciples would be leaders. We can assume then that Jesus wanted His disciples to serve one another as leaders. That is, Jesus was training them to do to one another as He had done to them.

This actually supports the concept of collegiate authority. You can learn more about the government of the Church from my book, ***"Church Government: Divine Order Produces Divine Presence."*** If the disciples were to treat one another in such humility and servitude, then they were not to exalt one person above another but rather serve one another. What would it look like if all leaders were of the mindset that they were servants to other leaders?

> *John 13:16-17 "Truly, truly, I say to you, a slave is not greater than his master, nor is one who is sent greater than the one who sent him. "If you know these things, you are blessed if you do them.*

Here is the same statement but in a different context of discipleship. This statement is used again after this one and it too is in a different context. Why I think this is so important is found in the fact that the statement, *"a disciple is not greater than their teacher or the one who sent them"* is found in the fact that it is used in three different contextual themes.

Discipleship in the Context of Student Relations

Luke 6:39-40 And He also spoke a parable to them: "A blind man cannot guide a blind man, can he? Will they not both fall into a pit? "A pupil is not above his teacher; but everyone, after he has been fully trained, will be like his teacher.

If one takes this in the teacher pupil relationship then it is without doubt that the student is seen as blind. However, when the leader is blind, the student really does not know because they are blind as well. This is why bad leaders are such a tragic reality of our time. What good leaders must do is point out the deeds of the bad leaders just as the apostle John did in his third letter.

The text takes a bit of turn at this point and begins to address the relationships between disciples. Note that we have dealt with the persecution of disciples and leaders, the relationships between leaders and now we answer the question, *"How should I treat my fellow student?"*

Luke 6:41-42 "Why do you look at the speck that is in your brother's eye, but do not notice the log that is in your own eye? "Or how can you say to your brother, 'Brother, let me take out the speck that is

in your eye,' when you yourself do not see the log
that is in your own eye? You hypocrite, first take
the log out of your own eye, and then you will see
clearly to take out the speck that is in your
brother's eye.

Recall that we started this section talking about the blind guides leading the blind student. In keeping with this theme Jesus now talks about a sliver and a log in the eye of the disciple. He cautions students to not be so quick to think that they see clearly to remove things in the lives of their fellow students.

It is about seeing. When we align our thoughts with those of the Creator, we see. Sight is walking in truth. Seeing is accessing reality. When we align our thoughts with the enemy, we walk in darkness and are blind. Blindness cannot access reality.

Luke 6:44-45 *"For each tree is known by its own*
fruit. For men do not gather figs from thorns, nor
do they pick grapes from a briar bush. "The good
man out of the good treasure of his heart brings
forth what is good; and the evil man out of the evil
treasure brings forth what is evil; for his mouth
speaks from that which fills his heart.

The result of blindness is that we produce bad fruit. The result of seeing is that we bear good fruit. What is found in the heart determines whether one is a good tree with good fruit or a bad tree with bad fruit. Blindness and seeing then is a matter of the heart. If it is a matter of the heart then we are talking about doctrine. Doctrine then has the ability to alter your behavior. The fruit of a tree represents our actions or behavior. Note the next thing Jesus says.

Luke 6:46-47 "Why do you call Me, 'Lord, Lord,' and
do not do what I say? "Everyone who comes to Me
and hears My words and acts on them, I will show
you whom he is like:

Jesus is talking only to disciples. This statement points
back to the good tree/bad tree statement. Bear in mind, the good
tree produces good fruit or behavior. Now we see what made the
bad tree, a bad tree. They hear what Jesus is saying but they do not
do what He says. If fruit or behavior is a condition of the heart,
then the student heard, but they did not believe. If they had
believed, they would have done.

Then Jesus brings the reader to the place where they can
see the result of these differences. Now He shows us the outcome
of the good tree and the bad tree. First we look at the good tree.

Luke 6:48 he is like a man building a house, who
dug deep and laid a foundation on the rock; and
when a flood occurred, the torrent burst against
that house and could not shake it, because it had
been well built.

We are talking about disciples. A good disciple, a good
tree, is likened to a person who digs deep into the Word and bases
his construction of his house upon the foundation rock. Note that
digging is needed to find foundation. We have a tendency to think
that foundation is the easy stuff. Think again. Foundation requires
a lot of work to solidify in one's life. Now let's look at the bad
tree.

Luke 6:49 "But the one who has heard and has not
acted accordingly, is like a man who built a house
on the ground without any foundation; and the

torrent burst against it and immediately it
collapsed, and the ruin of that house was great."

The bad disciple, the bad tree, is marked by the fact that he does not dig. He does not put any effort in his learning. He does just enough to get by. With no foundation there is nothing to anchor them and they have a fall. When disciples commit themselves to study, they are digging to find a foundation that will hold their building. Then when the storm comes, and it will come, they are able to stand.

Look at our culture today. There has been very little discipleship. In fact, during the sixties many church leaders were having difficulty with the questions that were being asked of the Christian faith. Because there was little foundation in the leadership, they did not have answers against the storms of Darwinism, secularism, or moral relativism.

Ephesians 4:14 As a result, we are no longer to be
children, tossed here and there by waves and
carried about by every wind of doctrine, by the
trickery of men, by craftiness in deceitful scheming;

As a result of what? What is it that brings us from the state of being easily deceived to seeing deception for what it was? It is discipleship. The equipping of the saints by the five-fold ministry.

Now we are going to shift again. We have looked at the three contextual themes surrounding the statement that a disciple is not greater than their teacher. Now I want to extend this a bit. The reason is that we need to read the Bible and understand where it is speaking to us and where it is not.

Chapters 13, 14, 15, and 16 of the Gospel of John are written to the disciple. A disciple is a disciple in the heart. It is a commitment to follow Christ and to give up our will and give heed to His will. I encourage you to read those chapters anew with the understanding that it is speaking to students of Christ. I would like to enumerate a few things that stood out to me though.

> **John 14:16-17** *"I will ask the Father, and He will give you another Helper, that He may be with you forever; that is the Spirit of truth, whom the world cannot receive, because it does not see Him or know Him, but you know Him because He abides with you and will be in you.*

The word *"helper"* is parakletos and it means *"one who pleads another's cause."* It is a word used for lawyer. Note also that Jesus used the term *"another"* to identify Himself as a parakletos as well. In fact the Bible does reveal Him in that role.

> **I John 2:1** *My little children, I am writing these things to you so that you may not sin. And if anyone sins, we have an Advocate with the Father, Jesus Christ the righteous;*

The word *"advocate"* is the same Greek word as *"helper."* Since Jesus is at the right hand of the Father in heaven, and the Holy Spirit is with us in the earth, we have a team of Lawyers fighting for us and the cause for which we are called. There are constant accusations being thrown at you by the devil.

> **Revelation 12:10** *Then I heard a loud voice in heaven, saying, "Now the salvation, and the power, and the kingdom of our God and the authority of His Christ have come,* **for the accuser of our brethren has been thrown down, he who accuses them before our God day and night.**

When we put it all together we get the picture of a court of law where you are the defendant and Satan is the plaintiff. The plaintiff is petitioning the court where the Righteous Judge, the Father sits. Our Advocate, Jesus, is there as our defense Lawyer to defend you against these accusations. This is a spiritual attack and is handled with complete success by our Advocate.

There is also a physical attack taking place against you as a Christian. As we have seen the world hates us as it did Jesus. Therefore we have human accusers in the earth and we need an Advocate here as well. Enter the Holy Spirit.

> *Mark 13:11* *"When they arrest you and hand you over, do not worry beforehand about what you are to say, but say whatever is given you in that hour; for it is not you who speak, but it is the Holy Spirit.*

Now let's shift to the next topic.

> *John 15:10* *"If you keep My commandments, you will abide in My love; just as I have kept My Father's commandments and abide in His love.*

> *I John 3:24* *The one who keeps His commandments abides in Him, and He in him. We know by this that He abides in us, by the Spirit whom He has given us.*

What did Jesus mean when He said, *"If you abide in me?"* The word *"abide"* means to dwell, continue, stay, sojourn, and rest in or upon. **It is being fixed and remaining there, continuing on and on in a fixed state, condition, or being.**

These statements of Christ are conditional statements. It is not enough for us to say that we abide in the love of God. **We must first keep His commandments.** Most people think immediately that this is speaking of the Ten Commandments.

Remember we are talking about disciples. We need to think beyond the commandments we have in writing.

> **John 14:31** *but so that the world may know that I love the Father,* ***I do exactly as the Father commanded Me.*** *Get up, let us go from here.*

Here the same Greek word is used but it is clearly speaking of Jesus following the purpose for which the Father had sent Him. Now, if we carry this forward to today, we can say that Jesus has commanded you for a specific purpose. If you love Him keep His commandments.

Note that the word *"commandment"* means an order, command, charge, precept, or injunction. Your charge is the very thing for which you were also created. If you love Him who set you free from sin, than do what He created you to do.

Reflection

At the moment Jesus began to teach on the vine, He was facing the most cruel and barbaric execution a man could face at that time. If that were not enough, many of His own followers had already left Him. Even His inner circle of disciples were going to reject Him and run for their lives. A betrayal was in progress from one of these close companions. The world He had come to save was about to crucify Him. Yet, with all of this hanging over His head, He was ready to teach His disciples another lesson.

This lesson however, would be a lesson that would stick with them for the rest of their lives. It may seem simple to the casual onlooker, but to the serious student of the Word these are Words of life! This story is one of relationship. Not only the relationship that Jesus has with His creation, but more importantly it points out the relationship His creation has with Him. As we step into this story, let the words of it go deep into your soul. Let the lessons learned here, direct your life from this day forward. Let this story bring life to your soul!

> **John 15:1** *"I am the true vine, and my Father is the husbandman."*

- **Jesus** is the Vine;
  - He is the genuine Vine, not a false or counterfeit vine.
- **God** is the Vinedresser or the Gardener;
  - He is the One who carefully planted the Vine (Christ) and He is the One who cares for the Vine and the branches. He is the One who prunes and purges, cleans and protects the Vine and its branches.
- **Men** are the branches.
  - They are all judged on the basis of how they relate to the true Vine.

There are two divisions. Division one is revealed in the fact that we have two types of branches, attached and unattached branches. This corresponds to those who are believers and those who are not. Division two is a subdivision of the attached branches and are revealed through being either **unfruitful** or **fruitful**.

> **John 15:2-3** *"Every branch in me that **beareth not fruit** he taketh away: and every branch that **beareth fruit,** he purgeth it, that it may bring forth more fruit. Now ye are clean through the word which I have spoken unto you."*

The Father deals differently with those who bear fruit and

those that do not. Those that do not are taken away. They are virtually cut off of the vine. We need to understand what this means and we will be sure to cover this in a bit.

> **John 15:4-5** *"Abide in me, and I in you. As the branch cannot bear fruit of itself, except it abide in the vine, no more can ye, except ye abide in me. I am the vine, ye are the branches: He that abideth in me, and I in him, the same bringeth forth much fruit: for without me ye can do nothing."*

Fruit bearing is the goal of the believer. Yet, the believer cannot bear fruit by themselves. They must be abiding in the vine and by that vine fruit is developed.

> **John 15: 6-8** *"If a man abides not in me, he is cast forth as a branch, and is withered; and men gather them, and cast them into the fire, and they are burned. If you abide in me, and my words abide in you, ye shall ask what ye will, and it shall be done unto you. Herein is my Father glorified, that ye bear much fruit; so shall you be my disciples."*

We have some among us that are believers, but they are *"UNFRUITFUL branches."* It would be wise of us to take note of what happens to these branches that are unfruitful. **They are taken away!**

They are actually abiding in the vine, yet they are producing nothing from that relationship. This means that as believers, they must have come to faith in Christ in order to be attached to the vine. They probably were also baptized and they might even be faithful members of a church. Yet they are not producing anything.

If we are to understand these things we need to seek the meaning of being unfruitful. If people can be Christians and yet unfruitful with results in their being cut off and taken away, I think it is vital for us to get the understanding so that we can make adjustments.

> **Matthew 13:22 (KJV)** *"He also that received the seed among the thorns is he that heareth the word; and the care of this world, and the deceitfulness of riches, choke the word, and he becometh unfruitful."*

Here is a clue to what Jesus is communicating to us. If the care of this world, the deceitfulness of riches are what causes unfruitfulness, then it could be argued that the absence of these qualities would produce an environment conducive to bearing fruit. That begs the question, what would that environment look like? We must go back to the Scriptures to find the answer.

> **Matthew 6:31-33** *"Do not worry then, saying, 'What will we eat?' or 'What will we drink?' or 'What will we wear for clothing?' "For the Gentiles eagerly seek all these things; for your heavenly Father knows that you need all these things. "But seek first His kingdom and His righteousness, and all these things will be added to you.*

The absence of those things that choke the Word is an environment produced by prioritizing the seeking of the kingdom of God. Jesus said to *"seek first."* That means that even the acquiring of food and shelter are to take a back seat to seeking the kingdom of God. Okay, so what does it mean to seek the kingdom of God?

Matthew 13:45-46 *"Again, the kingdom of heaven is like a merchant seeking fine pearls, and upon finding one pearl of great value, he went and sold all that he had and bought it.*

The Old Testament is full of statements about seeking the Lord. If you look at them you will get a sense that seeking the Lord means that you are learning of Him, seeking to know Him, and inquiring of Him for your needs. For instance, when faced with trouble, God wants you to seek Him first. When you lack understanding, God wants you to ask for wisdom from Him first.

The value of what you seek determines how diligently you seek for it. Those pearls are those great promises made by God on behalf of His creation. Note the last verse of our abiding in the vine Scripture.

John 15:8 *"My Father is glorified by this, that you bear much fruit, and so prove to be My disciples.*

Based upon that section of text, bearing fruit is the proof that you are His disciple. That means that being His disciple will also produce fruit. Bear with me on this, we are going somewhere. Not that the Father is glorified by our bearing much fruit. From this we can deduce further what it means to bear fruit.

John 17:4 *"I glorified You on the earth, having accomplished the work which You have given Me to do.*

Let's put it all together now. If glorifying God is accomplishing the work God has given you to do, and if bearing much fruit glorifies the Father, then bearing much fruit is accomplishing the work God has given you to do. Being unfruitful then is refusing to enter into one's calling and destiny to accomplish those things God has called them to accomplish.

Now it makes sense, the care of the world and the pursuit of riches makes me unfruitful precisely because I am focused on everything but my true calling and destiny. Now that we have identified what it means to be unfruitful, it is time for us to take an audit of our lives to see if we have fallen into unfruitfulness. I would urge you to take a moment and recommit yourself to the pursuit of the kingdom of God by picking up your purpose and begin doing the thing God created you to do.

This goes much deeper than I am able to go here in this writing. I just want you to be convinced of the importance in following your created purpose and the possible consequences in ignoring your created purpose. Now it is time to look at those consequences.

> *I John 5:16* "If anyone sees his brother committing a sin that does not lead to death, he will ask; and God will give him life for those whose sinning does not lead to death. There is sin that does lead to death; I am not saying he should pray' about that."

First, we must define the terms in order to understand what is being said here. To begin, let's define *"brother."* Brother clearly is referring to those who have come to a faith in Christ. It is a fellow believer. This means that a Christian can commit a sin that causes their untimely death. How many people have heard this preached from the pulpit? The Scripture is clear on this.

Examples of "Taken Away"

B. Moses because of sin was taken away.

Deuteronomy 32:48-52 (NKJV) *"Then the Lord spoke to Moses that very same day, saying: 'Go up this mountain of the Abarim, Mount Nebo, which is in the land of Moab, across from Jericho; view the land of Canaan, which I give to the children of Israel as a possession; and die on the mountain which you ascend, and be gathered to your people, just as Aaron your brother died on Mount Hor and was gathered to his people; because you trespassed against Me among the children of Israel at the waters of Meribah Kadesh, in the Wilderness of Zin, because you did not hallow Me in the midst of the children of Israel. Yet you shall see the land before you, though you shall not go there, into the land which I am giving to the children of Israel.'"*

C. Ananias and Sapphira because of sin were taken away.

Acts 5:1-11 (NKJV) *"But a certain man named Ananias, with Sapphira his wife, sold a possession. And he kept back part of the proceeds, his wife also being aware of it, and brought a certain part and laid it at the apostles' feet.*

But Peter said, "Ananias, why has Satan filled your heart to lie to the Holy Spirit and keep back part of the price of the land for yourself? While it remained, was it not your own? And after it was sold, was it not in your own control? Why have you conceived this thing in your heart? You have not lied to men but to God."

Then Ananias, hearing these words, fell down and breathed his last. So great fear came upon all those who heard these things. And the young men arose and wrapped him up, carried him out, and buried him.

Now it was about three hours later when his wife came in, not knowing what had happened. And Peter answered her, "Tell me whether you sold the land for so much?" She said, "Yes, for so much." Then Peter said to her, "How is it that you have agreed together to test the Spirit of the Lord? Look, the feet of those who have buried your husband are at the door, and they will carry you out."

Then immediately she fell down at his feet and breathed her last. And the young men came in and found her dead, and carrying her out, buried her by her husband. So great fear came upon all the church and upon all who heard these things."

D. Nadab and Abihu because of sin were taken away.

Leviticus 10:1-2 (NCV) " Aaron's sons Nadab and Abihu took their pans for burning incense, put fire in them, and added incense; but they did not use the special fire Moses had commanded them to use in the presence of the Lord. So fire came down from the Lord and destroyed Nadab and Abihu, and they died in front of the Lord."

E. The man who had slipped into a shameful, immoral sin was taken away.

I Corinthians 5:1-5 (ESV) "It is actually reported that there is sexual immorality among you, and of a kind that is not tolerated even among pagans, for a man has his father's wife. And you are arrogant! Ought you not rather to mourn? Let him who has done this be removed from among you.

For though absent in body, I am present in spirit; and as if present, I have already pronounced judgment on the one who did such a thing. When you are assembled in the name of the Lord Jesus and my spirit is present, with the power of our Lord Jesus, you are to deliver this man to Satan for the destruction of the flesh, so that his spirit may be saved in the day of the Lord."

Here we have examples of people of God who, because of sin, were taken away in physical death. We know from the Bible that being fruitful refers to **a refusal to enter in to the pursuit of one's purpose.**

Unfruitful Branches

I Corinthians 3:11-15 "For no man can lay a foundation other than the one which is laid, which is Jesus Christ. Now if any man builds on the foundation with gold, silver, precious stones, wood, hay, straw, each man's work will become evident; for the day will show it because **it is to be revealed with fire**, and the fire itself will test the quality of each man's work. If any man's work which he has built on it remains, he will receive a reward. If any *man's work is burned up, he will suffer loss; **but he himself will be saved, yet so as through fire."***

This is the proof that even if you happen to stand before Christ having been unfruitful, you will suffer loss, but you will be saved. That means the unfruitful Christian, could be cut off from the vine and find their works being judged. Even though there are no works from which to derive a reward, they are saved but as by fire.

Yet, would it not be better to abide in Christ while you have life here and allow the Spirit of God to cause your life to be fruitful rather than refusing to abide in Christ to the point of bearing fruit and having your life cut short? I want to remind you that without Christ you can do nothing. **Your good fruit is only an extension of God's work in you.**

Conclusion

> *Rev. 3:20 "Behold, I stand at the door and knock; if anyone hears and listens to and heeds My voice and opens the door, I will come in to him and will eat with him, and he [will eat] with Me."*

Jesus wants to be a part of your life, but He will not force you to do His will. You possess a free will. When you refuse to allow God to be a part of your life, God respects your decision. As long as you have breath, He will never stop knocking at the door of your heart.

That verse was speaking to those who were already Christians, yet He is on the outside knocking, inviting the person to open up and let Him in. He wants to be a part of you and for you to be a part of Him. Doing so will have the natural effect of producing fruit in your life.

> **Revelation 3:15-16** *'I know your deeds, that you are neither cold nor hot; I wish that you were cold or hot. 'So because you are lukewarm, and neither hot nor cold, I will spit you out of My mouth.*

Revealed in this verse is that the condition of being hot, cold, or luke warm is found by your deeds. God knows when we are half hearted in our show of works. Cold would be the outright denial of one's purpose in exchange for pursuing their own interests. Hot would be defined by full hearted energetic pursuit of God calling upon your life. Being lukewarm is defined as a half hearted attempt at destiny.

A tree does not struggle to produce fruit; it is the natural result of what type of tree it is and to what root it is attached. By abiding in Him, you will produce peace, contentment, love, and answers to prayers in your life. You will find your purpose and access destiny simply by abiding in Him. Abide in Him and become a fruit bearer today.

Buried With Christ

Chapter Seven

> *PURPOSE: In this chapter we will reveal the power of water baptism and the tangible effect that it has on one's life. You will discover the three-fold purpose that this rite serves from both an Old Testament and New Testament perspective.*

When men and women as students of the Word begin to discuss doctrinal issues there are bound to be some nuances that are not easily reconciled. That is much the case with the subject of baptism. When I first wrote this lesson, I realized when I read it back to myself that I had just repeated all of the clichés that are so often associated with water baptism. When I seen this I erased the entire lesson and cleared my mind of any preconceived ideas on baptism and approached it from a Hebraic perspective. I was so excited as to what I discovered that I could not wait to share them with you. Before I get into the material, I want to state that there are three major arguments in the Church concerning baptism.

1. Does baptism amount to salvation or is it simply an act of faith?
2. By what method, sprinkling or immersion, are we truly baptized?

3. Is infant baptism a valid choice or is adult baptism the only way?

My goal in this writing was not to settle these contentions but rather to identify what baptism is and in doing that, I believe we will answer those arguments listed above. As we move forward in this lesson, these things will become clearer, and it will be easy to answer all the questions concerning this issue of baptism. Then, at the end of this lesson, we will revisit these controversies to see if they are finally answered.

I want to stress how important it is to relinquish any preconceptions you may have on baptism until you have finished reading this chapter. Doing so will allow you to hear what is being said. I am not asking you to check your logic at the door, I am only asking that you hear what I have to say and then judge it. I think that when we are finished you will see how important this issue is to all of us, and what ramification it has on our Christian walk.

Definitions

In defining what is meant by the word *"baptism,"* we need to see if this is a concept that was understood by the Hebrews already or it is something new. If baptism is a practice that is already established in the Hebrew culture then we need to start with their understanding of it in order to get a thorough understanding of this practice.

The Hebrew people indeed were familiar with the concept of baptism. We can see this by the reaction of the Hebrews to John the Baptist. Even the religious leaders wanted to be baptized by him.

Kabac - *to wash*

Rachats - *to bath*

Mikveh - *It literally means a reservoir. It is from the root word that means to bind together.*

Baptize - *immersion or dipped. There is also the sense of washing as in the Hebrew.*

Baptism - *Our English word is obviously from the Greek and carries the same meaning, "to dip."*

All three definitions carry the idea of washing or taking a bath. This is an important concept to cling to when defining this Christian ceremony.

Old Testament Application

Baptism to the Jew had three major ideas: **purification**, **priestly rite**, and the **wedding**. When we read the New Testament, it is easy to forget that the terms and acts that were done at that time most always stemmed from a Jewish cultural understanding. There was no need to explain why they did certain things because it was culturally understood. That is why it is vital to our understanding that we go back to that culture to get a complete understanding of the topics that we study. Without doing so, we run the risk of misinterpreting them, and we can even unknowingly introduce heresy.

Baptism was not foreign to the Jew. It wasn't as if John was introducing a new concept to the Jewish people. If he had, he would have had to explain himself. Yet when we look at the story we see no attempt to explain himself. It was as if the people of that culture already understood what he was doing.

Purification

God instituted various ceremonial washings that were an act of purification. The idea of washing off the filth is of course only ritual as water is incapable of washing the soul. It was only a symbol of God's washing of the inner man. Here are some examples of symbolic washing.

- Lepers could not eat of the sacrifice until they washed their bodies.
- If a leper was healed, he was commanded to bathe before showing himself to the priest.
- Anyone who came in contact with an article of clothing or furniture of a person who had a sore that was flowing was to wash.
- After the High Priest sent the scapegoat away, he was required to wash his whole body.

This is not a complete list of ceremonial washings for purification. There are many more. Also, anyone who was not a Jew but wanted to convert to Judaism had to undergo a baptism before he would be considered a Jew. As we can see, baptism was not foreign to the Jew.

Priestly Rite

All those who entered the priesthood had to undergo a baptism before they were considered a priest. It was considered a rite of passage.

Jewish Wedding

When a wedding contract was agreed upon by the groom and the bride, (engagement or betrothal) the bride would take a bath. It is called the **mikveh**. This Hebrew word is from the root word translated *"wait"* or *"qavah"* but had the meaning of binding together.

> *Isaiah 40:31 (NKJV) But those who **wait** on the Lord shall renew their strength; they shall mount up with wings like eagles, they shall run and not be weary, they shall walk and not faint.*

It was a sign of consecration. The bride was saying that she was setting herself apart for her husband; that she was binding herself to him, and that she was to remain pure while waiting for his return. This was called *"kiddushin"* in Jewish culture (literally, *"being set apart for God"*).

This should firm up in your own mind that baptism was a regular practice by the Jew. This is why no one asked John what he was doing. They understood it from the start. Now let us look at the New Testament application.

John the Baptist brought baptism to the forefront right from the beginning of his ministry. It is important to note that John's baptism was called the *"baptism of repentance."*

> **Mark 1:4** *John the Baptist appeared in the wilderness preaching a baptism of repentance for the forgiveness of sins.*

The Greek word for *"repentance"* means to change your mind. With that definition, it was a baptism of changing your mind for the forgiveness of sins. The idea being that we are making a shift from the Old Covenant sacrifice to the ultimate sacrifice that ushers in a New Covenant. In order to have my sins forgiven by this New Covenant, it requires a change of my mind. I must now embrace Christ and what He has done for me rather than the ceremonial sacrifice of lambs.

When the Pharisees came to John to be baptized, John called them a den of vipers and told them that they need to bring forth fruits of repentance. They needed to demonstrate by their actions that they repented before he would baptize them.

> **John 3:25-30 (NKJV)** *Then there arose a dispute between some of John's disciples and the Jews about **purification**. And they came to John and said to him, "Rabbi, He who was with you beyond the Jordan, to whom you have testified—behold, He is **baptizing**, and all are coming to Him!"*
>
> *John answered and said, "A man can receive nothing unless it has been given to him from heaven. You yourselves bear me witness, that I*

*said, 'I am not the Christ,' but, 'I have been sent before Him.' He who has the **bride** is the bridegroom; but the friend of the bridegroom, who stands and hears him, rejoices greatly because of the bridegroom's voice. Therefore this joy of mine is fulfilled. He must increase, but I must decrease.*

In this one section of Scripture there is the tying together of purification, baptism, and being a bride. The language was such that the people understood what was being said. Nothing new is being presented, but John is preparing the way for Jesus to come. What does is mean *"to prepare the way?"* I believe it was to prepare people to think differently about the forgiveness of sins. In this, John was preparing the way for the message of Jesus.

Purification

In order for faith to be completed, there must be an action that is the proof of one's belief. In the Old Testament, that action was circumcision. In the New Testament, it is baptism.

> *James 2:22 You see that faith was working with his works, and as a result of the works, faith was perfected.*

Consecration

Consecration has the idea of setting something or someone aside. To consecrate yourself to God means that you make a conscious decision to set yourself apart to Christ. It is the action of baptism that says, I am setting myself apart to you Jesus; I believe in you and I am promising to keep myself pure. That is, I will not serve or worship any other. Hence, baptism is actually making a statement of devotion.

It needs to be noted that one is not baptized into an organization or denomination. I have heard people make declarations like that. If I am in a Baptist church and I am baptized there, it does not make me a Baptist. That is a pollution of the concept of baptism.

Priestly Rite

If baptism is just the washing away of sin, then why was the sinless Christ baptized at the age of thirty?

> *Matthew 3:13-15 Then Jesus arrived from Galilee at the Jordan coming to John, to be baptized by him. But John tried to prevent Him, saying, "I have need to be baptized by You, and do You come to me?" But Jesus answering said to him, "Permit it at this time; for in this way it is fitting for us to fulfill all righteousness." Then he permitted Him.*

Remember, John refused to baptize some because they had not repented of their sins.

> *Matthew 3:7-8 But when he saw many of the Pharisees and Sadducees coming for baptism, he said to them, "You brood of vipers, who warned you to flee from the wrath to come? Therefore bear fruit in keeping with repentance;"*

John's reaction to Jesus when Jesus asked John to baptize Him shows that John believed Jesus to be sinless. John refused at first and then said that it was he who needed to be baptized by Jesus. What then was the necessity of Jesus being baptized?

Some commentators say that Jesus just wanted to identify Himself with sinners. In Jesus' response to John, He makes the statement that He must be baptized to *"fulfill all righteousness."* If righteousness is the observance of the divine law, and Jesus has never broken any divine law, could it be that Jesus needed to be baptized in order to **operate legally** as a high priest? Note also that the baptism of Jesus marked the beginning of His ministry. Jesus is also at the age of thirty, and the Levite had to attain that age before they were allowed to minister as a priest.

Something else needs to be brought out here. John's father was a high priest. That means that they were Levites. Levites were a priestly tribe, and this would make John a priest as well. In order to be a priest, one had to descend from the tribe of Levi. However, Jesus was from the tribe of Judah. How then can Jesus be our High Priest if He is not from the tribe of Levi?

He could not without breaking His own Law unless there was a priesthood of another order. That is why in Hebrews it states that Jesus is a High Priest after the order of Melchizedek. This Melchizedek was the first priest mentioned in the Bible, and he existed even before the tribe of Levi or Levi himself for that matter. Could it be that John, being a priest after the Levitical order, needed to transfer the priesthood to another order, that of Melchizedek?

I believe this to be the case because Jesus uses the term *"us."* He said, *"...it is fitting for US to fulfill all righteousness."* Therefore, John was playing a very crucial role in fulfilling righteousness that Jesus could not fill alone. Jesus could not have entered the temple in heaven unless He was a High Priest. Becoming a high priest was necessary for Him in order to offer His own blood for our salvation, and in this He fulfilled all righteousness!

Baptism can be seen as a rite of passage from one thing to another.

Noah's flood is identified with baptism. He went from an environment where there was no rain, where there was a water canopy around the earth to an earth where it rained.

Moses' passing through the Red Sea is identified with baptism. The Jews went from a place of slavery, to a place of freedom on the other side of that sea.

Therefore, it would be in keeping with that theme that the priesthood was passing from the order of the Levites to the order of Melchizedek. Now we must deal with the question, *"What does the priestly rite of baptism have to do with us?"*

> ***Revelation 1:5-6 (NKJV)*** *and from Jesus Christ, the faithful witness, the firstborn from the dead, and the ruler over the kings of the earth. To Him Who loved us and washed us from our sins in His own blood, and **has made us kings and priests** to His God and Father, to Him be glory and dominion forever and ever. Amen.*

> ***1 Peter 2:9-10 (NKJV)*** *But you are a chosen generation, **a royal priesthood**, a holy nation, His own special people, that you may proclaim the praises of Him who called you out of darkness into*

His marvelous light; who once were not a people
but are now the people of God, who had not
obtained mercy but now have obtained mercy.

If we look at Melchizedek, we see that he was a priest and a king. It was the joining of the political and religious systems. Now we are called royal or kingly priests. We, too, are operating as priests after the order of Melchizedek.

Jewish Wedding

Again, the Jewish wedding is a picture of our complete relationship to Jesus. We believers are identified several times as the Bride of Christ. When we are baptized, we are setting ourselves apart to Christ just as a bride through the ritual of the mikveh is setting herself aside for her husband. We are telling Him that we are making the vow of chastity to Him as our husband. We are promising that He will be the one to whom we will be faithful. We are telling Him that we believe that He will come back for us just as the Jewish groom comes back for his wife.

Also, note that the bride does not take the ceremonial bath until she has entered into covenant with her husband and has agreed to be his bride. This is important to note because baptism has to be an act of one's free will. A bride commits adultery by joining herself to another man. How is it that we, being the Bride of Christ, can be unfaithful to Him as our husband?

*1 John 2:15-16 Do not **love** the world nor the things*
in the world. If anyone loves the world, the love of
the Father is not in him. For all that is in the world,
the lust of the flesh and the lust of the eyes and the

boastful pride of life, is not from the Father, but is from the world.

***James 4:4** You **adulteresses,** do you not know that friendship with the world is hostility toward God? Therefore whoever wishes to be a friend of the world makes himself an enemy of God.*

How we become adulterous, is by loving the world and the things of the world. After the bride takes her bath of consecration in the Jewish culture of that time, she would put on the veil for the first time and she would not take it off. The veil told the world of men that she was devoted to someone. Our confession of Christ is our veil. By confessing Him before men, we are saying that we are devoted to Him.

Other Pictures of Baptism

Noah and the Flood

***1 Peter 3:20-22 (NKJV)** who formerly were disobedient, when once the divine longsuffering waited in the days of Noah, while the ark was being prepared, in which a few, that is, eight souls, **were saved through water.** There is also an antitype which now saves us—baptism (not the removal of the filth of the flesh, but the answer of a good conscience toward God), **through the resurrection of Jesus Christ,** Who has gone into heaven and is at the right hand of God, angels and authorities and powers having been made subject to Him.*

We need to recognize the beautiful picture presented here. In the flood of Noah, water represents a baptism of eight people. Before we can bring clarity to this story, we need to understand the representation that is revealed. First, it must be understood that the water was actually the judgment of God upon the earth. Noah and his family safely traversed the floodwaters while God shut them up in the ark. Now if we apply that understanding to baptism, we see that it represents our passing safely through the water or judgment of God upon our sin without being harmed by it. Why are we not harmed by God's judgment on our sin? Look at the Scripture, it tells us that we were protected because of the resurrection of Jesus.

The resurrection of Christ represents the satisfaction of His sacrifice by the Judge of Heaven. The blood of Christ was payment enough for our sins. Thus, in baptism, we ceremoniously go through the water of God's judgment safely, while the wicked or unbeliever in us, is destroyed or left behind. This picture is repeated.

Moses and the Red Sea

I Corinthians 10:2 (NKJV) all were baptized into Moses in the cloud and in the sea,

The picture is the same as Noah. Moses and the nation of Israel passed safely through the Red Sea. When Pharaoh's army pursued them, they were drowned in the sea. God's people pass through His judgment (water) safely, while the wicked are consumed by it. Note also that this took place after the blood of the lamb had been applied to their houses.

Death by Drowning

*Romans 6:1-7 (ESV) What shall we say then? Are we to continue in sin that grace may abound? By no means! How can we who **died to sin** still live in it? Do you not know that all of us who have been baptized into Christ Jesus were **baptized into His death?** We were **buried therefore with Him by baptism into death,** in order that, just as Christ was raised from the dead by the glory of the Father, we too might walk in newness of life. For if we have been united with Him in a death like his, we shall certainly be united with Him in a resurrection like His. We know that our old self was crucified with Him in order that the body of sin might be brought to nothing, so that we would no longer be enslaved to sin. For one who has died has been set free from sin.*

The idea from this Scripture is in keeping with the thoughts of Noah and Moses concerning the flood and sea. When we are baptized, there is a part of us that dies and there is a part of us that lives. The wicked self is symbolically killed through drowning just as the wicked were killed in the flood and in the Red Sea.

Why is this important? This may make more sense once you read the chapter titled *"Amazing Grace."* For now, I will just say the import of baptism is found in the knowledge that we have not obtained all of our redemption presently. Being baptized then is a ceremony that celebrates that which is to come. Much as the ceremonial law is to the Jews of the Old Testament, baptism is to the people of the New Testament.

The true self that was made righteous by faith in Jesus symbolically passes through the judgment of God safely. When I am baptized, I am agreeing with God that my sins are judged in the body of Jesus and I pass safely through God's judgment. If God's judgment has come and I am still alive afterwards, then one can assume with great probability that they are saved.

Conclusion

Baptism is an act of purification.

When we willfully participate in baptism, we are making the decision to set our self aside from the rest of the world and we are giving our self wholly unto God.

Baptism initiates all believers into a royal priesthood.

When we willfully participate in baptism, we are each made into a kingly priest, joining both the political and religious systems. We rule and reign with Christ as our King.

Baptism is a sign of our betrothal to Christ.

When we willfully participate in baptism, we are betrothing ourselves to our Husband, Jesus. We are saying by the action of baptism that we will faithfully wait for Him to return for us and we will not adulterate ourselves with the world.

We gather from all of this evidence that baptism is not just a ceremony to be entered into lightly. We must first resolve ourselves to be faithful to Christ. Even though we are commanded to be baptized, it is still a willful choice on our part. We are also commanded to love, yet we do not always love. Baptism is your decision, but take note of its meaning and chose solemnly whether to proceed or not.

Arguments

Now that we have examined the reasons of baptism, let us revisit the controversies I mentioned in the beginning of this lesson. I would like to raise one problem that is associated with two of these arguments.

If we hold that baptism is the means of salvation, and then follow that doctrine with the doctrine of infant baptism, infant baptism then becomes a way of salvation for that individual.

- In this position, faith is eliminated.
- Works are then instituted as the means of salvation.
- This results in a false conversion.

If we hold that baptism is NOT the means of salvation, then infant baptism is harmless as a practice so long as there is no inference to salvation by infant baptism in the life of that individual. However, one must understand that this act has no validity in Scripture and that the parents possibly subject their child to a belief that their salvation is secure in their baptism as an infant rather than a faith in the Son of God.

One more problem is that infant baptism amounts to baptism by force; therefore, it cannot count on behalf of the individual being baptized. What I mean by that is, there was not a choice made by the infant to be baptized; therefore, they were baptized by force.

Is Baptism the Act of Being Saved?

If baptism is the act of being saved, then why do we need faith? It is the same controversy that is found in Judaism. Does circumcision make one a Jew or does faith make one a Jew? Does baptism make one a Christian, or does faith make one a Christian? Paul answers this for us in Romans.

> ***Romans 4:9-12*** *Is this blessing then on the circumcised or on the uncircumcised also? For we say, "Faith was credited to Abraham as righteousness." How then was it credited? While he was circumcised or uncircumcised? Not while circumcised, but while uncircumcised; and he received the sign of circumcision, a seal of the righteousness of the faith which he had while uncircumcised, so that he might be the father of all who believe without being circumcised, that righteousness might be credited to them, and the father of circumcision to those who not only are of the circumcision, but who also follow in the steps of the faith of our father Abraham which he had while uncircumcised.*

Paul reveals that circumcision took place after righteousness was credited because of faith. Likewise, baptism only makes sense after someone believes, not before. It is like circumcision in that it is a seal of our faith. The confusion over this argument is based on a translation of the text in the King James Version of the Bible. The Scripture in question is:

> **I Peter 3:20-21 ~KJV~** *Which sometime were disobedient, when once the longsuffering of God waited in the days of Noah, while the ark was a preparing, wherein few, that is, eight souls were* **saved by water**. *The like figure whereunto even baptism doth also now save us (not the putting away of the filth of the flesh, but the answer of a good conscience toward God,) by the resurrection of Jesus Christ:*

The word *"by"* in the phrase *"saved by water"* is the word in question. The word is also translated *"through."* This last sense is what the word denotes. That is, I am not saved **by** the water; I am saved **through** the water. If we look at the components of baptism, it brings clarity to the text. The problem is that the English word *"by"* can mean *"with the use of or help of"* or it can mean *"up to, beyond, or past."* The later is the sense used and we can prove that by looking closely at the flood.

In the story of Noah, the ark represented their safety and the water represented God's judgment. We are saved by the ark representation, not the water representation. Our problem is the presence of the water. The water is there to kill the sinner. It is the judgment of God. We are sinners and God's justice is found manifest in His judgment.

Baptism then becomes the picture of passing *"through, beyond, and past"* the judgment of God while safely hidden in Christ, our Ark. Look at how the New American Standard renders that same Scripture.

> *I Peter 3:20-21 who once were disobedient, when the patience of God kept waiting in the days of Noah, during the construction of the ark, in which a few, that is, eight persons, were **brought safely through the water.** Corresponding to that, baptism now saves you—not the removal of dirt from the flesh, but an appeal to God for a good conscience—through the resurrection of Jesus Christ,*

If we are to read it in the sense of being saved by water, then the components of the story of Noah no longer make sense. It only makes sense when we read it in tension with the flood of Noah. When we apply the components correctly to the story it brings meaning to the text.

To Sprinkle or Immerse

Which method is the valid method? First, we must understand that for the picture of being drowned to be retained, one must be immersed. The word *"baptism"* means to be immersed. However, in situations where one cannot be immersed, whether by lack of a body of water or the health of an individual, sprinkling is also acceptable.

> *Ezekiel 36:24-25 "For I will take you from the nations, gather you from all the lands and bring you into your own land. **Then I will sprinkle clean water** on you, and you will be clean; I will cleanse you from all your filthiness and from all your idols."*

Amazing Grace

> **PURPOSE:** *To give the reader a thorough knowledge of the provision of the cross in relation to his or her eternal life, sin, and works. Our goal is to eliminate any question that a reader may have concerning his or her position in Christ.*

The biggest change in my Christian walk came when I finally made sense out of the grace of God. The life changing principles that His grace offers us is sorely diminished in the idea of salvation today. Grace has either been diluted or removed completely from the Christian's life. It seems that there are two extremes regarding grace and it is these extremes that have predominated Christian teaching for too long. What I will try to do is spell out the concept of grace in an easy and understandable way; to bring clarity and balance to the subject. Above all, we want the truth to be exposed.

Before we begin if you are to receive the truth about grace, you are going to have to remove any **preconceptions** or **mind-sets** that you may already have. I have talked to many people on this subject, and even though they don't disagree with what I am saying, they will not accept the grace of God because of their mind-sets. They become immovable in what they believe, even when the truth is plainly in front of them. Let us all be teachable.

Introduction

What I am about to say is going to be very important for you to understand. Read it again if you need to so that you understand it.

Satan does not want you to have a relationship with God. If he could not stop you from having a relationship with God, then he will try to keep you from doing the work of God. He does this by keeping you busy either trying to overcome sin or wallowing in condemnation. If he can keep you busy with these, he has succeeded in keeping you from the purpose and destiny to which God called you. Any means Satan can use to distract you from doing what God has intended for you to do, believe me, he will do it!

The word *"grace"* very simply means *"unmerited favor."* It is an act done to the one shown grace that is not due them, but rather a kindness bestowed based on the loving kindness of the giver, not the receiver. **Grace is misunderstood because it flies in the face of logic and reason when we don't have all the facts.** Why would God overlook my sin? He is absolutely holy and absolutely just, and no sin can even dwell in His presence.

Many of God's people are not walking in the freedom that Jesus purchased through willfully going to the cross to suffer in their place. He shed His holy blood, that you and I might not live under the threat of the death penalty that we so earnestly deserve. Either that act is a powerful force in our lives or it is not. Either it took care of my past sin but not my present and future sins, or it is perpetual in its application and removes me from ever having sin put to my account again.

Objections

There are a number of reasons why there is confusion surrounding this issue, one of which is the terminology used in the New Testament. For example Galatians 5:19-21 describes for us the works of the flesh and the results of living according to them. Then the same author says that all things are lawful unto him in I Corinthians 10:23.

It would seem then that the apostle Paul is contradicting himself. First, he tells us what keeps people out of Heaven and then seems to say of himself that he could do any of those things without it affecting his status of going to Heaven.

> *Galatians 5:19-21 Now the deeds of the flesh are evident, which are: immorality, impurity, sensuality, idolatry, sorcery, enmities, strife, jealousy, outbursts of anger, disputes, dissensions, factions, envying, drunkenness, carousing, and things like these, of which I forewarn you, just as I have forewarned you, that those who practice such things will not inherit the kingdom of God.*

> *I Corinthians 6:12 All things are lawful for me, but not all things are profitable. All things are lawful for me, but I will not be mastered by anything.*

How do we reconcile these verses? When we understand the grace of God that is given to us, we can begin to make sense of these two Scriptures. We will revisit them later after we have explored the grace of God.

Most Christians will agree that they are saved by their belief, acceptance of, and confession in Jesus. Yet there are many opinions about what can remove that salvation, or if it can be removed at all. If we take a linear approach to this, we should be able to come to some conclusions concerning the application of God's grace.

The Law

If we are to understand our salvation we must put in question form, the things that we need to address. If Jesus has saved us and removed our sin from us, what do we do when we sin after we have been saved? Are we lost if we sin? Can we regain our salvation if we lose it? If we look at the other extreme of anything-goes-grace, then we must ask these questions. Does God just ignore my sin? Can I do anything without suffering any consequence for my actions? Can I lose my salvation if I am bad enough?

Understanding the Law of God will help us to place into proper tension the Grace of God. We know that God's Law is good and that it is the standard for righteous living. We also know that it is unwavering and if broken in just one area, guilt is transferred to the breaker of the Law and a sentence of eternal death is applied. Thus, we are all guilty of breaking the whole Law.

A problem arises in that we are all incapable of following God's Law perfectly. Moreover, if we have some kind of outside help in fulfilling that Law, then we can no longer take the credit for living according to God's Law. Let's look at some Scriptures that show us that we are incapable by ourselves of following God's Law.

Sin

Romans 3:9-18 (NCV) So are we Jews better than others? No! We have already said that Jews and those who are not Jews are all guilty of sin. As the Scriptures say: "There is no one who always does what is right, not even one. There is no one who understands. There is no one who looks to God for help. All have turned away. Together, everyone has become useless. There is no one who does anything good; there is not even one. (Psalm 14:1-3) Their throats are like open graves; they use their tongues for telling lies. (Psalm 5:9) Their words are like snake poison. (Psalm 140:3) Their mouths are full of cursing and hate. (Psalm 10:7) They are always ready to kill people. Everywhere they go they cause ruin and misery. They don't know how to live in peace. (Isaiah 59:7-8) They have no fear of God." (Psalm 36:1)

If this is the **pre-salvation** state of every human being that has ever, is now, or will ever live, than we must agree with the statement that, *"there is no one who does good always."* The problem is that we have this tendency to measure the level of sin in us by comparing ourselves with other humans. That will result in a false sense of being good. When we compare ourselves with God, we all find ourselves guilty under the Law of God that says that we deserve the sentence of death and separation from God. Not one human being can claim that they are righteous in accordance with God's Law.

This leaves all of humanity in a quandary, and it propels us toward the noteworthy question, *"What must I do then to be saved?"* **Understanding the reality of where you are will also give you a view to where you need to be.** Once that understanding is present in any life, then that life is able to find the answer that God so beautifully provided. If we have not seen our self in light of God's Law, you will not see the need to be saved.

> **Romans 3:19-20 (NCV)** *We know that the law's commands are for those who have the law. This stops all excuses and brings the whole world under God's judgment, because no one can be made right with God by following the law. The law only shows us our sin.*

This is a very important Scripture. It establishes that every person that will come into this world does so under God's Law. This means that every excuse that you or anyone else can come up with is stopped, and every person is held accountable to God for his or her life. It also states that not a single person will be justified by obedience to the Law, because not a single individual is able to obey it to the letter.

The purpose of the Law is to show us our sin so that we will look for the solution to our sin. The conclusion we must come to is that if the Law can only show us sin, we must never trust in the Law to remove our sin. God's solution has always been blood where sin is concerned. When Moses received the Law from God, he also received instructions for sacrifice. Only blood can remove sin, not obedience to the Law! You cannot do a good deed to erase a bad deed. If you have sinned, there is nothing you can do to pay your debt but to die for your own sins.

The idea that you can undo sin by doing something righteous would demand a judge who is willing to overlook the Law. That is not a picture of our God. Jesus can be the only answer to our sin. Why is Jesus the only answer? First, God's nature has to be preserved because it is impossible for Him to change. He is a good and righteous Judge. Since this is so, then He must judge all sin without partiality. That assures each one of us that we are doomed and lost without hope under the Law of God. Left in our sinful state, we would all be found guilty under the Law of God. God's perfect nature becomes the standard that He uses as the righteous Judge.

What if God came into this world as a human being? What if He went through the process of birth like any other person has? Of course, He would live a perfect law abiding life under the law that He created. What if God allowed His human blood to be shed and then died while completely innocent? Remember, the penalty for sin is death, and Jesus, who is God, has never sinned. Since Jesus was sinless, His death was an unjust one for He had not sinned.

Not only that, but if the penalty of sin is death, then wasn't it impossible for Him to die? But wait, His life was not taken from Him nor could it be, since He had not sinned. The Bible says that He gave His life up!

John 10:17-18 *"For this reason the Father loves Me, because I lay down My life so that I may take it again. **No one has taken it away from Me**, but I lay it down on My own initiative. I have authority to lay*

it down, and I have authority to take it up again.
This commandment I received from My Father."

That means that Jesus is the only human being that lived a perfect life; it is this fact that caused Him to give His life willfully. Because of this, there is a death of an adult human person in which there was no sin ever committed in that body. Because it was God that inhabited this body, He was able to apply His own judgment for all the sin of the whole world to His own body. He literally judged the sin of every person in His own body. Remember, the soul that sins shall die. That penalty was paid for every human being by the Son of God!

God's nature is uncorrupted in that He did punish every sin with death, it just happened to be Himself. This way, as one man sinned and brought death upon all, one Man's righteousness is able to bring life for all. He created a Way for anyone who wants to escape the punishment of their sins. Jesus can be the only way to eternal life. This shows us the dichotomy and synthesis of God's justice and God's mercy.

> **Romans 5:15-19 (ESV)** *But the free gift is not like the trespass. For if many died through one man's trespass, much more have the grace of God and the free gift by the grace of that one man Jesus Christ abounded for many. And the free gift is not like the result of that one man's sin. For the judgment following one trespass brought condemnation, but the free gift following many trespasses brought justification. If, because of one man's trespass, death reigned through that one man, much more will those who receive the abundance of grace and the free gift of righteousness reign in life through*

*the one man Jesus Christ. Therefore, as one trespass led to condemnation for all men, so one act of righteousness leads to justification and life for all men. For as by the one man's disobedience the many were made sinners, **so by the one man's obedience the many will be made righteous.***

This passage of Scripture forces us to consider that Jesus was not just any human being; He was also God in the flesh. Why? If this man Jesus was sinless, and if He were just a human like you or me, then He would only be an example of how the rest of us would be capable of living as well.

This would place all of us in a state of doom for we have all sinned. It only takes one sin for me to be separated from God for eternity. If one of us who are from the seed of Adam can live perfectly, then any one of us could have. On the other hand, if God was indwelling the body of Jesus who was born of the seed of God, that perfect life and death can be a substitution for all of us, rather than just an example of living, because He is **greater** than we are.

To summarize, the Law brings the knowledge of sin and places me in a state of death. In this state of death I am driven to look for a solution. If I am looking for a solution, I am faced with only one, a blood sacrifice. There is only one human sacrifice that is acceptable. Since all have sinned there are no human beings worthy of dying for someone else's sins. They can only pay their own debt through their own death. It takes an act of God becoming human, living a sinless life, dying an innocent death, and making that life an offering for the sin of every human being. There is then only one sacrifice for sin, it is Jesus.

Romans 2:14-15 (ESV) For when Gentiles, who do not have the law, by nature do what the law requires, they are a law to themselves, even though they do not have the law. They show that the work of the law is written on their hearts, while their conscience also bears witness, and their conflicting thoughts accuse or even excuse them.

Romans 2:23-24 (ESV) You who boast in the law dishonor God by breaking the law. For, as it is written, "The name of God is blasphemed among the Gentiles because of you."

It is important to understand the purpose of the Law so that we do not boast in keeping the Law. All we will accomplish by boasting in the Law is alienating the world from Christ. We have for too long acted as if we are better than the world. In reality, we are all sinners before God. We all fall short before His holy Law, and we find that we too are lawbreakers before God.

This is why we must stand humble before our God. His ways are much higher than ours. Think about this for a moment. If you were capable of living up to God's standards which are His ways, would that not make you as able as God regarding His ways? This is the insidiousness of thinking that we can be perfect regarding the Law and also why when we suggest that we can be perfect according to God's Laws to the world, the world sees us stumble and they blaspheme God.

Let's turn the table a bit. Suppose we had told the world how God knew that no one could keep His Law, and that we are all guilty of breaking the Law. Now, what can the world scoff at when they see a Christian break one of God's Laws? Absolutely nothing!

It is extremely important that we as Christians do not tell others that they, by their words and actions, have to be perfect...and we don't. No, we need to tell one another and the world that no one is perfect, not them, not us. What did Jesus say to the accusers of the woman caught in adultery, was it not, *"he who is without sin cast the first stone"*? **To our shame the world is quoting that passage to us.**

Legalism

I would like to take a moment to deal with the doctrines of legalism. First I would like to say that I am not very fond of the term legalism especially in light of the fact that God's Law is good and holy. By using the term legalism, we bring a negative light to God's Law and that is unfortunate.

We might be surprised to find that there may be an element of legalism in most every church and in most Christians. Legalism is what the apostle Paul struggled against so often in his time of ministry, and so it is his writings that show us the greatest arguments against legalism.

Summed up into a single sentence, legalism is a term that was given for the belief that God demands our works under the Law in order to retain our salvation after we have been saved. In Paul's day, Jews who had accepted Christ were attempting to place the Gentiles under the Law.

Paul argued against this and even called a council in Jerusalem to get a ruling from the apostles. The apostles ruled that the Law was not applicable to the Gentiles. This story is in the Book of Acts. What we will deal with in this section is the arguments of the legalist so that the contrast of their argument and the argument for grace will give a crystal clear picture of the grace of our Lord Jesus. Legalism disagrees with the clear instruction given to us in how we please God.

> *Hebrews 11:6 (ESV) And **without faith** it is impossible to please him, for whoever would draw near to God must believe that he exists and that he rewards those who seek him.*

It is not that doing the right thing does not please Him, it is doing so outside of faith that does not please Him. If I do well and yet do not believe on His Son, what pleasure does God have in my action? Yet if I do well **because** I believe in His Son, God is pleased.

Look at the Pharisees, they were trying to look holy through the works of the flesh, and Jesus said that they had the appearance of righteousness but inward they were rotting corpses. According to Jesus they had it backward. They were trying to clean the outside of the vessel but Jesus told them that they must clean the inside and then the outside will be clean as a natural result of your inward relationship.

> *I John 2:3 And by this we know that we have come to know Him, if we keep His commandments.*

Keeping His commandments is a natural result of a right relationship. In other words, it is submission that brings about relationship, which brings about obedience. Most people have this backwards, that is they try to be obedient to increase their relationship. Increase submission to Christ and that will bring about an increase in relationship and an increase in obedience.

God can be pleased by obeying His Laws, but not as an act of your strength. If you are doing it, then faith is not present and you will be unable to sustain that act of righteousness. Faith produces obedience so that it is no longer our action, but His action by His Spirit that is in us. Faith has a byproduct. It is the doing of those things that issue out of the heart, not the will of man. Why is this? It is so that we will have no reason to boast in ourselves.

> **Romans 3:27-28 (ESV)** *Then what becomes of our boasting? It is excluded. By what kind of law? By a law of works? No, but by the law of faith. For we hold that one is justified by faith apart from works of the law.*

> **Ephesians 2:8-9 (ESV)** *For by grace you have been saved **through faith**. And this is not your own doing; it is the gift of God, not a result of works, so that no one may boast.*

Let us conclude, then, that if we obey God's commands from our own strength or will power, we have reason to boast in our ability to do so. But if we obey God's commands by a natural desire that issues out of a changed heart because of faith, then we cannot boast because it is the work of God in us that produces this obedience.

Legalism falls on its face in light of the grace of God. There is nothing I can do to be accepted by God except believe in Him and what He says. My work only results in my boasting in myself which culminates in pride. It is because of this that the legalist will always be a proud faultfinder. We know that they cannot keep the whole Law of God, so they are faced with finding faults in others to make themselves feel justified.

Simplicity

I want to put this in the simplest of terms. There are two sides of the argument. It is the classic grace vs. works argument. I would like to present to you a third option.

That Jesus is the only way is irrelevant in this argument because both sides would agree with that. Here is the disagreement. The works crowd will see sin as a failure of salvation in the life of the believer. It is then necessary for the works crowd to ask for forgiveness or go to hell if they die before repenting. The grace crowd sees the sin equation as being answered in Christ. They conclude that any sin is already covered and depending on who you speak with there are many degrees of thought with regard to sin in the grace crowd.

Some say that because sin is dealt with by faith, they can do anything without consequence. Then there are those that resist sin but still do not see consequences as a result of sin. Then there are those that see the consequence but they really are conflicted between the argument of grace and the argument for Law or works.

Here is where I think we need to strike balance. First, if I cannot be saved by good works, what makes me think I can be unsaved by bad works? The conclusion of that argument by many is, that gives you a license to sin. Does it? If grace removed me from the Law, it also moved me under the Lawgiver. I may be separated from the written Law, but now I have a heavenly Father who disciplines me as His child for sin that I commit. He might even take my life because of disobedience, but He does not reject me as His child because of disobedience.

What was the name of the tree in the Garden of Eden that Adam and Eve were commanded not to eat from? **It is the Tree of the Knowledge of Good and Evil.** Who planted the tree?

> ***Genesis 2:8-9*** *The Lord God **planted** a garden toward the east, in Eden; and there He placed the man whom He had formed. Out of the ground the Lord God **caused to grow** every tree that is pleasing to the sight and good for food; the tree of life also in the midst of the garden, and the **tree of the knowledge of good and evil.***

Since God is the One that planted the Tree of the Knowledge of Good and Evil, who's standard of good and evil would be represented by that tree? It is obvious that it is God's standard of good and evil. In other words, the Tree of the Knowledge of Good and Evil is a representation of the Law of God.

Adam and Eve did not eat from the fruit of that tree; they lived from the fruit of the Tree of Life. But when they partook of the fruit of the Tree of the Knowledge of Good and Evil they became responsible for sin because they now had the knowledge of sin through the Law.

The reason this is important to note is so that you understand that God never wanted Adam and Eve to partake of His standards of good and evil, His Law. As long as Adam and Eve had access to the Tree of Life, there was no reason to partake of the Law which brings death.

> *Romans 7:9-11 I was once alive apart from the Law; but when the commandment came, sin became alive and I died; and this commandment, which was to result in life, proved to result in death for me; for sin, taking an opportunity through the commandment, deceived me and through it killed me.*

This is the same thing that happened to Adam and Eve when they partook of the forbidden tree. Because of sin, Adam and Eve were now forbidden to partake of the Tree of Life. This is the reconciliation that Jesus brings back to us. Remember that Adam and Eve was cast out of the garden precisely because they would have access to the tree of life as sinners.

> *Genesis 3:22-24 Then the Lord God said, "Behold, the man has become like one of Us, knowing good and evil; and now, he might stretch out his hand, and take also from the tree of life, and eat, and live forever"— therefore the Lord God sent him out from the garden of Eden, to cultivate the ground from which he was taken. So He drove the man out; and at the east of the garden of Eden He stationed the cherubim and the flaming sword which turned every direction to guard the way to the tree of life.*

What does the Tree of Life represent? It represents eternal life.

> *John 14:6 Jesus said to him, "I am the way, and the truth, and the life; no one comes to the Father but through Me.*

John 1:4 In Him was life, and the life was the Light of men.

John 11:25-26 Jesus said to her, "I am the resurrection and the life; he who believes in Me will live even if he dies, and everyone who lives and believes in Me will never die. Do you believe this?"

I John 5:20 And we know that the Son of God has come, and has given us understanding so that we may know Him who is true; and we are in Him who is true, in His Son Jesus Christ. This is the true God and eternal life.

Jesus is the Tree of Life! The Tree of Life is available again if we will partake of Him. In Him we have eternal life. God has always intended that man live under the blessing of eternal life apart from the Law. Even though the Law was in the Garden of Eden, they were not to partake of it because they were in their current state under a sentence of life. If they partake of this tree of the Law, they are under a sentence of death.

We must face the reality of this. If the tree of the Knowledge of Good and Evil is a representation of the Law of God, then it is indisputable that God did not want man to live under His righteous Law.

Why would God not want His creation to live under His Law? I think it goes to the fact that God's holiness is divine; it is infinite. Moreover, if we are created less than infinite, how could we hope to live up to a standard that is infinite? That is why we look at the Law of God and say it is good, it is holy, but I am but mortal flesh and cannot even hope to rise to a standard that is the infinite God's standard.

Think about the poetry. The God who did not intend for man to partake of His law which was in the form of a tree, defeated the hostility of the Law by nailing it to a tree.

> ***Colossians 2:13-14*** *When you were dead in your transgressions and the uncircumcision of your flesh, He made you alive together with Him, having forgiven us all our transgressions, having canceled out the certificate of debt consisting of decrees against us, which was hostile to us; and He has taken it out of the way, having nailed it to the cross.*

That certificate of debt, is the sentence of death that was a consequence of breaking the Law. With this understanding we need to visit grace.

Grace

Jesus gave up His life willfully so that His death would be a substitute for our death. If Jesus were just a man, He could only make substitution for another human being. But if He is God, then that death can be a substitution for all of mankind.

However, in order to partake of this extraordinary gift of life, it requires that we believe that God did this for all of us so that any of us could be spared the death penalty. It does one no good, if they do not believe this happened, for they cannot unwillingly apply it to their life. That is why the Word says:

> ***Romans 10:9-13 (ESV)*** *because, if you confess with your mouth that Jesus is Lord and believe in your heart that God raised him from the dead, you will*

be saved. For with the heart one believes and is justified, and with the mouth one confesses and is saved. For the Scripture says, "Everyone who believes in him will not be put to shame." For there is no distinction between Jew and Greek; the same Lord is Lord of all, bestowing his riches on all who call on him. For "everyone who calls on the name of the Lord will be saved."

We need to understand that in order to cleanse anyone from a sin, there must be the payment of the fine that sin incurred. Since God decreed that, *"the soul that sins shall die,"* there must be a death to make payment for the sin.

If your soul dies, that is payment for your sin, but then you are in an eternal state of separation from God. That is why in the Old Testament they brought a lamb without spot or wrinkle. This was to be a symbol of perfection and sinlessness. The lamb was slain and the innocent blood of that lamb was then sprinkled on the mercy seat of God located within the Holy of Holies beyond the veil in the temple.

This sacrifice was to be a picture of what Jesus was going to do for us. Since the innocent blood of animals cannot make restitution for the guilty blood of humans, God became the innocent sacrificial lamb by taking on human flesh, walking a sinless life, which also made Him completely innocent, and then allowing Himself to be slain.

By shedding His innocent blood, there is now the availability of the payment for sin, and each person who accepts that payment for his sin will have eternal life. When you do this, you are at that moment cleansed from the **guilt** incurred by your sin. In essence, somebody else suffered in your place. This is the only way for your sin to be removed because there is only one penalty for sin, and **it is death.** That means that there is a certificate of death with your name on it. By repenting, believing, and confessing the name of Jesus, your certificate of death is canceled. This is the only way that you can escape your own soul's death and spend eternity with God.

There has to be death wherever there is sin because God is perfectly holy and no sin can dwell in His presence. By accepting the death of Jesus, Who was also sinless, as the substitution for my own death, then my sin has been erased. All of my sin has been placed upon Jesus, Who willfully died in my place.

> *Romans 6:10 (ESV) For the death He died He died to sin, **once for all**, but the life He lives He lives to God.*

> *Hebrews 7:26-28 (ESV) For it was indeed fitting that we should have such a high priest, holy, innocent, unstained, separated from sinners, and exalted above the heavens. He has no need, like those high priests, to offer sacrifices daily, first for His own sins and then for those of the people, since He did this **once for all** when He offered up Himself. For the law appoints men in their weakness as high priests, but the word of the oath, which came later than the law, appoints a Son who has **been made perfect forever.***

> *Hebrews 6:4-6 (ESV) For it is impossible to restore again to repentance those who have once been enlightened, who have tasted the heavenly gift, and have shared in the Holy Spirit, and have tasted the goodness of the word of God and the powers of*

the age to come, if they then fall away, since they
are crucifying once again the Son of God to their
own harm and holding him up to contempt.

There are two things that need to be noted from these Scriptures. **First, there is only one sacrifice for sin.** That means that if I sin after applying the blood of Jesus to my life, either I have to have another sacrifice for that sin, or it is already covered by the blood of Jesus because of faith.

Secondly, this shows us that if we did lose our blood atonement, that it is **impossible** to put Jesus back on the cross. This would suggest that either all of us are lost because we have all sinned after salvation or that the blood is perpetual in its application.

Romans 5:13 KJV (For until the law sin was in the
world: but sin is not imputed when there is no law.

If sin is not put to our account when there is no Law, then we must prove scripturally that when you were born again, you were no longer under the Law. We must do this in order to make this claim for ourselves.

Romans 7:6 NLT But now we have been released
from the law, for we died with Christ, and we are
no longer captive to its power. Now we can really
serve God, not in the old way by obeying the letter
of the law, but in the new way, by the Spirit.

Since we are released from the Law, sin is no longer imputed to our account. It is a legal point that needs to be understood. If someone pays my fine, I am released from the Law that levied the fine.

*Hebrews 9:11-14 (ESV) But when Christ appeared as a high priest of the good things that have come, then through the greater and more perfect tent (not made with hands, that is, not of this creation) he entered once for all into the holy places, not by means of the blood of goats and calves but by means of his own blood, thus **securing an eternal redemption.** For if the sprinkling of defiled persons with the blood of goats and bulls and with the ashes of a heifer sanctifies for the purification of the flesh, how much more will the blood of Christ, who through the eternal Spirit offered himself without blemish to God, **purify our conscience** from dead works to serve the living God.*

We Christians get into trouble when we start resurrecting the Law in our lives. You see, the Law says, *"I must,"* but grace says, *"I desire."* If you try to replace the *"I desire"* with *"I must,"* you will also resurrect your bad conscience. Look, you could not by your own power live for God before you got saved. What makes you think you can live for God by your own power afterwards?

The only way I can live for God is to allow Him to live in me. **I must resign myself to the failure of my own efforts and surrender to the efforts of Christ in me.** The evidence is there. Jesus said, *"Without Me, you can do nothing."* We must abide in Jesus from Whom the power to live our lives for God comes.

When I believe in Jesus and what He accomplished for me, I move out from under the Law. This is important to note because the Bible says that the Law entices us to sin.

Romans 7:5 (ESV) For while we were living in the flesh, our sinful passions, aroused by the law, were at work in our members to bear fruit for death.

The only way to escape the Law is to die! That's what Christ did for you! Because He took your sin, His death becomes your death and in that state of death, the Law has no jurisdiction over you. So we not only accept His life as ours, but we must accept His death as ours also. That is why Paul says to consider yourselves dead to sin but alive to God. When you became a Christian, you became dead to the Law. As far as the Law is concerned, you don't exist. Dead people don't break the Law.

Let us look at this in our own laws. If a man were convicted of a crime that required his death, and if it were possible, another man went to the judge and said, *"Put me to death in his place."* According to the Law, the man that actually committed the crime is dead to the Law that was putting him to death.

Galatians 2:20-21 "I have been crucified with Christ; and it is no longer I who live, but Christ lives in me; and the life which I now live in the flesh I live by faith in the Son of God, who loved me and gave Himself up for me. I do not nullify the grace of God, for if righteousness comes through the Law, then Christ died needlessly."

God has provided a tree of life for us. Moreover, under the tree of life there is only life and the command not to partake of the Law (knowledge of good and evil). Jesus said, *"I came to give you LIFE, and to give it more abundantly."*

Hebrews 12:7-11 (ESV) It is for discipline that you have to endure. God is treating you as sons. For what son is there whom his father does not discipline? If you are left without discipline, in which all have participated, then you are illegitimate children and not sons. Besides this, we have had earthly fathers who disciplined us and we respected them. Shall we not much more be subject to the Father of spirits and live? For they disciplined us for a short time as it seemed best to them, but He disciplines us for our good, that we may share His holiness. For the moment all discipline seems painful rather than pleasant, but later it yields the peaceful fruit of righteousness to those who have been trained by it.

This discipline did not take place before you became a Christian. This means that Christians will not be able to just get away with sin like the world does. They are children of God, and God will discipline them for the wrong they do. This also becomes a deterrent to sinning. After experiencing the discipline of God, sinning just does not seem worth it. It is just too painful.

Contrast

Now, I want you to contrast what you have just learned in this lesson with what we often hear. We often are told that God has provided a free gift of salvation to all who will believe. There are no conditions other than just believing. Then, when we accept this gift, we are often told that we have to do things to keep this gift.

The logic found in these statements is obviously contradictory at best. I can only receive salvation by believing, but then I am told that I can lose it by only doing wrong. Either I do good to get it, and I do wrong to lose it, or I believe to get it, and I don't believe to lose it.

We find that many Christians are bound by the belief that they will be rejected by Jesus because of something they have done wrong as a Christian. We will be disciplined by God for doing something wrong, but we will not lose our relationship of son or daughter. I don't cease to be His son because of what I did wrong. God will deal with me for those things that I do wrong. Just as I did not cease to be my earthly father's son when I did wrong, I will not cease to be my heavenly Father's son; I am just disciplined for the wrong I did.

> **Galatians 2:19 (ESV)** *For through the law I died to the law, so that I might live to God. I have been crucified with Christ.*

The sacrifice of Jesus must be continuous or perpetual (unending) to the one who believes. The Bible says repeatedly that, *"the just shall live by faith."* I am not justified at any time in my life by what I do. I am only justified by what I believe.

Since I am saved by my faith in Christ, then to be unsaved after that means that I must come to a place where I no longer believe in my heart that Jesus came in the flesh. You see if I am saved by faith, then I can only be unsaved by having no faith. What I do is only a by-product of what I believe.

If you see me with a raincoat, then you can assume that I believe it is going to rain. So it is in the life of Christians. If they truly believe in Jesus, they will not justify their sin, and if they have a proper understanding of the grace of God, they will always turn from their sins in order to live for God. However, we will always struggle with sin.

The War

The apostle Paul developed this understanding for us in the seventh chapter of Romans. Paul, a Christian, was giving an example of his own life as a Christian, teaching us how and why there are two natures at work in a person. Let's take a look at what he says.

> *Romans 7:14-25 (ESV) For we know that the law is spiritual, but I am of the flesh, sold under sin. I do not understand my own actions. For I do not do what I want, but I do the very thing I hate. Now if I do what I do not want, I agree with the law, that it is good. So now it is no longer I who do it, but sin that dwells within me. For I know that nothing good dwells in me, that is, in my flesh. For I have the desire to do what is right, but not the ability to carry it out. For I do not do the good I want, but the evil I do not want is what I keep on doing. Now if I do what I do not want, it is no longer I who do it, but sin that dwells within me.*
>
> *So I find it to be a law that when I want to do right, evil lies close at hand. For I delight in the law of God, in my inner being, but I see in my members another law waging war against the law of my mind and making me captive to the law of sin that dwells in my members. Wretched man that I am! Who will deliver me from this body of death? Thanks be to God through Jesus Christ our Lord! So then, I myself serve the law of God with my mind, but with my flesh I serve the law of sin.*

Verse 25

The question in verse 24 appears to be a rhetorical one, with the answer "Nobody can" all too apparent. But Paul answers it with the joyful shout "Thanks be to God -- through Jesus Christ our Lord!" The victory is God's and he gives it through Christ. It is Paul's consistent teaching that God in Christ has supplied all our need and will continue to do so (cf. Phil. 4:19). Clearly Paul's words express gratitude for a present deliverance, but it is likely that they also have eschatological significance. The deliverance we have today is wonderful, but it is partial and incomplete. It is but a first installment of greater things to come, and Paul looks forward to that great day with his burst of thanksgiving.

"So then" introduces a logical summary of what Paul has been saying. This, then, is what it all adds up to. There is disagreement about this, it is true. Some exegetes feel that the outburst of thanksgiving cannot have been followed by a reference to being "a slave to the law of sin." Moffatt accordingly transfers this part of the verse to the end of verse 23, a rearrangement that is accepted by Dodd and others. There is no support for this in the MSS, but Dodd says, "we cannot avoid trusting our own judgment against their evidence". But is hazardous to set our view of what Paul ought to have said against all the evidence. It *is better to view the second half of verse 25 as a summary of the preceding argument before going on to the triumph of chapter 8. As Cranfield puts it, "it sums up with clear-sighted honesty . . . the tension with all its real anguish and also all its real hopefulness, in which the Christian never ceases to be involved so long as he is living this present life." Notice that Paul does not shrug off his responsibility; he does say that his mind serves God while his flesh serves sin. He uses the emphatic pronoun "I". It is what he has been saying all along. While there is that in him which approves God's way there is that in him also which follows the paths of sin.*

There is no doubt in my mind that, like me, you too have struggled with sin, and you have wondered, *"Why am I doing the things I do not want to do?"* Let me assure you that we all have had to deal with this and are continuing to do so.

The importance of this section of Scripture cannot be understated. Here is the picture of a man that is a Christian, and he has the desire to do what is good, but he finds that he fails at doing it. So the conclusion that Paul comes to is that if he is doing something that he does not want to do, then it is not he (and by *"he"* he means his spirit) that is doing it, but rather sin that dwells in him.

Moreover, he very well cries for us all, *"Oh what a wretched man that I am!"* What shall we say then; shall we just give up and let the sin that dwells in us drive us to do wrong? NO! How can we when our inner man is screaming NO! DON'T DO

IT! Paul delivers the ultimate proper question, *"Who shall deliver me from this body of death?"*

It is important to take note that Paul is laying the blame of his sin upon the body of flesh. The answer to deliverance from that body is Jesus! He will deliver us from this body of death, this mortal body. We just don't have possession of it yet. It is when we finally put on those bodies of immortality that we will no longer struggle with sin. Until then, we are in a war.

> **Galatians 5:17 (ESV)** *For the desires of the flesh are against the Spirit, and the desires of the Spirit are against the flesh, for these are opposed to each other, to keep you from doing the things you want to do.*

The original Greek did not capitalize letters to show deity. I think that when we understand our redemption, this Scripture makes sense only in the context of our spirit, not the Holy Spirit. There you have it; we are in a war and the battleground of that war is within each one of us. Notice that when Paul mentioned that Jesus was the One that would set us free from the body of death, his meaning was not to be taken to mean now, but rather our total deliverance from sin will only be accomplished by the changing of our mortal flesh (body of death) into immortal flesh.

That has yet to be accomplished; therefore, Paul's statement after this declaration of victory through Christ was a statement of present fact. *"So then, I of myself serve the law of God with my mind, but with my flesh I serve the law of sin."* In this statement, Paul states that he recognizes that he will still contend with the flesh as long as that flesh is mortal. This is the very idea that is so foreign to Christians currently. In the next chapter of Romans, Paul reveals this idea in a more detailed fashion.

This Scripture shows us that our bodies are not redeemed yet. Our spirit man is redeemed, and it is that change that caused the war against our flesh to be initiated in the first place.

By understanding this, do you not have a better picture of the sacrifice of Christ and its ability to perpetually cover your sins? Can we now go on and do the work of God without always worrying that we are no longer saved because of our weaknesses? We are called to freedom! We already have within us as Christians, the safety mechanism that keeps us from just sinning to our body's content.

When I, in my body of death, do something that is against God's Law, my spirit cries out relentlessly and without ceasing, to stop and repent from doing it. That is why Paul said, *"all things are lawful for me but not all things are profitable."* That is why Paul tells us that if we live after the spirit, we will not fulfill the desires of the flesh.

This is where the differences between true Christianity and casual Christianity are defined. Those that are serious about their relationship with God will not be satisfied in this life until all sin is eradicated from their beings.

There is a distinct difference between the act of sin and the will to sin. The true Christian no longer has the **will to sin**, yet they still sin as we just read in Romans chapter seven. However, as Paul stated, he was a wretched man because he found himself doing that which he did not want to do. He was not satisfied just wanting to do well in the inner man, he wanted to perform it with the body as well.

That is where we find the break down; it is in the ability to perform what is good at all times that we find difficult to accomplish. **Again, it is because we have a changed spirit living** in an unchanged body, which produces a war for supremacy in the mind. So, Christians will to live after the Law of God, but find it hard to perform at every instant.

> *Hebrews 10:26-27 For if we go on sinning willfully after receiving the knowledge of the truth, there no longer remains a sacrifice for sins, but a terrifying expectation of judgment and the fury of a fire which will consume the adversaries.*

We are not alone in our fight against sin. We not only have the action of our spirit man crying out against it, but we also have the Holy Spirit that will empower us to live holy lives. God and man are in an alliance that culminates in walking out the will and purpose of God for that life.

We overcame by the blood of the Lamb! This is not of our own self-power or self-will, not of our own self-desire, and not even by our own good works. No, we overcame by the blood of the Lamb that we applied by faith.

The blood that was shed by Christ on the cross is our exoneration from the death sentence due us eternally. How can we say that we are saved today and then lost tomorrow? God is greater than that! He is able to keep each one of us, and no one is able to pluck us out of His mighty hand. Therefore, let us not proclaim ourselves as holy by our own ability. Rather, proclaim yourself holy by the blood of Jesus, which makes you holy apart from your works.

> *Galatians 5:13 (ESV) For you were called to freedom, brothers. Only do not use your freedom as an opportunity for the flesh, but through love serve one another.*

I Peter 2:16 (ESV) Live as people who are free, not using your freedom as a cover-up for evil, but living as servants of God.

What is the implication of those two verses? Is it not that we have such freedom in Christ that if we sin, we are not lost? If I am commended not to use my freedom as a cover-up, does that not suggest that I can?

We must get this idea of grace in our minds so that we will be in the right frame of mind to do the work that God has called us to do. If we are always trying to overcome a sin, we will feel inadequate to perform the function or work God desires of us. The issue of sin has been answered by the blood of Christ. As He said on the cross, *"It is finished!!"*

It is done, and we must understand who we are in Christ that we might be even more effective in being the light that God called us to be. We are not to be men and women that have a pretense of piousness or holiness, but rather having a pretense of wretched sinners saved by the blood of Christ. With the latter attitude, you will be able to win the lost, but if you project yourself as without sin, then you make yourself a liar in their sight, and they will only see hypocrisy.

Additions

Just after Paul writes Romans 7:25 he writes 8:1. Now think about this for a moment. Paul just said, *"so on the one hand, in my mind, I serve that law of God but on the other, with my body I serve the law of sin."* Then Paul goes into this great statement.

> **Romans 8:1** *Therefore there is now no condemnation for those who are in Christ Jesus.*

Even when Paul realizes that in his body he sins, he makes the statement that there is now no condemnation for those who are in Christ Jesus. Now some versions add to this verse the following text, *"that do not walk after the flesh but after the Spirit."*

Many versions have left this phrase off without so much as an explanation because it contradicts verse nine. It is also clear that the earlier dated manuscripts did not have that phrase in it.

> **Romans 8:9** *However, you are not in the flesh but in the Spirit, if indeed the Spirit of God dwells in you. But if anyone does not have the Spirit of Christ, he does not belong to Him.*

If Paul can say that we are not in the flesh if the Spirit of God dwells in us, then you cannot say in verse 8:1 that those that are in Christ can be in the flesh.

Revisit

It is now time to revisit those Scriptures that we talked about in the beginning of this chapter.

> **Galatians 5:19-21** *Now the deeds of the flesh are evident, which are: immorality, impurity, sensuality, idolatry, sorcery, enmities, strife, jealousy, outbursts of anger, disputes, dissensions, factions, envying, drunkenness, carousing, and things like these, of which I forewarn you, just as I have*

forewarned you, that those who practice such
things will not inherit the kingdom of God.

   I Corinthians 6:12 All things are lawful for me, but
not all things are profitable. All things are lawful for
me, but I will not be mastered by anything.

The idea is that if you are bought with the blood of Christ through faith, then you are not practicing the deeds of the flesh because the *"I"* is your spirit man not your body. This is brought out in a number of places but none so pertinent than what Paul said just before he said that all things were lawful to him.

   I Corinthians 6:9-11 Or do you not know that the
unrighteous will not inherit the kingdom of God? Do
not be deceived; neither fornicators, nor idolaters,
nor adulterers, nor effeminate, nor homosexuals,
nor thieves, nor the covetous, nor drunkards, nor
revilers, nor swindlers, will inherit the kingdom of
God. **Such were some of you; but you were**
washed, but you were sanctified, but you were
justified in the name of the Lord Jesus Christ and
in the Spirit of our God.

Paul says the same thing that he says in Galatians chapter 5, but this time he clarifies that we are washed, sanctified, and justified in the name of Jesus. No longer are our spirits sinning; sin is now just in our bodies. Our spirit man is free from sin forever through faith. This idea will be further explained in the next chapter, *"Overcoming Sin."*

Conclusion

- We have laid out for you from point to point the concept of the grace of God.
- We have found that the blood of Christ is perpetual through faith.
- We have taken a look at the Law to see what its function is toward us.
- We have shown the fallacy of legalism.
- We have discovered that God has never intended for us to live under the Law or the Tree of the Knowledge of Good and Evil.
- We have discovered that God does intend for us to live under the Tree of Life which is Jesus.
- We have shown how unless there is a sacrifice there is no forgiveness of sins.
- We have shown that in Jesus there is only one sacrifice.
- We have looked at the contrast between what we hear from some pulpits and what the Scriptures are saying.
- We have revealed the war between the flesh and the spirit.
- We have shown that it is by faith, not the Law, that we are saved.

Therefore beloved, live in the faith to which you were called, having full assurance that you are in right standing with God. Present your bodies to do the will of God, and live in the awesome freedom and wonderful love of God.

My prayer for you is that you see yourself as God sees you. He sees you as a son or a daughter if you are saved. Do you see yourself that way, or do you see yourself as an outsider? If you have faith in the blood of Christ, He has set you free. So live as freemen, doing good to your neighbor. Live being honest with yourself, others, and God about your weaknesses so that you do not bring reproach upon the blood of Christ.

We cannot go on looking at what we have done right or what we have done wrong as a means of getting or losing our salvation. God is not saving you determined on that basis. Instead, He is looking to see if you have faith in the sacrifice of Christ. If you do, then you are saved! God has poured out upon you His favor. The fact that it was undeserved or unmerited speaks of the magnitude that the grace of God exhibits toward us.

> *Ephesians 2:7-9 (The Message) Now God has us where he wants us, with all the time in this world and the next to shower grace and kindness upon us in Christ Jesus. Saving is all his idea, and all his work. All we do is trust him enough to let him do it. It's God's gift from start to finish! We don't play the major role. If we did, we'd probably go around bragging that we'd done the whole thing!*

Overcoming Sin

> PURPOSE: *This is a detailed study about sin and how one overcomes it. The reader will learn where sin gets its power and how to deal with sin in a biblical way in order to overcome it. This lesson puts sin in the proper perspective in order to free the reader to do the work of God.*

Romans 6:14 For *sin shall not be your master, because you are not under law, but under grace.*

Have you ever read that verse and realize that it isn't working in your life? That is exactly what happened to me several years ago. When I read that verse I realized that something was wrong because sin was my master, and I was its slave. So I prayed and asked God what it was that I was doing wrong. I wanted to be in that place where sin was not my master. I wanted to experience Romans 6:14, not just read about it.

I know that I am not alone; others, like me, like you, have weaknesses that need to be dealt with. You look at Romans 6:14 and you have to wonder, if this is true, why do I still sin? We all war against the flesh, and we all desire, *that is, you should if you are a Christian,* to do good. You see the word sin in the Greek means ***"to miss the mark."***

We do not want to sin; as Christians we want to be obedient to the Law of God. We even get frustrated and angry with ourselves when we do not rise to that standard that we so badly want to attain. I know personally how absolutely frustrating it is to want to do well and wind up falling short instead.

> ***Romans 7:15-25** For what I am doing, I do not understand; for I am not practicing what I would like to do, but I am doing the very thing I hate. But if I do the very thing I do not want to do, I agree with the Law, confessing that the Law is good. So now, no longer am I the one doing it, but sin which dwells in me. For I know that nothing good dwells in me, that is, in my flesh; for the willing is present in me, but the doing of the good is not. For the good that I want, I do not do, but I practice the very evil that I do not want. But if I am doing the very thing I do not want, I am no longer the one doing it, but sin which dwells in me.*
>
> *I find then the principle that evil is present in me, the one who wants to do good. For I joyfully concur with the law of God in the inner man, but I see a different law in the members of my body, waging war against the law of my mind and making me a prisoner of the law of sin which is in my members. Wretched man that I am! Who will set me free from the body of this death? Thanks be to God through Jesus Christ our Lord! So then, on the one hand I*

myself with my mind am serving the law of God,
but on the other, with my flesh the law of sin.

You can see that the apostle Paul struggled with sin as well. God has written His Laws upon our hearts. It is part of our nature to know God's moral code, and all of us know when we break that code.

I have heard missionaries tell their stories of cultures that were cannibalistic. Even though they did not have any access to the Bible or any knowledge of God's moral requirements, they knew that what they were doing was wrong. Their conscience bore witness with the law of God that they were sinning.

The Power of Sin

Sin has power. We all know this, or none of us would have sinned. If asked where sin gets its power, most of us would say the old sinful nature. However, we need to let the Bible answer this question.

I Corinthians 15:56 *The sting of death is sin, and* *the **power of sin is the law**;*

According to Theological Dictionary of the New Testament, the Greek word *dýnamis "power"* means, *"ability,"* *then "possibility," then "power" both physical and intellectual or* *spiritual.*[6]

---

[6]Kittel, Gerhard ; Friedrich, Gerhard ; Bromiley, Geoffrey William: *Theological Dictionary of the New Testament.* Grand Rapids, Mich. : W.B. Eerdmans, 1995, c1985, S. 187

The ability, the possibility, and the power of sin is God's Law. Now some of you may say, *"That's not fair; God created us this way, so how can He hold me up to His standard when He knows that I cannot attain it?"* To answer that you must realize that Adam and Eve were not created that way; they were created in a way in which they were able to live with and satisfy God's moral standard. *"How so?"* you may ask. It is by the fact that Adam and Eve were created in a state of perfection; **they were created without the knowledge of good and evil.**

Yet, they were also created with free will. Free will demands choice. The choice available to them is to disobey God's will or to submit to it. Adam and Eve disobeyed it, and thereby brought sin into a sinless world. All of creation was affected by their action.

You might think that this is unfair. After all it was Adam and Eve, not me. Why do I have to suffer because of their mistake? Why doesn't God give me a chance to live without taking from the tree of the Knowledge of Good and Evil? The answer to that is that something happened to Adam and Eve when they partook of that tree. They were changed, and that change passed on from Adam to every generation infecting all human beings.

So, if the Law represents the knowledge of good and evil, Adam and Eve had what is termed a *"pure conscience"* until they partook of the tree. Why was their conscience pure? It is because they did not have the knowledge of good or evil. There was no written code that told them what was right and what was wrong. They were in the same state as a small child is in today.

A small child feels no shame in running around naked. Remember that after partaking of the tree of the knowledge of good and evil, Adam and Eve felt shame for being naked and tried to cover themselves. We must find out what this tree of the knowledge of good and evil really is if we are to understand the power of sin.

> **Deuteronomy 1:39** *'Moreover, your little ones who you said would become a prey, and your sons, who this day **have no knowledge of good or evil**, shall enter there, and I will give it to them and they shall possess it.*

This Scripture was describing the punishment of the nation of Israel for believing the ten spies who brought back a bad report rather than the two spies who said that God would give them the land. The punishment was that Israel would wander in the wilderness for 40 years until that generation who did not believe was dead, and then their children would go in and possess the land.

This verse shows us that children are just like Adam and Eve were before their fall. They are without the knowledge of good or evil. Children have no shame in nakedness. This is another reason we can say that if a child dies, they go to heaven. They have no knowledge of good or evil. It also brings to light something Jesus said.

> **Matthew 18:3** *and said, "Truly I say to you, unless you are **converted** and **become like children**, you will not enter the kingdom of heaven.*

Jesus was saying that the conversion process puts you in a state of being like little children. That means that God makes us innocent like little children; we do not make ourselves into little children. God makes us just like Adam and Eve before the fall.

Adam and Eve's conscience was pure because they were without the knowledge of the Law. We can say they were without the knowledge of good and evil because we know that God has written His law upon the conscience. Thus, if there is no law written upon the conscience, then their conscience was pure because they could not violate it. When they partook of the tree of the knowledge of good and evil, their conscience was written upon with God's law and changed them and their posterity forever.

Let's consider again *I Corinthians 15:56. ("The sting of death is sin, and the power of sin is the law.")* Now it makes sense. The power of sin is inexorably tied to our knowledge of good and evil. If we make a substitution, it will read like this, *"and the power of sin is the knowledge of good and evil."*

When Adam and Eve took of that tree, it produced a conscience that would enslave them and their posterity for the rest of their lives. Not only that, but the earth was cursed as a result of Adam and Eve's sin The knowledge of good and evil, or the Law, gave sin power, strength, and ability.

> *Hebrews 10:22 let us draw near with a sincere heart in full assurance of faith, having our hearts sprinkled clean from an evil conscience and our bodies washed with pure water.*

An evil conscience is a conscience that has been defiled by sin. That means you become aware of sin through the Law, and that awareness produces a conscience that says you are evil. That evil conscience is eliminated through faith in Jesus with the knowledge of God that states all of your sins have been punished in Christ. This has the effect of purifying your conscience so that it is quieted.

Since all your sin has been judged by God through the body of Jesus on the cross, the voice of your conscience is quieted even though your conscience still has the knowledge of good and evil. It is by faith that your conscience is quieted. The problem is that so many Christians do not understand the grace of God and as a result their conscience is condemning them.

A Good Law

Romans 7:12 So the law is holy, and the command is holy and right and good.

If the Law is good and holy, how can it give sin its power or strength?

Romans 8:3 For what the Law could not do, weak as it was through the flesh, God did: sending His own Son in the likeness of sinful flesh and as an offering for sin, He condemned sin in the flesh,

Since the Law was made weak by our sinful nature, then we are right back where we started. The Law is weakened by our sinful nature because the Law cannot stop us from sinning.

*Romans 7:5 For while we were in the flesh, the sinful passions, which were **aroused by the Law**, were at work in the members of our body to bear fruit for death.*

The Law is powerless in its ability to bring us to righteousness. All the Law can do is point out to us that we are not righteous at all. Indeed, that is why the written Law was given, to show us that we are exceedingly sinful and that we have a need for a solution.

Romans 7:13 Has then what is good become death to me? Certainly not! But sin, that it might appear sin, was producing death in me through what is

*good, **so that sin through the commandment
might become exceedingly sinful.***

Our sinful nature is strengthened by the Law because of how the sinful nature works. I call it the cookie jar syndrome. It works like this. A cookie jar full of cookies has no power over you as long as it is lawful for you to eat the cookies. However, let the law be laid down that forbids you to eat those cookies and the thoughts of eating those cookies will consume you.

It is when we are told we can't do something that we want to do it the most. Now keep in mind that the cookies were always sinful, but there was no law written that made it so. When the law came it increased the desire for the cookies.

The Conflict Within

*Romans 7:20-23 Now if I do what I do not want, **it is no longer I that do it, but sin** which dwells within me. So I find it to be a law that when I want to do right, evil lies close at hand. For I delight in the law of God, in my inmost self, but I see in my members another law **at war with the law of my mind** and making me captive to the law of sin which dwells in my members.*

Those verses are describing a Christian, not an unbeliever. How do we know? First, it is written by the apostle Paul who was a Christian at the time it was written. Secondly, it is written in the present tense. If Paul were trying to describe himself as an unbeliever, he would have used past tense in this section of Scripture.

The next verse that I am about to quote is one that is misquoted often. I want us to take a closer look at it and get an idea what it is saying to us. It is the answer to Paul's question.

> **Romans 7:24-25** *Wretched man that I am! Who will deliver me from this body of death? Thanks be to God through Jesus Christ our Lord!* **So then, I of myself serve the law of God with my mind, but with my flesh I serve the law of sin.**

Most ministers quote verse 24 and the first half of verse 25. They always avoid the sentence that starts with, *"So then, I of myself...."* The reason they do not quote it is that they do not understand that our spirit man has experienced redemption but our body or flesh has not.

Here we have the answer to our deliverance. What is important to note is that Paul does not declare that we can live sinless lives, but that we have victory over sin through Jesus Christ. After asking the question, *"Who will deliver me from this body of death?"* speaking of his fleshly body which by sin produces death in us, he states that he thanks God through Jesus Christ. That is not the real time solution to his problem of sin, but it is **RECOGNITION** of the ultimate victory that we have through Jesus.

Now look at the last part of that verse. This is very important to grasp! Paul says that, *"I of myself serve the law of God with my mind."* Now look at verse twenty again. *"If I* [myself] *do what I* [myself] *do not want to do, it is no longer I* [myself] *that do it, but sin which dwells in me."*

It is important to grasp that there is a separation in Paul's own mind about his own identity. Paul realizes that he, the inner man, was made good (born again) by the regenerated work of the

Holy Spirit. He also realizes that the body that houses his spirit was not regenerated yet. He realizes that we have regenerated spirits but not regenerated bodies. He identifies with his spirit in the use of the personal pronoun *"I"* but does not include his body. It is important to note that we will have regenerated bodies when Jesus comes back for us and we are raised incorruptible. Look at this next verse that bears this out.

> *Romans 8:22-23 We know that the whole creation has been groaning in travail together until now; and not only the creation, but we ourselves, who have the first fruits of the Spirit, groan inwardly as* **we wait** *for adoption as sons,* **the redemption of our bodies.**

We are waiting for the completion of our redemption. We have received a down payment of it in the form of a regenerated spirit, but its completion will not happen until we have received new bodies. That is why the Word states that the spirit wars against the flesh, and the flesh wars against the spirit.

Catch 22

Now we need to revisit *I Corinthians 15:56.* What we have is a closed system where one thing feeds off of the other and neither is able to get free of the other. Our sinful nature **weakens the Law,** and the Law **strengthens the sinful nature**. We are in a quandary, or a catch 22. What hope do we have if this closed system is feeding each other and causing greater weakness in our lives? It is no wonder Paul said that we are sold as slaves to sin.

> *Romans 7:5 For when we were controlled by the sinful nature, the sinful passions* **aroused by the**

law were at work in our bodies, so that we bore fruit for death.

Romans 5:20 *The law was added **so that the trespass might increase**. But where sin increased, grace increased all the more,*

I want you to notice something here. It says, *"**when** we were controlled by our sinful natures."* This denotes a position in us whereby there was a time, at some point in the past, when we were controlled by our sinful natures, but more importantly this also denotes that there is a point in our lives when we are no longer controlled by our sinful natures! The Law was given to show us just how lost we really are and that we cannot hope to meet the demands of the Law through our own works or ability.

Romans 3:20 *Therefore **no one will be declared righteous in His sight by observing the law;** rather, through the law we become conscious of sin.*

You should, at this point, have a good indication that we are lost under the Law and that sin is actually increased by knowledge of the Law. Therefore, the Law gives power to our sinful natures. This addresses the need that we have for Christ. **Jesus breaks this catch 22 effect.** It reaches to the very core issues of our lives! We want to live godly! We need to live godly! We can live godly! Through Christ is the power over the sinful nature. So how does bringing Jesus into our lives break sin's power?

Remember the very first verse that I quoted, *"Sin shall not have power over you"* (Romans 6:14)? **That is a stated fact not a proposition!** If sin has power over me and I am a Christian, **then I must not understand something.** Maybe I am living inside of a shack that is inside of a mansion. I will say that again. Maybe I am living inside of a shack that is inside of a mansion. Perhaps I just don't SEE that I am free, and I have, in a sense, bound myself, because I do not believe in this freedom that was purchased with God's blood.

I can tell you that I was very much like a man who was in a jail cell, but in reality the door was not locked. **I assumed it was locked**, but I never really tried to open the door. Let me assure you, saints, Jesus has unlocked that door!

You just have to see and believe that you are free before you can actually walk in that freedom. **The Word states that we walk by faith.** Our very walk every day is by faith. So let us walk as a people that are free from sin. You may suffer a weakness, but remember you walk by faith. God has delivered you from sin. By faith you can live as though you do not sin.

I want you to understand what I am saying. I am not saying that you should hide your weaknesses so everyone else thinks you're holy. I am saying I want you to walk by faith, knowing that your sin is erased by God's blood applied to your life. I want you to walk as if sin has no power over you! Because, if you are a blood-washed, Spirit-indwelled Christian, then sin has been dealt with once and for all, and it is time that you quit letting sin hold you back from the service to which God has called you!

*God was pointing out to Satan how righteous Job was. One of the attributes that God mentioned was that Job turned away from sin. Notice that God didn't say that Job did NOT sin, but that he TURNED AWAY from sin. This is the mark of a true Christian. A true Christian is **not** one that never sins, but one who recognizes that he has sinned and turns away from it. He repents and turns from sin.*

The Picture of Freedom

Okay, so the Law strengthens sin in us, and we, by our sin, weaken the law. You have to understand that when we were dead in sin, that is, we had not received Christ yet, both our spirits and our flesh were unregenerate. Our spirits had no power to prevent us from sinning. Let's look at our astonishing deliverance.

*__Romans 7:4-6__ In the same way, my brothers and sisters, your old selves died, and you became **free from the law** through the body of Christ. This happened so that you might belong to someone else-- the One who was raised from the dead-- and **so that we might be used in service to God**. In the past, we were ruled by our sinful selves. The law made us want to do sinful things that controlled our bodies, so the things we did were bringing us death. In the past, the law held us like prisoners, but our old selves died, and we were made free from the law. So now we serve God in a new way* *with the spirit, and not in the old way with written rules.*

Now you can see why sin is not supposed to be your master. Sin gets its power from the Law, but you are not under the Law. You are under Grace! In addition, you are dead; that is, your old nature is dead. The Word tells us to **CONSIDER** ourselves dead. As a Christian, you have been freed from the Law!

Many Christians are living their lives as if they are under a system of Law and as if they are ruled by their sinful nature. They are still in the mansion but they are living in a shack inside that mansion. They do not see their beautiful surroundings. They have requirements that they feel they have to fulfill to please God. Does this sound like you?

Grace

What is grace? In short, it is a special favor shown to you by God when you believed. It is the **APPLICATION** of holiness and righteousness applied to your life. This special favor applies to you the very righteousness of God when you did not deserve it or earn it. **Through grace, the way we look to God is as if we have been completely obedient our whole lives to the Law.** It applies to you the complete compliance and obedience under the Law, even though you were and are a lawbreaker. In grace, God makes you righteous so that you can again have a relationship with Him. Christ has fulfilled the Law in you so that you may be used in service to God.

If you understand what true grace is, and what it is like to live under it, I am convinced that if you did go back to a life of sin, you would not remain there for long. This is because it is under grace where we experience freedom; it is under grace where we experience the fullness of life. Under the Law we feel condemned, under the Law we feel weak, and under the Law we feel hopeless. We are no longer under the Law! Our Redeemer obeyed the Law for us!

In Christ, we are free; we are called to freedom. We are God's very own children. If God is holy, doesn't it follow that His children are holy also? I mean, a cow's offspring are still cows with the same attributes as the cow. Although we are not gods or able to ascend to the awesome power of almighty God, we can expect that some of God's nature is applied to us through faith since He calls us sons and daughters.

*II Corinthians 3:17-18 Now the Lord is the Spirit, and where the Spirit of the Lord is, there is liberty. But we all, with unveiled face, beholding as in a mirror the glory of the Lord, **are being transformed into the same image** from glory to glory, just as from the Lord, the Spirit.*

Since we are made holy by Christ, then we ought to show it in our everyday lives, and we can. We were given the Holy Spirit on the day of Pentecost. That is the same day that Moses received the Law from God on the mountain. The fruit of the Holy Spirit is the effect that He has on our lives as He dwells in each of us.

Galatians 5:22-23 But the fruit of the Spirit is love, joy, peace, patience, kindness, goodness, faithfulness, gentleness, self-control; against such there is no law.

What a wonderful life our God has provided for us, but we must believe in it in order to walk in it. We walk by faith. If we do not believe that we are free from the Law, we will walk as if we are not free. We will constantly be looking for a way to atone for our own sins. We will make up laws for ourselves that will sooth our consciences, like read the Bible more, pray more, or witness more. When we live in the freedom that Jesus purchased, it has the effect of causing us to want to read our Bibles more, pray more and witness more.

Made Holy

*Hebrews 13:12 So Jesus also suffered outside the city **to make his people holy with his own blood.***

Since we are made holy we have access to things that we never had access to before. We have access to God's holy nature. We have access to God's throne, to which we are told to approach boldly. This can only be done if you are holy—without sin of any kind—or totally clean. You can only come to His throne if you **are made holy, made clean, or made righteous.**

If you have been released from the Law, then sin does not have power over you. You are free from the punishment that your sin deserves. Here is a very important statement that is necessary for you to grasp. **Where there is no law, there is no sin imputed to your account.**

*Romans 4:15 because the law can only bring God's anger. **But if there is no law, there is nothing to disobey.***

*Romans 5:13 Sin was in the world before the law of Moses, **but sin is not counted against us as breaking a command when there is no law.***

Sin still exists, but it is not put to your account as a child of God. You will still suffer for committing sin, but it is in this earthly life. In eternity, you will also suffer rewards lost for not doing God's will, but you will be saved. You might be thinking; *"Wouldn't that just give us a license to sin?"*

In a sense it seems that way, but you must remember that the truly converted does not want to sin! They have a regenerated spirit that hates sin. That is, God installed His nature within the true believer. It is no longer *"I can't,"* but *"I don't want to."* It is no longer *"I have to read my Bible,"* but *"I want to read my Bible."* It is no longer *"I have to pray,"* but *"I want to pray"*. The law says, *"I shall not sin,"* but grace says *"I don't want to sin"*.

Moreover, we do not want to enter into a period of discipline in our life. Since God is our Father, He treats us like children. When we do wrong, He exposes it and DISCIPLINES us, and this is painful. So, we don't get away with sin, rather we are even more exposed to God's light, and we get away with less then what the world does. This is because those who have not believed are not adopted children of God.

I remember telling my children that since they all have accepted Jesus into their lives, they are not as apt to get away with the same things that their unsaved co-workers are able to. This is because God will expose our sin and discipline us for it, since we are His children and He wants His best for us.

> *I Corinthians 6:12* "I am allowed to do all things," but all things are not good for me to do. "I am allowed to do all things," but I will not let anything make me its slave.

What a powerful statement! Paul understood the entirety of his freedom in Christ. He understood that he was not under sin's power anymore and that he was set free by the blood of Christ to live in the fullness of life in which God intended for us to live.

Sin has no benefit at all. It only causes hurt and destruction. A universal and biblical Law states, *"I will reap what I sow"* (Galatians 6:7). Sin will still cause pain for those who have believed but not the fear of being eternally lost. There is also an expectation of discipline from the Father of our spirits when we sin.

> ***Hebrews 12:4-11*** *You are struggling against sin, but your struggles have not yet caused you to be killed. You have forgotten the encouraging words that call you His children: "My child, don't think the Lord's discipline is worth nothing, and don't stop trying when He corrects you. The Lord disciplines those He loves, and He punishes everyone He accepts as his child." So hold on through your sufferings, because they are like a father's discipline. God is treating you as children. All children are disciplined by their fathers.*
>
> *If you are never disciplined (and every child must be disciplined), you are not true children. We have all had fathers here on earth who disciplined us, and we respected them. So it is even more important that we accept discipline from the Father of our spirits so we will have life. Our fathers on earth disciplined us for a short time in the way they thought was best. But God disciplines us to help us, so we can become holy as He is. We do not enjoy being disciplined. It is painful, but later, after we*

*have learned from it, we have peace, because we
start living in the right way.*

Overcoming Sin

Okay, so how do I not sin? How do I get to a point in my life where sin does not have any power over me?

> *Romans 6:13-14 Do not offer the parts of your body
> to serve sin, as things to be used in doing evil.
> Instead, offer yourselves to God as people who
> have died and now live. Offer the parts of your body
> to God to be used in doing good. Sin will not be
> your master, because you are not under law but
> under God's grace.*

Sin does not have power over you! That is a fact! Only you can let sin rule your life now. You see, submission is the key in your fight against sin. Sin now becomes a barometer of the relationship that you have with God, and your relationship is the barometer of the amount of submission that you have toward God.

If the sin in your life is **high**, it is because your relationship with God is low, and your relationship with God is low, because your submission of yourself to God is low.

If the sin in your life is **low**, it is because your relationship with God is high, your relationship with God is high, because the amount of yourself that you submit to God is high.

The higher one's relationship is with God, the lower the incidents of sin are. Surrender to God determines your relationship with God.

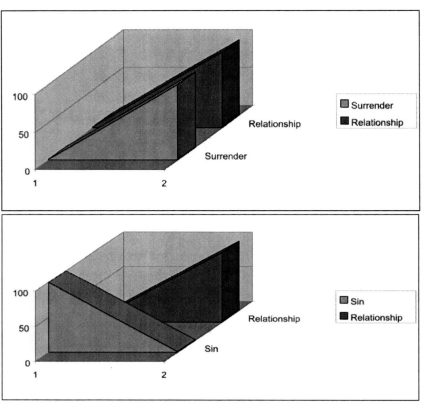

I hope that makes sense to you. See for yourself if this is not true! If you also want to conquer weakness, fear, and bondage, you can! You do this by an offering of yourself. You can do this by just praying a prayer like this and truly meaning it.

"Father, I approach Your throne with a request
for my life. I request that You make me into the
person that You created me to be. I want to fulfill
the purpose that You sent me here to accomplish.
I give You permission to do this without any
regards to my family, my finances, or my body. I
give You all of me. I give You permission to
remove anything in my life that is not pleasing to
You. I give my will up for Your will to be done in
me. I am Yours to do with what You want, Father.
In Jesus' name—Amen."

I hope you prayed that prayer with me and meant it. In a spiritual sense, it can bring the greatest change in your life that you will ever see. God never intended for man to live under a system of law. Adam and Eve lived under a system of grace. God only gave them one requirement, which was do not partake of the tree of the knowledge of good and evil. That was the one and only thing they were forbidden to do. The only thing that they needed to do in order to stay under grace was to NOT partake of the tree of the Knowledge of Good and Evil.

Look at what Christ has done for us. We can now partake of life again and live under the shadow of the Almighty. There is only one thing that will keep a person from being in God, not partaking of the Son of God. We are again under only one requirement for salvation, which is to believe in the Son of God, Who loved us and gave Himself for us. I want you to take a look at Romans again.

*Romans 3:20 Therefore no one will be declared righteous in his sight by observing the law; rather, **through the law we become conscious of sin.***

Now compare that with the name of the tree of which God forbade Adam and Eve to partake. *"Through the law we become conscious of sin"* and *"the tree of the knowledge of good and evil."* Do you see the similarity?

Law defines what is acceptable and unacceptable moral behavior, or the knowledge of good and evil. Adam and Eve lived under a system of grace. They lost this state when they partook of the tree of the Knowledge of Good and Evil, thereby plunging the entire human race under a system of Law.

Jesus brought us back under a system of grace. Under a system of grace, God looks at us as children, and even though we do things wrong at times, He will discipline us but not reject us eternally. That means our destiny is sealed in Him in Whom we believe.

Sealed

We, as children of God, need not fear our eternal destiny as it is sealed in the work of Jesus. What we do need to fear as God's children is what happens to us when we sin. God's discipline is painful. Sin also has built in pain. It will cause harm to your life and your loved ones' lives. That is what Paul meant when he said, *"All things are lawful for me, but not all things are profitable"* (I Corinthians 6:12a).

Paul knew that since he was not under a system of Law, logic follows that all things are lawful. However, he also noted that even though he would not be judged by the Law, he would fall under the discipline of the Father. Again, we go out from under the Law to be under the Lawgiver. Even though God's discipline will produce righteousness eventually, it will cost you in other things: finances, sicknesses, and troubles of all sorts.

Review

Sin is not profitable. So what do we do with our weaknesses? How do we overcome that we might live in the prosperity that God wants us to live in? How do we access prosperity in health, prosperity in our soul, and prosperity in our finances? It starts with being rightly related to grace. If I do not believe that Jesus has set me free from the power of sin, I will walk as if I do not believe it, and I will be a slave to the Law.

First, as I stated earlier, you have to surrender. This surrender is not just with the mind, but with the spirit, mind, and body. Secondly, you need to be baptized. Third, you need to confess your faults to God. Fourth, you need to confess your faults to one another. Fifth, you need to increase in the knowledge of God. So let's go over these individually. Please bear with me if I repeat some of what I have said; I feel that it is important enough to repeat.

Surrender

Just what is it that you are surrendering? God gave each human the gift of free will. We all have a will of our own. When you tell God that you only want to do what you were created to do, in effect, you are giving Him your free will. You are submitting to His will for your life and not your own. Since you possess free will, God will not override your will. It is something that you have to give up; otherwise, it would not be free will.

By giving up your free will, you are allowing God's will to be done in your life. God can now freely work in your life and bring you to the greatness of His calling. In this, you will partake of His peace, joy, and love. You will find contentment and fulfillment with your life because of this surrender. That is why it is the first step in overcoming sin. God is now free to work out things in your life that are holding you back from achieving the greatness of His calling. You must also surrender the members of your body for the service of the gospel. This will help you produce fruit and allow God to work in your body to accomplish His will.

The importance of offering your members to righteousness cannot be understated. When you make a conscious effort to do God's will each day, God undergirds your weak areas. What a wonderful thought! I have at my side the very Creator of all things; His strength at my side. Is it any wonder that Jesus said to Paul, *"My strength is made perfect in your weakness"* (II Corinthians 12:9)? When I am aware of my weaknesses, and others are aware of them too, and when they see those weaknesses turned to strengths, people can rejoice in what God is doing in me.

You must also let the mind of Christ be in you. Let God fill your mind with His desire and His thoughts. Refuse thoughts that you know are against what you know is God's truth.

Baptism

Baptism will quiet the sin that dwells in your body. You are laying the old man to rest in death and coming up a new person out of the judgment of God as represented by the water. Baptism represents the purification from sins in your body.

Confess your faults to God

Confessing your faults to God will help to bring honesty into your relationship with God. It will also allow God to work in those areas where you are weak. Confession is not only acknowledging your wrongdoing but also acknowledging your desire for God to take that weakness out of your life. If you let Him, God will do just that.

Confessing your faults one to another

Confessing your faults one to another is something that is difficult to do, and because of its difficulty, it is usually not done. However, there is a benefit in confessing your faults to each other. We all have faults, but because we do not confess them to one another, we have this tendency to internalize them and feel as if we are alone in our faults. That is the great benefit of confessing our faults; it allows us all to know that we are all struggling with the flesh. Yes, some of us struggle more than others, but we all struggle.

This is how we can build each other up and how we can pray for one another and see deliverance from things that used to easily tear us down. At church we must quit putting on airs as if we are perfect. We are only perfect in the sense of the applied righteousness of God, but that is by grace. You did not earn it or work for it; therefore, you cannot take credit for it. You know the world scoffs at God because we put up this front that says, *"All is well; nothing is wrong; I have everything under control."* Then the world sees us as we come apart and fall. We have to begin to be transparent with God and each other. It is beneficial to you and the body of Christ.

Increase in the knowledge of God

Increasing in the knowledge of God will have the effect of bringing holiness to your life. The more of the knowledge of God you acquire, the easier it becomes not to sin. The primary knowledge of God necessary to start upon this road is the knowledge of grace. If people do not understand the grace of God, they will have a false idea of their position in Christ.

Conclusion

Dear saint, God said that He came to give us life and to give it more abundantly (John 10:10). The Greek word for *"abundantly"* means *"over and above, more than is necessary, superadded, something further, more, much more than all."* Now consider these questions. Are you experiencing life in this manner? Do you have a life that has greater joy than normal, greater peace than normal, greater contentment than normal, and greater fulfillment than normal? It is accessible to every Christian; it can be possessed even in the greatest of human trials. God came to give you life more abundant. Think about the meaning of that statement. If God desires that we experience life abundantly, and we are not, the fault must lie with us.

Remember that the enemy comes only to kill, steal, and destroy. If he can keep you feeling half-saved and hell-bound, then you will not be an effective vessel for God's use. On the other hand, if you dare to believe what God says in His Word, then you can live an abundant life. David wrote about it in Psalms. Being led beside still waters and green pastures, having a table prepared in the presence of my enemies, and not fearing even in the shadow of death, sounds like abundant life to me.

My prayer for all of you is that you learn that your enemy has no power over you as long as you don't hand it to him. When you fear, you give him power; when you doubt, you give him power; when you lack faith, you give him power. But when you walk in faith, you destroy the power of the enemy in your life.

I pray for your weaknesses, and as you confess them, I stand with you in the Spirit and say for all to hear, you are the very righteousness of God. I pray that the enemy's work in your life will be destroyed. I declare that his power is broken by the power of the Spirit of God and through the name of Jesus. God has a designed, specific purpose for your life. Walk in it, and you will have abundant life. God bless you richly in your Christian walk.

Healing: The Life Force of God

Chapter Ten

> *PURPOSE: This is a powerful presentation of the mandate for healing the sick. This chapter will prove without a doubt that God desires and empowers us to heal the sick. It will also build a sound foundation upon which you can build your faith to live in the blessing of health provided by the covenant promise of God.*

I
n discussing the subject of supernatural healing there are a myriad of responses. Too many people who consider themselves to be Christians will respond that those who believe in supernatural healing are in need of psychological assistance. Others will respond that if God does heal, it is a rarity. Few Christians respond by stating that if God wills one can get healed. Still fewer others affirm that God still heals supernaturally today.

We find about as many different opinions as we can find words in a dictionary concerning this subject. What I will make an effort to accomplish is to bring some clarity to this issue and lay out a biblical case for supernatural healing. I will attempt to avoid the chatter from the extreme wings on both sides of this subject and stay on an even keel toward biblical understanding. Having raised these issues let us begin.

According to I Corinthians 12, we find that the Holy Spirit has given to the Church spiritual gifts; one of which is called the gifts of healings. Therefore, in order to get a feel for the pulse of the American Church, we need to look at the mindset of the American Church. George Barna did some interesting research concerning spiritual gifts that will give us some insight into why American Christians respond the way they do about the subject of supernatural healing.

Knowledge of Spiritual Gifts

Barna Research Group	Born Again Adults	Protestant Pastors
Listed biblical gifts only.	30%	74%
Listed a combination of biblical and other, non-biblical gifts.	8%	19%
Listed non-biblical gifts only.	16%	4%
Claim they have no gifts or are not sure of their gifts	46%	4%
Sample size	455	601

From the above chart we find that 30% of Christians have a biblical working knowledge of what spiritual gifts are. That does not mean they believe they are operating today, only that they have a knowledge of them.

What is shocking is that seventy percent of Christians do not have a biblical working knowledge of spiritual gifts. That means that seven out of ten people are likely to think differently concerning spiritual gifts than what the Bible reveals. I think it is safe to say that there is a huge disconnect between what the Bible says and what Christians are thinking concerning spiritual gifts.

For instance, the following are some of the *"non-biblical"* spiritual gifts listed by Christians who were asked to list their spiritual gifts. *A sense of humor, listening, patience, a good personality, friendliness, poetry, going to church, being likeable, drawing, survival, observation, and being a good person.* There were several dozen *"non-gifts"* mentioned according to Barna's study.

"QUOTE"

Barna Research Group

"The big change relates to people's perceptions of what gifts God has given to them. Among born again adults, the percentage that say they have heard of spiritual gifts but do not believe God has given them one jumped from 4% in 1995 to 21% in 2000."

Concerning the gifts of healings specifically, 3% of senior pastors reported to have this gift, and 4% of born again adults claim this gift. I think from this research it would be safe to say that less than 30% of all Christians will be *"friendly"* toward this gift.

I wanted to show the mindset of the Church in America before I presented my case. I hope to show by the end of this chapter that a gap has been created between what the Bible declares about healing and what the Body of Christ is believing about healing.

There are numerous belittlements thrown at those who claim to have this gift or even those who claim to believe in it. These are simply ad hominem attacks which are baseless and delivered because of the inability of the attacker to defend why they believe there are no supernatural spiritual gifts of healings. In other words, the environment in the Church is hostile concerning this subject.

Natural Presentation

In order to deliver a proper perspective we must put the mind of Christ into the context of this argument. If one would be honest with himself and answer the following question with careful thought, I think he could be brought to the place of discovery and inquiry concerning the supernatural gifts of healings. The question is this: *"If Jesus were to come to earth today, do you think He would heal the sick?"*

If Christians would be honest concerning that question, I believe there would be a considerably higher percentage of Christians coming into agreement concerning this issue than the less than 30% found in George Barna's research. The obvious answer to that question is a resounding *"Yes!"*

God does not change. The works He did two thousand years ago would be done today if He were to again walk among humanity. But wait a minute! He does walk among humanity today! How does He walk among humanity today? It is through you and me!

I Corinthians 12:27 Now you are Christ's body, and individually members of it.

You see, if you answered yes to the question I gave earlier, you have a problem. The body always does what the Head tells it to do.

> *Colossians 1:17-18 He is before all things, and in Him all things hold together. **He is also head of the body,** the church; and He is the beginning, the firstborn from the dead, so that He Himself will come to have first place in everything.*

If the Head (Jesus) of the Body (the Church) would heal the sick if He were here, and you and I are His represented presence in the earth, it is therefore only logical to conclude that it is the will of Jesus to heal the sick through the members of His Body, the Church! Now, if this is the case, that is, Jesus wills to heal the sick today through His Body, the Church, then we should be able to provide ample evidence from the Bible to support this. Even though we have not started our biblical presentation concerning the gifts of healings, we have a very strong argument concerning the heart of God toward His creation as it concerns healing the sick.

Biblical Presentation

The Will of God

In discussing the desire of God for all of mankind, could we even think that God does not will that His healing be given to the people of the earth? The problem is that certain biblical truths do get lost over time because of cultural movements and/or social conditions. It is not surprising that these things happen; however, it is surprising how much opposition is found when we try to restore these truths. In contemplating healing for today we must start with the will of God. We must first show that it is the will of God to heal the sick at any time.

> **Luke 10:2-9** *And He was saying to them, "The harvest is plentiful, but the laborers are few; therefore beseech the Lord of the harvest to send out laborers into His harvest. "Go; behold, I send you out as lambs in the midst of wolves. "Carry no money belt, no bag, no shoes; and greet no one on the way. "Whatever house you enter, first say, 'Peace be to this house.' "If a man of peace is there, your peace will rest on him; but if not, it will return to you. "Stay in that house, eating and drinking what they give you; for the laborer is worthy of his wages. Do not keep moving from house to house. "Whatever city you enter and they receive you, eat what is set before you; and heal those in it who are sick, and say to them, 'The kingdom of God has come near to you.'*

Note that Jesus commands his apostles to heal the sick. Moreover, He told his apostles to reveal something to those who were just healed. It is revealed only after the miracle of healing took place. It is the statement, *"The kingdom of God has come near to you."* If the miracle of healing was a *"sign"* that the kingdom of God has come near, do we no longer need to have the evidence that the kingdom of God has come near us? What does it mean to have the kingdom of God be near?

> **John 14:12** *"Truly, truly, I say to you, he who believes in Me, the works that I do, he will do also; and greater works than these he will do; because I go to the Father.*

Jesus parsed His Words very carefully. There is no ambiguity in the meaning of this text. Jesus is plainly saying that the works that He did will continue through those who would believe upon Him. This was not a message only for the apostles; notice the phrase, *"he who believes in Me."* **This statement is not time specific. It is faith specific.** We must remember that Jesus is also God. Anything God says is absolute! God cannot change, and His Word is sure and fixed. Therefore, we can only conclude that those who believe in Jesus will do the works that Jesus did and in a greater measure.

Now note this immutable fact. Those who believe in Jesus are also included in the term *"the Body of Christ."* The physical presence of Jesus on the earth is made up of those who believe in Him. His will is to be accomplished through that body of believers.

> *Mark 16:17-18 "These signs will accompany those who have believed: in My name they will cast out demons, they will speak with new tongues; they will pick up serpents, and if they drink any deadly poison, it will not hurt them; they will lay hands on the sick, and they will recover."*

This is the accomplishment expected by Jesus of His body, the assembly of believers in Him. If these are to be the *"signs"* of the believers, then it is also the will of the One doing those signs through His believers. These signs cannot be argued to have ceased if they are the very signs by which believers are revealed.

One cannot dismiss healing based upon their personal experience of seeing no manifestation healing take place no more than I can dismiss the space shuttle because I have not seen it. Rather, we should not only be seeing miracles take place, but they should be taking place through each of us. If the Word of God is true, and let there be no confusion on this matter, it is true, then we, the followers of Christ, are endued with power to work miracles in accordance with the will of God the Father!

> **Acts 10:38** *"You know of Jesus of Nazareth, how God anointed Him with the Holy Spirit and with power, and how He went about doing good and healing all who were oppressed by the devil, for God was with Him.*

If sickness and disease are a result of oppression from the devil, we must make a decision, a decision of such import, that lives could be won or lost depending on which way one chooses to believe. ***Does Jesus will the destruction of sickness and disease, which are oppression from the devil?***

The way you answer this question will force you to either attack sickness or endure it. It will change the way you pray for the sick. You will either command that sick body to respond to the healing force of God, or you will pray for the person to respond to the sickness with endurance. Which way is God's way?

> **Exodus 15:26** *And He said, "If you will give earnest heed to the voice of the Lord your God, and do what is right in His sight, and give ear to His commandments, and keep all His statutes, I will put none of the diseases on you which I have put on the Egyptians; **for I, the Lord, am your healer."***

The Lord is the healer, and Satan is the oppressor. We have a God Who is a healer. He is not the oppressor! We have an enemy who seeks to kill, steal, and destroy. It is so amazing that when disaster strikes, everyone blames God, but when good things come, they call it luck. Yet the Bible tells us that every good and perfect gift comes down from the Father of lights (James 1:17). It is God's will to see us healed. It is His will to heal the sick. Jesus has transformed us from the curse of the Law to the blessing of the Law by becoming a curse for us.

This is where the statement, *"the kingdom of God has come near you"* makes sense. The Bible says that Satan is the god of this world. This is his kingdom. Even Jesus did not dispute that when Satan offered the kingdoms of this world to Jesus if He would worship him.

The kingdom of the devil is called the kingdom of darkness. It is full of deceptions, lies, murders, abominations, death, sickness, heartache, and every kind of evil. Most who are in that kingdom do not know they are in that kingdom. The kingdom of God is full of light, salvation, redemption, love, joy, peace, hope, faith, healing, restoration, and every kind of good.

When Jesus commanded His twelve to say, "the kingdom of God has come near you" he was demonstrating His superiority to the kingdom of darkness. If the King of this kingdom can destroy a work of the king of that kingdom, then the kingdom of God is superior and outranks the kingdom of darkness.

Covenant Right

Now that we have established God's will concerning healing the sick, it would seem to follow that healing would be a covenant right to the believer. God's will for humanity is found in His covenants with humanity. The covenants show us what God promises to do and what God expects of mankind. If mankind would hold up its part of the covenant than the covenant is enforceable because we know God will hold up His end.

We have two covenants. We know them as the Old Testament and the New Testament. The conditions of each covenant are different. The Old Testament was a contract that required **action** on the part of humanity.

Old Covenant

> ***Deuteronomy 28:1*** *"Now it shall be, if you diligently obey the Lord your God, being careful to do all His commandments which I command you today, the Lord your God will set you high above all the nations of the earth...*

"If" is the condition, and *"the Lord your God will"* is the fulfillment of His part of the contract. Yet we know that we have a problem because humanity is incapable of doing all His commandments. Therefore, we have a breach of contract before we even get started. We must not forget that God established the sacrificial laws to address the inability of humanity to live according to His Laws. By following the sacrificial Laws the people could fulfill the Law of God through the sacrifice and thereby enter into the blessings of God for obeying the commandments. To simplify this we need to understand that there are two sides to the Law.

> ***Deuteronomy 28:15*** *"But it shall come about, if you do not obey the Lord your God, to observe to do all His commandments and His statutes with which I charge you today, that all these curses will come upon you and overtake you:*

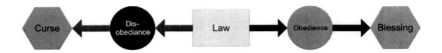

The way to the curse of the Law is through disobedience and the way to the blessing of the Law is through obedience. The way into the blessing of God then is only available through the sacrificial law that took man's disobedience out of the way.

> *Leviticus 16:29-30 "This shall be a permanent statute for you: in the seventh month, on the tenth day of the month, you shall humble your souls and not do any work, whether the native, or the alien who sojourns among you; for it is on this day that atonement shall be made for you **to cleanse you; you will be clean from all your sins before the Lord.***

Thus, the atonement through animal sacrifice was able to go around the disobedience of man and **make him obedient** through that sacrifice. Note also that in Leviticus 14:18, the priest is commanded to offer atonement for the leper. This would also suggest that healing is in the atonement.

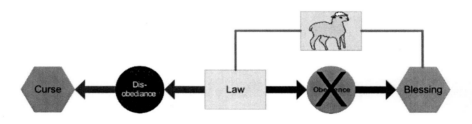

Now, then, there are two paths to the blessing. Either you could be obedient **absolutely** to the Law of God, or you could go by way of the sacrifice provided to cover your sins. One way was impossible, which in reality left only one way into the blessing, and that way was through the **blood** of the lamb.

By following the sacrificial system through **actions**, a person was able to access God's blessings, but this had to be done once a year and there also had to be a temple in which to do the sacrifice. The blood of that lamb had to be sprinkled on the lid of the Ark of the Covenant inside the Holy of Holies in order for the sacrifice to be legitimate.

> ***Psalm 103:1-5*** *Bless the Lord, O my soul, And all that is within me, bless His holy name. Bless the Lord, O my soul, And forget none of His benefits; Who pardons all your iniquities,* ***Who heals all your diseases;*** *Who redeems your life from the pit, Who crowns you with lovingkindness and compassion; Who satisfies your years with good things, So that your youth is renewed like the eagle.*

This was a description of the blessings of the Law. In this description we find that God heals all of our diseases. One could say then that **by the lamb taking the guilt and sin from the people, that lamb also bore all the sicknesses and diseases of the people since sickness was a result of sin.** They had access to healing because the lamb carried their sin away from them.

> ***Leviticus 16:21-22*** *"Then Aaron shall lay both of his hands on the head of the live goat, and confess over it all the iniquities of the sons of Israel and all their transgressions in regard to all their sins; and he shall lay them on the head of the goat and send it away into the wilderness by the hand of a man who stands in readiness. "***The goat shall bear on***

*itself all their iniquities to a solitary land; and he
shall release the goat in the wilderness.*

It should be clear from this Scripture that the goat or lamb
carries the sins of the people and is sent away from the people.
What they did to the goat after that is not found in the Bible. They
would then chase the goat off the edge of a cliff so that the goat
would not wander back into the camp with all of the sins of the
people.

New Covenant

Understanding the Old Covenant is vital in making sense of
the New Covenant and vice versa. However, we still have the same
problem. We still have the issue of sin, and we still have the issue
of sacrifice. Now enters a different sacrifice. Whereas in the Old
Covenant, we find that animals were needed to take sin away on an
annual basis, in the New Covenant we find that a human sacrifice
has taken sin away once and for all through faith.

*Romans 5:1-2 Therefore, having been justified **by
faith**, we have peace with God through our Lord
Jesus Christ, through whom also we have obtained
our introduction **by faith** into this grace in which we
stand; and we exult in hope of the glory of God.*

*Galatians 2:16 nevertheless knowing that a man is
not justified by the works of the Law but **through
faith** in Christ Jesus, even we have believed in Christ
Jesus, so that we may be justified **by faith** in Christ
and not by the works of the Law; since by the works
of the Law no flesh will be justified.*

When we believe in the sacrifice of the New Testament, we have access to the benefits of the New Testament. Jesus became the sacrificial Lamb Who took away the sins of the people; only this time the sacrifice took away the sins of the whole world, not just the nation of Israel.

> *I John 2:2* *and He Himself is the propitiation for our sins; and not for ours only, but also for those of the whole world.*

Not only this, but the sacrifice of the Lamb of God was not something that had to be done over and over every year; it was done once and for all.

> *Hebrews 9:24-26* *For Christ did not enter a holy place made with hands, a mere copy of the true one, but into heaven itself, now to appear in the presence of God for us; nor was it that He would offer Himself often, as the high priest enters the holy place year by year with blood that is not his own. Otherwise, He would have needed to suffer often since the foundation of the world; but now once at the consummation of the ages He has been manifested to put away sin by the sacrifice of Himself.*

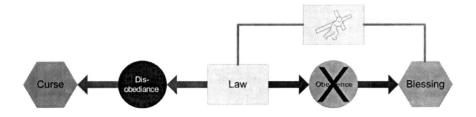

Now the cross has become *"the way"* to the blessings of the Law. In Christ the Law is completely fulfilled, and we are set free from the bondage of sin through His obedience. He literally bore our sins in His body that He might take away the ordinance that was hostile to us, making access possible to the blessing.

> *I Peter 2:24 and He Himself **bore our sins in His body** on the cross, so that we might die to sin and live to righteousness; for by His wounds you were healed.*

Now, if Jesus carried our sins in His body, can we conclude that the Lamb of God also bore our sicknesses and diseases since He has taken the curse of the law out of the way? Jesus demonstrated this concept in His prayer for the paralytic.

> *Matthew 9:2-8 And they brought to Him a paralytic lying on a bed. Seeing their faith, Jesus said to the paralytic, "Take courage, son; your sins are forgiven." And some of the scribes said to themselves, "This fellow blasphemes." And Jesus knowing their thoughts said, "Why are you thinking evil in your hearts? "Which is easier, to say, 'Your sins are forgiven,' or to say, 'Get up, and walk'? **"But so that you may know that the Son of Man has authority on earth to forgive sins"—then He said to the paralytic, "Get up, pick up your bed and go home."** And he got up and went home. But when the crowds saw this, they were awestruck, and glorified God, who had given such authority to men.*

In this passage Jesus was addressing the Scribes. They knew what Jesus meant when He made the statement *"so that you may know that the Son of Man has authority on earth to forgive sins.* " This was not just a show of power in healing the sick to prove Jesus had the power to forgive sins. Rather, Jesus was demonstrating that He could forgive sins by the fact that He also healed the man. Jesus demonstrated that by forgiving sins, the man now had access to healing since he was made righteous by Jesus.

> *Galatians 3:13 Christ redeemed us from the curse of the Law, having become a curse for us—for it is written, "Cursed is everyone who hangs on a tree"—*

> *Matthew 8:16-17 When evening came, they brought to Him many who were demon-possessed; and He cast out the spirits with a word, and healed all who were ill. This was to fulfill what was spoken through Isaiah the prophet: "He Himself took our infirmities and carried away our diseases."*

Hallelujah! Jesus carried our sins away and, since we are made His righteousness, sickness is also carried away and defeated!

The Brazen Serpent

The story of the brazen serpent is one that we must visit. It gives us a strong indication of the fact that Jesus provided health through the cross.

> *Numbers 21:6-9 The Lord sent fiery serpents among the people and they bit the people, so that many people of Israel died. So the people came to Moses and said, "We have sinned, because we have*

spoken against the Lord and you; intercede with the Lord, that He may remove the serpents from us." And Moses interceded for the people. Then the Lord said to Moses, "Make a fiery serpent, and set it on a standard; and it shall come about, that everyone who is bitten, when he looks at it, he will live." And Moses made a bronze serpent and set it on the standard; and it came about, that if a serpent bit any man, when he looked to the bronze serpent, he lived.

I want to parallel healing with this passage. First, sickness came through sin; the fiery serpents that bit the people came through sin. The people asked Moses to ask God to take away the fiery serpents, but God did not do that; instead, He provided a way to be healed from the bite of the serpents. However, it required faith. Sickness is not taken out of the world, but a remedy is provided by God; the Son of God was lifted up on the cross. However, it requires faith. In both cases, people are healed.

John 3:14 *"As Moses lifted up the serpent in the wilderness, even so must the Son of Man be lifted up;*

Jesus makes the parallel with Himself. The result is unmistakable. Some may argue that this has to do with salvation only. Well, yes! Salvation includes healing of the spirit, mind, and body of man.

The Importance of Faith in Healing

There is a term which has really become a derogatory statement for ministers who are moving with faith in the healing of God's people. It is *"faith healer."* This, however, is an inaccurate statement. One needs faith to operate in healing. For instance, one would not even attempt to pray for healing if they did not believe in it. Yet it is not always enough to just have faith by one's self. If the crowd being prayed for lacks faith, healing would not be able to take place. We could say that Jesus was a man of perfect faith. There was no lack in Him. He not only believed the Word, He was the Word. Yet Jesus was hindered by a lack of faith from the very ones to whom He desired to minister.

> *Matthew 13:58 And He did not do many miracles there because of their unbelief.*

If the Son of God was hindered by a lack of faith, then so are we. The reason that a lack of faith is so detrimental to the miracles of God, is the principle of free will. If we refuse to believe in the provision God has made, He will not force that provision upon us. This is understood in a number of places in the Bible but none more clearly than the following.

> *Psalm 103:1-5 Bless the Lord, O my soul, And all that is within me, bless His holy name. Bless the Lord, O my soul, **And forget none of His benefits;** Who pardons all your iniquities, Who heals all your diseases; Who redeems your life from the pit, Who crowns you with lovingkindness and compassion; Who satisfies your years with good things, So that your youth is renewed like the eagle.*

What is so important about us not forgetting any benefits? If we forget them, or refuse to believe them, we will not have access to them. God will not force us to believe; He invites us to believe. To believe means that I can now access His power for healing.

> **II Peter 1:4** *For by these He has granted to us His precious and magnificent promises, so that **by them you may become partakers of the divine nature,** having escaped the corruption that is in the world by lust.*

> **Luke 5:17** *One day He was teaching; and there were some Pharisees and teachers of the law sitting there, who had come from every village of Galilee and Judea and from Jerusalem; **and the power of the Lord was present for Him to perform healing.***

The reason I dislike the term *"faith healer"* is precisely because it is Jesus Who is supplying the power that produces the healing. Even though faith is required to access healing, the Healer has always been and will always be Jesus. It must be said that even though you have faith for healing and you pray for someone to be healed, they may not get healed due to their lack of faith. Only God knows your heart and the heart of the one who is sick. The Bible mentions that there are those with great faith, little faith, or no faith. There are different levels of faith.

Even when we know a person may be lacking enough faith, by joining our faith with the faith of that person, we are able to facilitate the miracle of healing. We find an example of this in the Bible with the story of a paralytic man and his friends. Some friends took their sick friend to Jesus, and, since they could not get through the crowd, they dug a hole in the roof where Jesus was and lowered their friend down to Jesus. Look what Jesus said when He healed this paralytic man.

> **Mark 2:5** And Jesus **seeing their faith** said to the paralytic, "Son, your sins are forgiven."

You see, Jesus could see the conglomeration of all their faith, and it was enough to facilitate healing. There can be no doubt; healing is only accessed through faith, just as any other benefit is accessed by faith.

True Faith Produces Expectation.

When we have a genuine faith, it will produce an expectation concerning the benefit in which we have faith. For instance, we will lead someone to Christ for salvation, and we go away with a sure knowledge that the person is now saved. We are so convinced in the power of God to save one from eternal damnation that we do not doubt that the person is saved. Yet, when we pray for a person to be healed, we often enter into a *"hope so"* kind of faith.

Peter did not pray with a *"hope so"* kind of faith. Peter declared, *"...in the name of Jesus, rise up and walk"* (Acts 3:6). Peter expected a result before he even prayed, and that expectation was revealed through his words. Today, most of us are afraid to pray like that because we are not really sure of the provision of healing. We think, *"What if they don't get up and walk?"* That is doubt. Yet, we usually don't think when we pray for salvation, *"What if they don't get saved?"*

We are **so** sure of salvation as a covenant right through faith that we actually thank God for the salvation. We need to get our faith for healing to the level where we thank God for healing that person no matter what we see. Do you see healing as a covenant right or not? If healing was a covenant right in the Old Testament, then it should be a covenant right of the New Testament. Look what Jesus tells a Gentile looking for healing.

> **Mark 7:26-30** *Now the woman was a Gentile, of the Syrophoenician race. And she kept asking Him to cast the demon out of her daughter. And He was saying to her, "Let the children be satisfied first, for it is not good to **take the children's bread** and throw it to the dogs." But she answered and said to Him, "Yes, Lord, but even the dogs under the table feed on the children's crumbs." And He said to her, "Because of this answer go; the demon has gone out of your daughter." And going back to her home, she found the child lying on the bed, the demon having left.*

Jesus called the healing from demon possession the children's bread. This is important when taken in context. The term *"children"* presupposes a parent. In this case the parent is the Father and the children are the sons' and daughters' of Israel. Bread, then, is the right of the children. It was a covenant right for every citizen of Israel to be free from the molestation of demonic spirits. Healing is still a covenant right, but it has to be accessed by faith based upon the surety of God's Word.

If the children's bread is a provision of the covenant promise, then we need to decide if it is something that is already there or something we have to generate now. If it is something already there, then all we need to do is access the provision. This may be pictured as walking to the cupboard and taking a piece of bread. The bread was already there.

I Peter 2:24 and He Himself bore our sins in His body on the cross, so that we might die to sin and live to righteousness; **for by His wounds you were healed.**

This is a reminder from Isaiah 53. What is interesting about it is the tense. In Isaiah 53:5, the phrase is *"we are healed;"* whereas, here we find it is *"you were healed."* What has changed that would cause the tense to change? Could it be that Jesus bore the sins and consequently the sicknesses of the believer?

Yet we often pray **not** as if the provision has already been made. We beg and ask for healing as if it is something in our future. What would you think of your child who would beg and ask for a piece of bread when they could walk into the kitchen and get a slice for themselves? There is only one reason why the child would not take that slice of bread; namely, the child does not really believe you that the bread is there, so he continues to ask and beg.

Luke 9:1-2 And He called the twelve together, and **gave them power and authority over all the demons and to heal diseases.** And He sent them out to proclaim the kingdom of God and **to perform healing.**

Was this power temporary? Was it just for a season after which it would cease to function? Or was this something that was meant to continue throughout every generation? I think in light of Mark 16 where Mark penned the words, *"These signs shall follow them that believe; …they shall lay hands on the sick, and they shall recover."* Almost every Christian pastor would not argue against the idea that every Christian has power over demonic spirits. Yet many do argue against the belief that healing power is available to Christians today.

In one case they say that healing power was only given to the apostles and therefore died out when the last apostle died. Yet they do not apply that same standard when talking about demonic spirits.

What we don't hear them say is that sickness is a curse. If sickness is a curse, and specifically a curse of the Law, then all we need to prove is that we are free from that curse through Christ. We already found in Galatians 3:13 that Jesus became a curse for us. This was to free us from the curse of the Law. If sickness is a curse of the Law, then we are free from that curse. Remember, though, that everything is accessed by faith. Without faith we can't get anything.

To put this into perspective, let's look at the lottery. Someone buys a lottery ticket and wins the lottery. This person does not wait to receive the money before he starts celebrating. He starts celebrating immediately even though he does not have one more penny than he did the minute before he won the lottery. Why, then, is he celebrating? He is celebrating the promissory words written upon that ticket. He has full faith and trust in those promised, written words. With this faith, he began celebrating before even receiving the manifestation of money.

How much more sure are the Words of our God? Yet we pray for people to be healed, and we don't expect it to happen, and we don't celebrate before it happens. Instead we wait for a sign that healing is taking place before we celebrate. In effect, we are saying by our actions that we really don't believe.

Walk by Faith and Not by Sight!

> ***II Corinthians 5:7*** *for we walk by faith, not by sight—*

This is an important statement. If we were to walk by sight, we would require the manifestation of a thing before we believed it. This would preclude the faithfulness of God, Who says a thing to be so. If we wait to see it, we are telling God, *"I will not believe unless I first see."* Let me explain why this distinction is so important.

We know that when God says something, it is absolute, because He is absolutely powerful, absolutely trustworthy, and absolutely faithful. He cannot change, and He cannot say one thing and then do another. He cannot say one thing and then change His mind. Since God has all foreknowledge, for Him to change His mind is for Him to admit that He did not know something. If He did not know something, He is not God.

This is why it is so important that we take God at His Word before we actually see the manifestation of it. We do this without thinking concerning salvation and the resulting eternal life. We do not have the manifestation of eternal life, but we do not doubt it. This is taking God at His word. Well, if we can take His word on one thing, we can take it on all things. He is absolutely faithful.

> ***Jeremiah 1:11-12*** *The word of the Lord came to me saying, "What do you see, Jeremiah?" And I said, "I see a rod of an almond tree." Then the Lord said to me, "You have seen well, for I am watching over My word to perform it."*

This seems to make no sense. What does seeing an almond tree have to do with God watching over His Word to perform it? The answer lies in the Hebrew word for *"almond."*

DEFINITION

שָׁקֵד *m*—*(1) the almond tree; so called because of all trees it is the first to arouse and awake from the sleep of winter, Jer. 1:11 (where allusion is made to the signification of haste and ardour, which there is in this root).* [7]

COMMENTARY

1:11. *God's first confirming vision caused Jeremiah to* **see the branch of an almond tree.** *The Hebrew word for "almond tree" is šāqēḏ, from the word "to watch or to wake" (šāqaḏ). The almond tree was named the "awake tree" because in Palestine it is the first tree in the year to bud and bear fruit. Its blooms precede its leaves, as the tree bursts into blossom in late January.*

1:12. *The branch represented God who was* **watching to see that** *His* **word is fulfilled.** *God used a play on words to associate the almond branch with His activity. The word for "watching" is šōqēḏ,*

[7] Gesenius, Wilhelm ; Tregelles, Samuel Prideaux: *Gesenius' Hebrew and Chaldee Lexicon to the Old Testament Scriptures.* Bellingham, WA : Logos Research Systems, Inc, 2003, S. 847

related to the Hebrew noun for "almond tree."
Jeremiah's vision of the "awake tree" reminded him
that God was awake and watching over His word to
make sure it came to pass.[8]

Therefore, when God says something, He is awake and watching to make sure His Word is performed. God puts great weight upon His Word for His Word speaks of His character.

Psalm 138:2 ~NKJV~ I will worship toward Your
holy temple, And praise Your name For Your
*lovingkindness and Your truth; **For You have***
magnified Your word above all Your name.

God puts such importance upon His Word that it is promoted above His name. In other words, if He does not perform His Word, then He is not God. That is what He is saying. If God has established healing as a covenant right for the children of God, then He has to perform it, if we have faith in His Word.

F. F. Bosworth author of, *"Christ the Healer"* states that God has so ordained things that there is not a harvest until there is first a seed. This means that God requires that the seed of His Word reside in our heart before we are to experience the harvest that seed will produce. Jonah did this from the belly of the great fish. He began to pray for God's mercy and notice what he says.

Jonah 2:9 ~NKJV~ But I will sacrifice to You With
the voice of thanksgiving; I will pay what I have
vowed. Salvation is of the Lord."

---

[8]Walvoord, J. F., Zuck, R. B., & Dallas Theological Seminary. (1983-c1985). *The Bible Knowledge Commentary: An Exposition of the Scriptures* (1:1131). Wheaton, IL: Victor Books.

Earlier in this passage it states that Jonah was about to lose consciousness in the belly of the fish, and yet here he offered a sacrifice of thanksgiving to God in spite of what he was experiencing bodily. This shows us that Jonah was walking by faith and not by sight.

> **Proverbs 4:20-23 ~NKJV~** *My son, give attention to my words; Incline your ear to my sayings. Do not let them depart from your eyes; Keep them in the midst of your heart; For they are life to those who find them, And health to all their flesh. Keep your heart with all diligence, For out of it spring the issues of life.*

The Word of God is health to all our flesh! God has provided for your healing, but you must give attention to His Words. How many times have people cried out to God for healing and found none because they were not willing to give attention to His Words? Oh, that we would put the Word of God in the midst of our heart and receive from it health for our souls and our bodies!

What Do the Senses Have to do With It?

The problem in accessing healing comes when we believe the senses over and above the Word of God. We feel pain in sickness, and we allow the feeling of pain to cloud what God has said. I don't want this concept to determine how we respond to those whose faith may not rise to the place of healing. There are and always will be some who have more or less faith than others. That is not a reason to look down upon or to criticize the person who is struggling.

Just as Jesus did, we must always have compassion upon the sick. It was often said of Him, *"He had compassion on them and healed them all."* Compassion alone cannot heal. It must be coupled with faith. We must remember that the senses belong to the natural, not the spiritual man. For this reason we must not suggest that a person stop taking medications or stop seeing a doctor. God will manifest the healing when faith is present.

Notice that we do not feel better and then get saved. We believe, which produces the manifestation of salvation, which produces the feeling of being saved. If we become double minded in the matter, we will lose the manifestation which is by faith. If we start out double minded, then we will not receive anything.

> *James 1:5-8* But if any of you lacks wisdom, let him ask of God, who gives to all generously and without reproach, and it will be given to him. But he must ask in faith without any doubting, for the one who doubts is like the surf of the sea, driven and tossed by the wind. For that man ought not to expect that he will receive anything from the Lord, being a double-minded man, unstable in all his ways.

When we get God's Word into our hearts, we will not doubt the thing for which we ask. The double-minded person will say, *"By His stripes I am healed"* and *"Why doesn't God heal me?"* God has healed him; he just needs to access it by faith.

> *Mark 11:24-25* "Therefore I say to you, all things for which you pray and ask, believe that you have received them, and they will be granted you. "Whenever you stand praying, forgive, if you have anything against anyone, so that your Father who

is in heaven will also forgive you your
transgressions.

Notice what the condition of receiving is. It is believing that we **HAVE** received when we ask. It doesn't say to wait until you receive to believe. The problem is that we think we believe when we actually do not. True belief does not waver in the face of opposing argument. The devil will argue with your faith. He will tell you that every ache and pain is a disease from which you will die. When you really believe, you will dismiss the voice of the devil in favor of the Word of God, providing truth to dispel the lies.

Jesus is telling us to come away with Him and to lighten our load through trusting in Him. He is telling us to come closer to hear what He is saying. Jesus is telling us to consider Him faithful, to learn of Him, and to find rest. Silence the voice of the enemy by believing in fullness on His provision. Bring health to yourself and health to those who are sick.

If the Body of Christ is to come to a place of faith concerning healing, they are going to have to be taught. If you don't know you have a promise from God, you will not be able to access it. If you believe a lie concerning God healing the sick, then you will not be able to access it. Let us all walk into faith concerning His provision of healing!

Obstacles to Healing

In this section we are going to look at some of the most common obstacles to healing that we find in the Body of Christ. This is not meant to answer every question. In fact, we may not have answers to every question as to why some do not get healed or why some have lost their healing after receiving it. This is also a sensitive subject therefore we will broach it with the utmost sensitivity.

There are many reasons that people have come up with to explain why some do not get healed or others who have lost a healing. The first thing that must be clear in your thinking before we even start to take a look at them is that we cannot impugn God or His nature. God's nature is unchangeable. We can be assured that God is just; God is merciful, God is love, and God is right in His dealings with us. Keep these things in the very front of your thinking. I have seen too many people blame God for a sickness or a death as if He were unjust. This cannot be the case.

Job provides for us a case where there were no reasons for his sickness. He did not understand why he was sick. There was a spiritual reason for it, but Job was unaware of it. We too, are unaware of things taking place spiritually that might, by no fault of our own, cause suffering in our lives. Now let's get to those obstacles.

Absence of Faith

Absence of faith is probably the number one reason why healing does not take place. I touched a bit on this earlier so I will just highlight some things. How many times have we heard, *"If it is God's will, healing will take place?"* That is a position of non faith. One is saying in that statement that if the person is not healed than God is not willing that the person be healed.

If we just look at some facts I think we can put this to rest. First, it is said of Jesus in Acts that He went about doing good, healing all who were oppressed of the devil. If a sickness is from the devil, does it not go against the nature of God to say that it is not His will for us to be healed? After all doesn't God want to destroy the works of the devil? If we say that it is not God's will, and the sick person is not healed, then using that philosophy God has a part in the person being sick. Sickness is a result of rebellion. It is initiated by the devil. It is a consequence of sin.

If we entertain that idea for a moment, we can see that it too leads nowhere. If God were causing a sickness, what set of circumstances would exist that would result in God making one sick? If you say sin, I will ask, does not God want them to repent and be healed? If you say to accomplish His will, than I will ask, does God need to use sickness to accomplish His will? Does that not make for a weak and ineffective God?

God has revealed that there are certain conditions that will bring about sickness, but this is no different from me telling you not to stick your hand in the fire or you will be burned. I did not cause the burn; I only revealed its cause. Let us look for a moment at the Lord's prayer. In the Lord's prayer there is the statement that says, *"...your will be done on earth as it is in heaven."*

Are there any sick people in heaven? Can we gain some insight from this? If there is no sickness in heaven and God's will is being accomplished in heaven, then we must conclude that it is His will to eliminate sickness on earth as well. We do not think that if someone did not get saved after hearing a message of salvation that it was not God's will for them to be saved. Yet we find many in the Church that are willing to say this about healing.

We do not put the responsibility on God for a person's salvation do we? God has already done His part to save all of humanity. The burden of salvation now lies with us alone to believe, to have faith which will give us access to the manifestation of salvation. Jesus has already carried our sickness and disease, therefore it is up to us to enter into faith to access it.

> *Ephesians 1:18-19 I pray that the eyes of your heart may be enlightened, so that you will know what is the hope of His calling, what are the riches of the glory of His inheritance in the saints, and what is the surpassing greatness of His power toward us who believe. These are in accordance with the working of the strength of His might*

I want to take you through these verses very slowly so that you will have the impact intended by them. First, Paul is praying. What is he praying for? He is praying for people to be enlightened; to understand; to know something. Paul wants us to know what is the surpassing; exceeding greatness of His power toward us who believe. Could it be that the Church to which He is writing was falling short of the benefits that were theirs because of a lack of knowledge? Not let us continue.

> *Ephesians 1:20-21 which He brought about in Christ, when He raised Him from the dead and seated Him at His right hand in the heavenly places, far above all rule and authority and power and dominion, and every name that is named, not only in this age but also in the one to come.*

Next, Paul establishes the authority of Jesus over the kingdom of darkness. He is above every rule, every authority, every power, and every dominion. He is above every name that is named; past, present, and future. He is above cancer; He is above heart disease; He is above MS; He is above diabetes; He is above everything. There is nothing that is above Him and He has authority over all things.

Ephesians 1:22-23 And He put all things in subjection under His feet, and gave Him as head over all things to the church, which is His body, the fullness of Him who fills all in all.

Now Paul reveals that not only is Jesus above everything, but He gave Him to us, the Church to be our Head. Notice however the last statement. It reveals that we, the Church, are the fullness of Him who fills all in all. If we are the fullness of Jesus corporately in the earth, then it stands to reason that we should be doing those things He would be doing if He were here. I find it interesting that many have more faith in the devil to make them sick than in God to heal them.

Unforgiveness

Unforgiveness will place us in the position of retaining the right of vengeance after God has forgiven us all that we have done wrong. By not forgiving someone, we are open to those tormenting spirits that only seek our destruction.

Mark 11:22-25 And Jesus answered saying to them, "Have faith in God. "Truly I say to you, whoever says to this mountain, 'Be taken up and cast into the sea,' and does not doubt in his heart, but believes that what he says is going to happen, it will be granted him. "Therefore I say to you, all things for which you pray and ask, believe that you have received them, and they will be granted you. "Whenever you stand praying, forgive, if you have anything against anyone, so that your Father who

is in heaven will also forgive you your
transgressions.

Note the condition that we must believe. Keep in mind that He said believe that it is "going to happen." That means that you count God so faithful, that when you ask for something from Him, you know He will do it. This means that if I am on the blessing side of the Law, there are certain things that have already been done for me. Notice that when Peter quotes from Isaiah the prophet, he changes the tense of the verb. Isaiah said that, "By His stripes we are healed" and Peter says, "By His stripes we were healed."

But also note the obstruction of unforgiveness to faith. Unforgiveness will stop faith in its tracks. That means that you can have the faith to move mountains but if you hold unforgiveness, that faith will not move so much as a grain of sand. Many people are so adamant in holding onto their unforgiveness that they would suffer sickness to do so rather than to forgive and be healed. Unforgiveness must be moved out of the way before healing can take place.

In order to receive from God, we have to make peace with every other person that we have had aught against and enter into forgiveness. There will be times that we will not remember some of the people that we have held unforgiveness toward. God is faithful to reveal these suppressed or forgotten incidences if you will ask Him to so that you can walk in freedom.

It must be remembered that forgiveness is not a feeling, it is a choice. You will hardly ever "feel" like forgiving someone, but you can make a willful choice to forgive someone. Feelings are derived from knowledge. That means the feeling of forgiveness will only come after you make the choice to forgive.

Unrepentant

Unrepentance causes us to enter into a reaping stage where I begin to receive in my body the things I have done against the Law of God.

> *Psalm 32:3-5 When I kept silent about my sin, my body wasted away Through my groaning all day long. For day and night Your hand was heavy upon me; My vitality was drained away as with the fever heat of summer. Selah. I acknowledged my sin to You, And my iniquity I did not hide; I said, "I will confess my transgressions to the Lord"; And You forgave the guilt of my sin. Selah.*

What does it mean to acknowledge my sin? It means that I come into agreement with the Law of God to measure my actions and intentions by it so that I will call those things that I do in opposition to the Law, sin. By looking at myself and condemning my sins as sin, I am saying that the Law of God is right and true. We get into difficulty when we start justifying our sin which really means that I have come out of agreement with God.

Not only is there the aspect of reaping in unrepentance but there is also the aspect of God's discipline. It must be noted however that God no more takes pleasure in disciplining you than you would take pleasure in disciplining your child. When you discipline your child it is with remorse that you do so but you do so because of the outcome it has upon the child. The outcome of repentance is restoration.

This begs the question, *"Will God make someone sick as a form of discipline?"* Not directly, however, He will take His hand of protection from you which opens you up to sickness because you are unrepentant. In actuality, you are making yourself sick by removing your life from the protection of God because you love sin more than you love God.

Absence of Knowledge

> ***Isaiah 5:13*** *Therefore My people go into exile for their lack of knowledge; And their honorable men are famished, And their multitude is parched with thirst.*

The people of God suffer from bondages through lack of knowledge. This can be a broad scope of things, but I want to concentrate on healing. Sickness is a bondage brought about by the enemy who desires to destroy the people of God. If people are unwilling to believe or are ignorant of the fact that their physical healing was paid for by Jesus through the cross, then they will not possess the faith necessary to access healing.

This is also where we find the consequences of family sins. What are family sins? They are sins committed by the fathers and mothers who then by their lack of repentance in committing those sins teach their children to do the same. As the children mature, they are faced with a temptation that is irresistible because their parents actions and lack of repentance make it permissible for them to commit those same sins.

Take smoking for example. Parents will often tell their children that they are not allowed to smoke. Yet, when questioned by the child as to why, the parents will not impugn themselves and resort to an excuse that amounts to saying it is only for adults. Well guess what, your child is going to grow up to adulthood in which the environment of smoking then becomes permissible.

In this example, the child lacks knowledge because of the actions viewed by the child. They are faced with false knowledge that certain adult behaviors are seen by God as acceptable. That somehow it is unacceptable as a child, but as an adult there is some mysterious shift in the code of morality that makes that behavior acceptable to God.

This why we see that statistical data will show that if a father commits suicide the likelihood of the child doing so goes way up. If the father is an alcoholic the likelihood of the child being one goes way up. There is a direct correlation to parental sins and generational continuance of that sin though the posterity of the parent. If parents would only see and believe the harm they do to their children through modeling, I think they would be less likely to engage in it to begin with.

Looking for the Miracle Rather Than the Healing

We are instructed from the Scriptures that looking for a sign is actually evil. This is so because it is a belief that requires God to prove Himself faithful before we trust Him. Imagine the thing created saying to the Creator that, "I don't trust you, prove yourself that you are who you say you are." That is folly in action.

Yet I want to address something that is not normally discussed in regard to healing. Too many are looking for a miraculous healing while ignoring the miracle of progressive healing. The gift of working of miracles is demonstrated in immediate results with visible transformation. How many have gone from a prayer line after receiving prayer for healing thinking that because they did not receive an instantaneous healing that they were not healed. That kind of think sabotages the gifts of healing where we find healing is progressive from the point of prayer.

Often times people are healed over time by a progressive miracle. A progressive miracle may not be as dynamic as an instantaneous manifestation of the power of God, but it is nonetheless as much of a miracle. How many more people would become healed because they entered into faith and placed their trust in the God who created them to heal them progressively?

Looking to Man Before Looking to God

When we become sick, the first thing we often do is go directly to the doctor, then when the doctor is unable to help us we cry out in desperation unto God. It is as if we believe that God is only to be invoked as a last resort only after we have no hope in man to help us. How does God feel about this?

> *II Chronicles 16:12 In the thirty-ninth year of his reign Asa became diseased in his feet. His disease was severe, yet even in his disease he did not seek the Lord, but the physicians.*

God desires us to seek Him first. He is not opposed to seeking the help of physicians, but He would like our trust in Him to be such that we seek His help first.

Irrational Understanding About God

There are some that have an irrational understanding of God which forces them into irrational beliefs about healing. For instance, many think that God is not willing that they be healed. However, if God is willing to heal one person, He is willing to heal all people.

Think of this in terms of salvation. Is God will to save all people? Did not Jesus say that God so loved the world that He gave His only begotten Son, that whosoever believes on Him should not perish but have everlasting life? Does that sound like God wants to save the whole world? Do you think that God could save one person without wanting to save all people? Face it, God does want to heal you, but it has to be on His terms just like salvation.

I have personally heard from people that basically say that they are sick for the glory of God. I heard from one Christian who said that God gave her cancer and it was her cancer and it was for her good. God is the Creator of life not death. Death and sickness are a result of a cursed world. It is the enemy who makes sick.

Look at the story of Job, God does not make him sick, the devil does. Who was it that touched Job's body to make it sick? It was Lucifer. Jesus went about doing good healing all who were oppressed of the devil. God heals, Satan destroys. Jesus said that the devil comes only to kill, steal, and destroy. But He has come to give us live and to give it more abundantly. Let this fact be perfectly clear. God does not and I would even argue that He could not make you sick. How can God create anything that is not good?

Others say that they will be healed if it is God's will. This suggests that sometimes it is not God's will to heal. Let's clarify this. I do believe that sometimes it is not the time to be healed, but God wants me to be healed at His time. Jesus asks us to pray, "thy will be done on earth as it is in heaven." That means that we are to seek to have God's will done in the earth exactly as His will is accomplished in heaven. Let me ask you, are there any sick people in heaven? No? Then if God's will would be done in earth would there be any sick people on earth?

Unhealthy Lifestyles

There are many things that we know are harmful to our bodies and we engage in them knowing full well what they are capable of doing to us. God is not obligated to heal us when we engage in known harmful activities.

The Authority to Heal the Sick

As a Christian, you have the authority to heal the sick. It is easy to make a statement like that but can it be backed up Scripturally? First if the devil is responsible for all sickness then we must first establish our authority over the devil.

> *Luke 10:18-19 ~NKJV~ And He said to them, "I saw Satan fall like lightning from heaven. Behold, I give you the **authority** to trample on serpents and scorpions, and over all the power of the enemy, and nothing shall by any means hurt you.*

In order for you to have authority, someone must have delegated it to you. We call that delegated authority. All authority is derived from another source. A soldier derives authority to carry out a mission from his commanding officer. If we have authority over the devil then it must have been delegated to us by someone who is in authority over the devil themselves. You cannot delegate authority you do not have. Therefore, Jesus delegated His authority to us for the purpose of carrying out His will in the earth.

That makes you and me a delegate. A delegate is *"A person authorized to act as representative for another; a deputy or an agent."* That means if someone gives you their authority to act on their behalf, you have been deputized to enforce the authority of the one who gave it to you. Notice that Jesus established His authority over the devil by first saying that He saw Satan fall from heaven like lightning.

Exousia is the Greek word used for "authority". In that one word is the assumption of right and ability. That is if I have been given authority, I possess not only the right to use it but with that right I have the ability to enforce it.

Peter was a man that denied Jesus in the face of possible persecution and even arrest. He had a desire to be courageous but he was unable to muster the ability to be what he thought he was. I am sure he felt like a total failure, a loser, an idiot. All of the others heard him proclaim that he would die for Jesus and yet when given the chance he ran just like the other. At least the others did not make that nefarious proclamation.

There is no sense in going on, I may as well go back to doing what I was doing before He found me. I have blown it. I have failed. Then three days later Jesus arose from the dead. He appeared to His disciples and found Peter fishing again. Jesus called to Him and Peter was restored when Jesus revealed to him that he would not be rejected for that failure.

Have you felt like God has rejected you because of a failure? I assure you He has not rejected you. He sees your humanity, He sees your weakness. He does not condemn you, He invites you to work with Him in spite of yourself.

Then something happened. Peter and the other ten were told to go to Jerusalem to wait to be endued with power. They complied and on the day of Pentecost, they were filled with the power of the Holy Spirit. Peter went out and preached a sermon even calling those who killed the Christ murderers. What happened to Peter? He was afraid to face these same people earlier. The difference was power.

II Corinthians 5:20 ~NKJV~ Now then, we are ambassadors for Christ, as though God were pleading through us: we implore you on Christ's behalf, be reconciled to God.

An ambassador is a little different than a delegate. An ambassador is, *"a diplomatic agent of the highest rank accredited to a foreign government or sovereign as the resident representative of his or her own government or sovereign."*

That means as an ambassador of Jesus, you represent the government of heaven on earth. An ambassador is someone who has been sent by the ruler of a country to be his voice in another country. The power of an ambassador is to deliver the message of the king to the ruling authorities of another land.

This is powerful in and of itself. Paul uses that term in the context of being a minister of reconciliation. That is, to declare the message of the King that will set people under the rule of Satan free from his hold.

A delegate however is different. **A delegate is endued with authority to enforce the king's authority.** Jesus deputized us when He passed that authority to His disciples.

An ambassador is able to contend as a representative of the King. A delegate is able to demand action on behalf of the King. Behold, I give you power!! Not just power, but power over all of the power of the devil and nothing shall by any means harm you. You have the power to enforce the Kingdom of our King!

However, before I continue it must be noted that it is one thing for God to give me authority, it is another thing for me to believe it. If I believe that God did give that authority to me, then I will submit to that authority. If I do not, I will not move in that authority. Faith is a necessary element in moving in the authority of Christ. If I don't believe in the authority to heal, no one will be healed.

> *Luke 9:1-2 ~NKJV~ Then He called His twelve disciples together and gave them power and authority over all demons, and to cure diseases. He sent them to preach the kingdom of God and to heal the sick.*

How can I preach the kingdom of God without demonstrating the kingdom of God? What one must ask themselves then is if Jesus gave this kind of power to His apostles, does that mean that we also have that same authority today?

> *John 17:18-21 ~NKJV~ As You sent Me into the world, I also have sent them into the world. And for their sakes I sanctify Myself, that they also may be sanctified by the truth.*

"I do not pray for these alone, but also for those who will believe in Me through their word; that they all may be one, as You, Father, are in Me, and I in You; that they also may be one in Us, that the world may believe that You sent Me.

That little word **"as"** ("as You sent Me into the world") means a lot.

- As (adverb) to the same degree or amount
- As (conjunction) in or to the same degree
- As (preposition) in the capacity, character, condition, or role of

Any way you slice it, the disciples were sent in the same manner as Jesus was sent. They were given the authority to carry out the mission of Jesus. But not only the disciples but Jesus prayed for us too who would come to believe their message. According to verse twenty, we too that believe in Jesus are also sent and are to be one with the disciples.

Ephesians 6:10 ~NKJV~ Finally, my brethren, be <u>**strong**</u> *in the Lord and in the* <u>**power**</u> *of His* <u>**might**</u>*.*

*Strong—**endynamóō** to render strong*

That means that you are not naturally strong, but you are made strong by the power of God.

*Power—**krátos** This word, denoting the presence of strength, means a. "natural strength," b. the "power" that one has, or with which one is invested*

You are given access to the natural strength of God.

*Might—**ischýō** exceptional capability, with the probable implication of personal potential—'capability, strength*

That verse could be rendered, "Be rendered strong in the Lord and in the natural power of His capable strength." Reading it like that really brings forward the idea that this is something we access that is not ours by nature. Only the representatives of the King have the right to tap into supernatural power. In fact the King is a supernatural King and as His representatives I have legal access to His supernatural power to enforce His kingdom in the midst of the kingdom of darkness!

> **Ephesians 1:18-23 ~NKJV~** *the eyes of your understanding being enlightened; that you may know what is the hope of His calling, what are the riches of the glory of His inheritance in the saints, and what is the exceeding greatness of His **power** (dunamis) toward us **who believe**, according to the working of His **mighty** (kratos) **power** (ischyo) which He worked in Christ (natural strength demonstrated in power) when He raised Him from the dead and seated Him at His right hand in the heavenly places, far above all principality and power and might and dominion, and every name that is named, not only in this age but also in that which is to come.*

In other words we that believe, note the necessity of the element of faith, are to have access to His natural power by means of His capability. What would happen when someone came to Jesus and asked him for a healing? He healed them! The Bible declares that everything that was created was created by Him. That is the natural strength that you have access to by faith.

> **Ephesians 1:22-23** *And He put all things under His feet, and gave Him to be head over all things to the church, which is His body, the fullness of Him who fills all in all.*

> **Ephesians 1:22-23 ~JNT~** *Also, he has put all things under his feet and made him head over everything for the Messianic Community, which is his body, the full expression of him who fills all creation.*

> **Ephesians 1:22-23 ~MESSAGE~** *He is in charge of it all, has the final word on everything. At the center of all this, Christ rules the church. The church, you see, is not peripheral to the world; the world is peripheral to the church. The church is Christ's body, in which he speaks and acts, by which he fills everything with his presence.*

You, the Church, are collectively Christ in the earth. We can conclude from this that God gave Jesus authority, Jesus gave the church that same authority. What would the physical body of Jesus be doing if He were here on earth now? You are that body!

- We are to be Jesus in the earth.
- We are to minister as He would minister.
- We are to love as Jesus would love.
- We are to heal the sick as Jesus would heal the sick.

> **I Corinthians 12:12 ~NKJV~** *For as the body is one and has many members, but all the members of*

*that one body, being many, are one body, **so also is Christ.***

This verse literally calls the many Christians united as one body, Christ. Can you get a hold of that? Can you believe that with your brothers and sisters you are to be ministering to the world and one another just as Jesus would?

> *Matthew 10:7-8 ~NKJV~ And as you go, preach, saying, 'The kingdom of heaven is at hand.' Heal the sick, cleanse the lepers, raise the dead, cast out demons. Freely you have received, freely give.*

Here is the sixty-five thousand dollar question. *"If the kingdom of God is visible only by healing the sick, cleansing the lepers, raising the dead and casting out demons, has the kingdom of God disappeared or have its representatives quit believing and enforcing it by the power of the King?"* Jesus was sending his disciples out on a ministry trip. This is not their commission into ministry, this is a training exercise by Jesus the Mentor.

Would Jesus send them to do something that they would be forbidden from doing as ministers? Would Jesus send them to do something that they would be unable to do as ministers? Would Jesus say that the works that He did would be replicated by His disciples and not follow that up with power and strength to accomplish it?

How Do I Access God's Power, Natural Strength, and Capability?

It is one thing to say that I have at my disposal, the authority to use God's power, and it is another thing to actually access it or possess it. This begs the question then, How do I access God's power, God's natural strength which is demonstrated in God's capability?

II Peter 1:2-4

2 Grace and peace be multiplied to you in the knowledge of God and of Jesus our Lord;

*3 seeing that His **divine** (God - Theos) **power** (dunamis) has granted to us everything pertaining to life and godliness, **through** the true knowledge of Him who called us by His own glory and excellence.*

- **Divine=God.** so it is the God explosive power that granted everything.
- **Granted=Means.** That means that it is provided but not necessarily taken.
- **Through=Taken by Way of.** That means that it is taken by way of – the knowledge of God.
- **Glory=doxa={good} opinion.**
- **Excellence=arête=fame or excellence.**

We have a grant. A grant is basically a present. It is given with no thought of a return of something. It is given freely and without any strings. Note that this grant is by God power. It is then the power of God that makes this grant possible. This means that God power is actually in the grant.

What is granted are all things pertaining to life and godliness. Godliness is a compound Greek word that means "well" and "to be devout." It gives us the sense of a walk that is holy. Did you know that to walk holy is granted to you?

Is good health something that pertains to life? Note also that we have access to these through, or by way of, the knowledge of God. Knowledge is something believed to be true. Therefore the knowledge of Him are those things we believe to be true about Jesus. If we do not believe that God still heals the sick, we do not have access to that grant. Your Creator invites you to believe.

*4 For **by these** He has granted to us His precious and **magnificent** (megistos is a superlative of megos) promises, so that **by them** you may become partakers of the **divine** (God - Theos) **nature**, having escaped the **corruption** that is in the world by lust.*

- **By These**=Either Our calling by Jesus' good opinion and fame or the knowledge of Him.
- **Granted**=Again means something offered but not necessarily taken.
- **Megos** is where we get the word and prefix, *"mega"* as in megaphone for a device that makes sound louder. Megos means large or great. A superlative is a word that brings its root word to the highest degree.
- **By Them**=The promises, i.e. the knowledge of God.
- **Divine=God**
- **Nature=God's Natural Endowment**
- **Corruption=Hebrew=Withering or Fading Away**

I think that "by these" points back to the knowledge of Jesus. Knowledge can be plural as it can denote more than one piece of knowledge. Notice that we have a second grant. The first grant is by God power, whereas this second grant is by knowledge. That makes sense because this grant consists of promises.

A promise is a sure guarantee. So it is by knowing Jesus that we discover the sure guarantees that will be accesses into God nature. God nature points back to Ephesians were we learned that it is the natural endowment of God. We are given access to the natural endowment or the God nature by learning of His sure guarantees found in the Word of God. What is the natural endowment of Jesus? What is His natural strength?

If He has flung the stars into the universe and created the cosmos and traced courses for the rivers on earth and created the mountains and the seas and the created things in them from the littlest bug to the biggest dinosaur, that is His natural endowment. We can become partakers of His natural endowment. When we are weak, He is strong.

When I traced the Greek word corruption back to Hebrew I found that means to wither away. Isn't that a picture of what sickness does? When we partake of the God nature we escape the withering away that is in the world by lust.

II Peter 1:5 Now for this very reason also, applying all diligence, in your faith supply moral excellence, and in your moral excellence, knowledge,

"For this reason" what reason? It is that we can access the God nature by the sure guarantees discovered by finding the knowledge of Jesus. Now that you know the reason, you see the importance of applying diligence which is steady effort in the face of resistance to acquire the thing sought. It is speaking to us about increasing or growing our faith. If we supply steady application to acquire faith, we can add moral excellence to our lives. In our moral excellence, we can actually supply more knowledge. How can this be?

It is the seed principle at work. In the parable of the sower, Jesus identifies the associations. The seed is the word of God. When the seed or Word fell upon good ground it produced fruit. Fruit is the resulting work that the seed or Word caused. We know that fruit is our works. When we put it all together we see that as we learn of Jesus we acquire knowledge of Him, that is seed in our hearts. That knowledge of Him will create a natural walk based upon the principle learned. Now, where do you find more seed? More seed is found in the fruit. As we walk out the belief we open ourselves to get more seed or knowledge.

> *II Peter 1:6 and in your knowledge, self-control, and in your self-control, perseverance, and in your perseverance, godliness,*

Inside knowledge is the ability of self-control, inside self-control is the ability of perseverance, inside perseverance is godliness. My ability to walk in godliness has nothing to do with me, but believing.

> *II Peter 1:7 and in your godliness, brotherly kindness, and in your brotherly kindness, love.*

Inside of godliness is brotherly kindness and inside of brotherly kindness is love. Love is the end result of it. I can't lay hands on the sick without love. Jesus saw the sick and had compassion on them and healed them all. He was driven by His love for them.

II Peter 1:8-9 For if these qualities are yours and are increasing, they render you neither useless nor unfruitful in the true knowledge of our Lord Jesus Christ. For he who lacks these qualities is blind or short-sighted, having forgotten his purification from his former sins.

Here is the problem. When we forget the foundation knowledge of the grace of God, we cannot go further into faith because we are not walking or bearing fruit in the first seed we received. Salvation is the first seed. When we walk in that we are open to receive more seed.

II Peter 1:10-11 Therefore, brethren, be all the more diligent to make certain about His calling and choosing you; for as long as you practice these things, you will never stumble; for in this way the entrance into the eternal kingdom of our Lord and Savior Jesus Christ will be abundantly supplied to you.

This is the only place in the Bible that reveals the condition whereby if created we will never stumble. If we will get a hold of what Peter is saying here and apply them through believing, we will never stumble. Your authority to heal the sick, your ability to tap into the power to heal the sick is clear. Now go and do it!

What About Suffering?

How can people grow their faith in healing when they see the leadership sick? Can a body grow their faith in healing when their leader is suffering and sick? Healing by faith can sometimes produce a cold atmosphere toward others who are sick. I have seen this in charismatic circles. It is as if the one sick is in a deficit with regard to faith and therefore they are to be avoided. That sounds like nonsense and it is but it is still a very real problem.

> **Psalm 34:17-22** *The righteous cry, and the Lord hears And delivers them out of all their troubles. The Lord is near to the brokenhearted And saves those who are crushed in spirit. Many are the afflictions of the righteous, But the Lord delivers him out of them all. He keeps all his bones, Not one of them is broken. Evil shall slay the wicked, And those who hate the righteous will be condemned. The Lord redeems the soul of His servants, And none of those who take refuge in Him will be condemned.*

Right away, we have a scenario that goes antagonistically against some of the teachings we have heard that somehow we are to live above suffering. I think it has done a lot of damage to the Body of Christ. I have seen people rejected by the body because they went through something. Because of being sick the others in the body would not associate with that person because they seen their plight as a lack of faith or as a result of something that they had done wrong.

It has been taught by some that the righteous, that is those filled with faith, never suffer. When we look at Psalm 34 we see that indeed the righteous can suffer, but they are delivered. That, I think is the missing component. We need to give room for the righteous to suffer, but we must also hold fast to the faith that they will be delivered.

Read the story of Job and you will discover that God pointed Job out because he was such a good model of faith. Job suffered and he was called the most righteous man on earth. What do we do with this story? Some may try to argue that Job made the statement, "what I have feared the most has come upon me." That this statement was a statement of fear and because he was full of fear, the thing feared overcame him.

Let me make this very clear. The Bible does reveal that Job was fearful. But his fear was not of losing his family or losing his prosperity or even losing his health. Job's fear was a fear of God. Job knew that he did not live up to God's standards. This is why the Bible tells us that Job was careful to sacrifice, even for his children. Job feared God! Job figured that God had did this to him, thus in his mind his fears were realized.

Even God stated to Satan that he had incited God against Job without a cause! Without a cause! What God allowed to come upon Job was without a cause! (Job 2:3) How can one argue that Job feared sickness and because of His fear, sickness came upon him when God stated that He was incited against Job without a cause?

Psalm 34 does not say that God delivers you from going through tribulations, but He delivers you out of everyone of them. This gives us hope that when we enter into a trial there is an exit point. I want to destroy this notion that men and women of faith do not have things happen to them or they don't get sick. I think we are spiking people's goofy meter when we make claims like that. Then when a man or woman of God does get sick, in order to protect the false notion, they are maligned by those who believe it cannot happen to them.

Is it any wonder that the charismatic church suffers from an image problem among their fellow brothers and sisters? I am strong in believing in miracles. I am strong in believing in praying for the sick, but we must bring things back to reality so that we are more effective in our ministry and our message. Divine health is very real to me and I will not compromise my faith in it.

I have a firm knowledge of God's desire and will to heal the sick. Imagine my surprise when in April of 2008 I found myself in the hospital with a clogged artery. I was at once faced with my faith in healing. I was in a crisis. Before I go on, I want to make sure that you understand that I am not disparaging those who have by faith live healthy their whole lives. I celebrate their faith and their results. I commend them.

Yet, the reality of my condition was something that I had to face. I began to step back and look at my reactions almost as if I were a bystander looking on. I noticed the quiet strength in my spirit man but my mind and body were reacting in a completely surprising manner. How is it that I can know what I believe and am strong in that, even in the face of death. I am satisfied with knowing that my God has my life in His hands to do with as He pleases, yet I am a basket case. Why am I acting this way when I know what I believe?

As I was questioning myself, God interrupted and asked, "Didn't you teach this?" It was then that I remembered one of the lessons I taught my students. The concept is that we are dual natured. We have a spiritual nature and we have a physical nature. The spiritual nature is a reality for both the believer and the unbeliever. When a person dies there spirit does not die. Even the wicked man lives on. Because the spirit never dies, it does not possess a survival instinct. The spirit of man does not resist death. It may resist the destination at death, but it does not resist the death of the body.

The body however is afraid of death. Because the body does not live forever it has a survival mechanism that is very strong when one is faced with death. The body will do everything in its power to survive. It will fight death to the very end. It is only when God's grace is given at the end of a person's life that their flesh is quieted. Through every sickness and every disease, the body fights, through every injury it fights because it does not want to die.

The spirit of the Christian is quietly confident that it will be present with Christ the moment the body dies. As I thought about this, I said to myself, "Okay, I see what is going on here." It is the same problem I had when I started preaching the gospel. I had a strong desire in my inner man to preach the gospel, yet I was so terrified that I would become crippled from doing so. I would cry out to God and tell Him that I desire to preach His Word, I desire to fulfill my call but my flesh will not cooperate. Then I asked Him to deliver me from this.

When I asked Him to deliver me, I will never forget this, in one single moment He delivered me by giving me one simple statement. This is what He told me. "Mark, you are not here to impress anyone and they are not here to impress you." As I would get ready to preach before a group of people and I would feel my stomach begin to churn and my bowels begin to get agitated, I would say to myself. "I am not here to impress anyone, and they are not here to impress me. I am here to deliver a message and that is all." Instantly I was filled with courage and all of the physical symptoms of fear would cease.

My spirit man is willing but my flesh is weak. That means you can act completely different from what you believe in a bad situation. But given time and prayer and contemplation, God will deliver you. When we do react differently than what we believe, we can have a tendency to kick ourselves over it.

> **Philippians 2:25-27** *But I thought it necessary to send to you Epaphroditus, my brother and fellow worker and fellow soldier, who is also your messenger and minister to my need; because he was longing for you all and was distressed because you had heard that he was sick. For indeed he was sick to the point of death, but God had mercy on him, and not on him only but also on me, so that I would not have sorrow upon sorrow.*

Here apostle Paul is revealing that one of the fellow soldier is sick. Even to the point of death. Notice that Paul did not disparage this person's lack of faith, but pointed out that God had mercy on him and delivered him from the sickness.

Notice also that Paul states the obvious. The man is sick. In many charismatic circles this is looked down on as if to state the obvious is an admission of death. Jesus never asked anyone to refuse the reality of their current condition. Jesus healed them when they stated their current condition.

Can you imagine if the two blind men in Matthew twenty after being asked what was wrong with them by Jesus, they said nothing? But you are blind, I won't confess that. Can you see the lunacy of this. They won't confess that they are blind yet they can't see. Do you think Jesus knew they were blind before asking them what they needed. Sometimes God asks us to come to the reality of our situation so that He would be empowered in us to heal us.

When are we going to come to the reality that I am weak? You see we need to confess what is before we can access what

God wants. When I am weak, then I am strong. When I am strong I don't need Him so I never want to think that I am strong for I need Him at all times.

II Timothy 4:19-20 Greet Prisca and Aquila, and the household of Onesiphorus. Erastus remained at Corinth, but Trophimus I left sick at Miletus.

Did Paul just say that he left one of his fellow workers behind because he was sick? Well Paul, why didn't you lay hands on him and heal him? We don't always know what God's purposes are or what He is doing. When faced with my own illness, I asked God, what is going on? His reply was instantaneous. He said, "Protect My nature." I knew exactly what He meant by that. I knew what I had to do.

You see, God's nature cannot be altered, yet many times when we suffer we have a tendency to change God's nature to fit into our circumstances, instead of seeing God's nature as unchanging in spite of my circumstances. God is still my Healer even though I am laying in the hospital bed. He still heals the sick. Why that very instant, I could have prayed for someone to be healed and they would not have been denied simply because I was suffering.

God is unchanging in His nature. If He is the God that healeth thee in the Old Testament, He is the God that healeth thee now! He is my healer and He has not changed! It matters not that I am in a hospital bed, He is the God that heals! Protect His nature in spite of your circumstances!

I asked Him again, what is going on. This time He replied, "I am making you stronger." I am thinking, "You got a funny way of doing that, how am I made stronger by being made weaker?" Oh I stepped into that one.

II Corinthians 12:7-10 Because of the surpassing greatness of the revelations, for this reason, to keep me from exalting myself, there was given me a thorn in the flesh, a messenger of Satan to torment me—to keep me from exalting myself! Concerning this I implored the Lord three times that it might leave me. And He has said to me, "My grace is sufficient for you, for power is perfected in weakness." Most gladly, therefore, I will rather boast about my weaknesses, so that the power of Christ may dwell in me. Therefore I am well content with weaknesses, with insults, with distresses, with persecutions, with difficulties, for Christ's sake; for when I am weak, then I am strong.

How many times have brothers and sisters turned their face from the one who was weak because they seen is as a defect of faith? Well I think it is time for us to begin to understand that God deals with people on different levels and with different ways. When are we going to begin to admit that we are weak so that we will be filled with the power of God.

Once Paul wraps his brain around that concept he even proclaims that he will boast in his weakness. God spoke to my spirit in that hospital and He said, *"You need to remember that you are weak and I am the strong One. And if you will remember that you are weak, then you can walk in power."* If I do not recognize my weakness, than I will not see His strength.

II Corinthians 13:4 For indeed He was crucified because of weakness, yet He lives because of the power of God. For we also are weak in Him, yet we

will live with Him because of the power of God
directed toward you.

As charismatic churches go, they will never confess weakness. This is unfortunate. We are weak in Him… We are insufficient, we are unable, we are without power, we are weak. But we are in Him and because we are in Him, the power of God is directed toward us.

> ***II Corinthians 11:23-28*** *Are they servants of*
> *Christ?—I speak as if insane—I more so; in far more*
> *labors, in far more imprisonments, beaten times*
> *without number, often in danger of death. Five*
> *times I received from the Jews thirty-nine lashes.*
> *Three times I was beaten with rods, once I was*
> *stoned, three times I was shipwrecked, a night and*
> *a day I have spent in the deep. I have been on*
> *frequent journeys, in dangers from rivers, dangers*
> *from robbers, dangers from my countrymen,*
> *dangers from the Gentiles, dangers in the city,*
> *dangers in the wilderness, dangers on the sea,*
> *dangers among false brethren; I have been in labor*
> *and hardship, through many sleepless nights, in*
> *hunger and thirst, often without food, in cold and*
> *exposure. Apart from such external things, there is*
> *the daily pressure on me of concern for all the*
> *churches.*

Now if a minister got behind the pulpit and confessed what Paul just stated they would run him out of town. Reality is the quality of what is as defined by God. In other words if it I am suffering I don't need to hide and act as if I am not. What I need to do is to confess the obvious and believe the impossible.

Purpose of Strength

>*Romans 15:1-7 Now we who are strong ought to bear the weaknesses of those without strength and not just please ourselves.*

How is it that too often the strong in faith see it as beneath them to bear the weaknesses of those without strength? We are all on different levels in our journey. Some are just beginning and find their lives full of different weaknesses, then there are those that have learned and strengthened their faith. The strong ought to bear up the weak.

>*II Corinthians 1:3-7 Blessed be the God and Father of our Lord Jesus Christ, the Father of mercies and God of all comfort, who comforts us in all our affliction so that we will be able to comfort those who are in any affliction with the comfort with which we ourselves are comforted by God.*

The purpose of strength is not for you to make a name for yourself. The purpose of strength is not for you to draw attention to yourself. The purpose of strength is to comfort those who are weak.

How Should We Relate to Those Who Are Sick?

>*Matthew 25:34-40 "Then the King will say to those on His right, 'Come, you who are blessed of My Father, inherit the kingdom prepared for you from*

the foundation of the world. 'For I was hungry, and
you gave Me something to eat; I was thirsty, and
you gave Me something to drink; I was a stranger,
and you invited Me in; naked, and you clothed Me; I
was sick, and you visited Me; I was in prison, and
you came to Me.' "Then the righteous will answer
Him, 'Lord, when did we see You hungry, and feed
You, or thirsty, and give You something to
drink? 'And when did we see You a stranger, and
invite You in, or naked, and clothe You? 'When did
we see You sick, or in prison, and come to You?'
"The King will answer and say to them, 'Truly I say
to you, to the extent that you did it to one of these
brothers of Mine, even the least of them, you did it
to Me.'

Jesus called them brothers. That means these are believers He is talking about. When they are sick we are to visit them. What does that mean really. The Greek word for visited is to look upon or after. It is not just a short visit but a visit that affords the sick a person who is genuine in their affections toward them.

It is a common practice of some to scamper away when someone becomes sick. This is a result of false faith. They believe that the person got sick because they lacked faith and they do not want to be pulled down to that same position or be forced to look upon those who are sick.

Would you take stock this moment and look at those who you know are brothers and sisters who are sick? Would you go to them, would you pray for them? Would you minister to them and their needs? Would Jesus say to you, I was sick, and you visited Me?

***Psalm 69:20-25** Reproach has broken my heart and I am so sick. And I looked for sympathy, but there was none, And for comforters, but I found none.*

If we are transparent with one another we can be weak with one another and we can comfort one another.

The Treasure Within

$$\left[\begin{array}{c} \textit{PURPOSE: To instill in the reader the} \\ \textit{understanding of how they are created so that they} \\ \textit{will begin to look to their Creator for their needs.} \end{array} \right]$$

Genesis 1:26-27 *Then God said, "Let Us make man in Our image, according to Our likeness; let them have dominion over the fish of the sea, over the birds of the air, and over the cattle, over all the earth and over every creeping thing that creeps on the earth." So God created man in His own image; in the image of God He created him; male and female He created them.*

Why did God give man dominion over the earth? One reason is that God intended for man to accomplish God's will upon the earth as it is in heaven thereby establishing mankind's authority and relationship to God. I think that we take too lightly the truth that we are created in God's image. What an honor and what glory we should give God for His marvelous works!

Did man lose his dominion when he sinned? No, man did not lose authority or dominion but God lost something. If I work for Bob, then Bob is able to develop his business through me, since I am his employee and have submitted myself to him. But if I quit and go across town and work for Jerry, then Jerry can develop his business through me.

This is what happened in the Garden of Eden. Man made the choice to work for a different boss. That is why when Satan tempted Jesus in the wilderness; he offered all the kingdoms of the earth to Him. Jesus did not dispute this claim because man had **rejected** God and **accepted** Satan as his superior.

You might be asking how did man actually choose Satan? They did so the same way we choose God today—by faith. It is believing the word of the enemy that caused God to be rejected and Satan to be accepted. If you investigate what Adam and Eve did, they chose a different path through faith and their actions were predicated on their beliefs.

Because God will not force us to work for Him by reason of the way He created us, He will allow us to work for a different boss. What is important to note is that I make the person I work for my king or ruler. Every ruler knows that his power is found in the people, not in his military force.

The Makeup of Man

When we look at the composition of our creation, we find that man is multi -natured. Our design is revealed as body, mind (soul), and spirit with each component acting and reacting on the whole of our being. When we examine each aspect of our makeup, we find that we are designed to function according to God's standards, but we also find that we are **not actually functioning** up to those Godly standards.

God's standards are designed to bring us wholeness emotionally, spiritually, and physically. We find then that when we are not living up to these Godly standards, it creates in us distresses. These deviations from Godly standards are called *"gaps,"* and it is these *"gaps"* that cause many of the problems we all are experiencing today.

Spirit

When God created Adam, He first designed the physical body, then He breathed into man the breath of life and man became a living soul. Adam literally had the life of God put inside him! This is what we understand as the spirit and mind of man. God is Spirit and when He breathed into man, He breathed in His image of spirit and man became a spiritual being.

When Adam fell through sin, something happened to his spirit. To better understand this, we can look at the temple of God that Moses was instructed to build. We find that this temple is a model of our makeup. This makes sense because God has always intended to live within us and if you notice something about God, He likes the furniture in His house one way and one way only.

The first temple of God was built as a replica of the one in heaven. We conclude from this that God wanted things arranged on earth for His presence here to be arranged as it was in heaven. Then add to that, we are the temple of God.

I Corinthians 3:16 Do you not know that you are a temple of God and that the Spirit of God dwells in you?

If God arranges things the same way where He intends to dwell, then we should see some similarities between how we are created and how God commanded the temple on earth to be created. Then, when we see those similarities we will understand that we are, as David succinctly said, fearfully and wonderfully made.

*Psalm 139:14-16 I will give thanks to You, for **I am fearfully and wonderfully made**; Wonderful are Your works, And my soul knows it very well. My frame was not hidden from You, When I was made in secret, And skillfully wrought in the depths of the earth; Your eyes have seen my unformed substance; And in Your book were all written The days that were ordained for me, When as yet there was not one of them.*

The part in the temple that corresponds to our spirit man is the Holy of Holies. It is interesting to note that just as the Holy of Holies in the temple was built so that it had no access to natural or manufactured light, so our spirits are in a state of darkness without

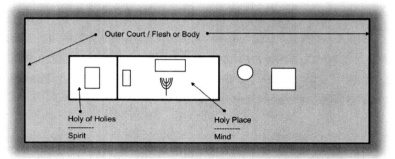

the presence of God. In the structural temple, when the Spirit of God showed up there was light in the Holy of Holies! This was not manmade light, nor was it natural light; this was the light of God called the *"kabod"* glory of God!

The gap that our spirits experience when separated from God is that they dwell in darkness. This dwelling in darkness is a picture of life experienced within our spirits without God's presence. When God comes into our spirit, His light also comes into our spirits. The only way this gap can be overcome is by inviting the Son of God who redeemed you, who reconciled you, who saved you, to take up residence in your temple and renew and enlighten your spirit man through faith.

Furniture in the Holy of Holies

There are items of furniture in each room that represent something that is part of the component it represents in us. The only furniture in the Holy of Holies is the Ark of the Covenant. The lid of this ark is called the *"mercy seat"* and it is a representation of the throne of God both in the heavenly Temple and in the temple on earth.

In addition, God created **us** in such a way that His throne is also located in us and He wants to dwell in our holy of holies, which is our *"spirit man."* The question then, is who is on that throne right now? It was made for God to sit in authority over lives, but some of us like to sit on that throne and rule in the darkness. How many of us try to take God's place on that throne within ourselves?

Inside the ark are three items. The first item is the two stones with the Ten Commandments written on them. The second item is the manna in a jar. The third item is Aaron's rod that budded and bore fruit. **Note that all three items inside the ark is something that God made. There are no man-made items in the ark.**

The Ten Commandments

The Ten Commandments under the throne of God represents His rule and authority. He is the King, the Judge and He judges righteously. His Law is a representation of His nature. The Law was also called His ways. What is interesting is that God also writes His Laws in our hearts which represents the **conscience** in each person's life. This conscience has the Law of God written upon it and it informs us when we do wrong. Your conscience then is located in your spirit. I think intuitive knowledge of right and wrong is one of the greatest proofs of God's existence.

> *Romans 2:15 in that they show the **work of the Law written in their hearts, their conscience** bearing witness and their thoughts alternately accusing or else defending them,*

Jar of Manna

When the children of Israel were wandering in the wilderness, there was not enough food to sustain them. God provided their food and gave instructions concerning it. This bread became metaphoric in application.

In the sixth chapter of the gospel of John we find that the Jews were looking for a sign that Jesus was who He claimed to be. What is interesting is what is not said. There is much assumed as knowledge in the audience that could hear this conversation. When asking Jesus for a sign, they said that their fathers ate manna in the wilderness. The assumption of this was actually pointing back to Moses who they attributed this sign to. This is so because Moses prophesied of the Messiah to come, which was called *"that prophet."* Look how Jesus responded.

John 6:31-33 *"Our fathers ate the manna in the wilderness; as it is written, 'HE GAVE THEM BREAD OUT OF HEAVEN TO EAT.'" Jesus then said to them, "Truly, truly, I say to you, it is not Moses who has given you the bread out of heaven, but it is My Father who gives you the true bread out of heaven. "For the bread of God is that which comes down out of heaven, and gives life to the world."*

Note that Jesus immediately corrected them. It wasn't Moses who gave the bread or sign, it was the Father. Now also notice the metaphoric shift. The bread comes from God out of heaven and gives life to the world. No longer is the bread being seen as sustaining the nation of Israel in the wilderness, but now the bread Jesus is talking about is giving life to both Jew and Gentile. Now Jesus brings it to the completion He had in mind.

John 6:34-35 *Then they said to Him, "Lord, always give us this bread." Jesus said to them, "I am the bread of life; he who comes to Me will not hunger, and he who believes in Me will never thirst.*

Jesus is the bread that came down out of heaven. Jesus is also the Word.

Deuteronomy 8:3 *"He humbled you and let you be hungry, and fed you with manna which you did not know, nor did your fathers know, that **He might***

make you understand that man does not live by bread alone, but man lives by everything that proceeds out of the mouth of the Lord.

Matthew 4:4 But He answered and said, "It is written, 'Man shall not live on bread alone, but on every word that proceeds out of the mouth of God.'"

The word in Greek for *"word"* here is *"rhema."* This manna represents the *"rhema"* word that is speaking to our spirit from God. This would be a good place to discuss quickly the difference between the *"rhema"* Word of God and *"logos"* Word of God. Both Greek words are translated *"word"* in the bible. Rhema is the spoken Word of God. It is therefore a *"right now"* Word spoken into your spirit by God. Logos is the written Word of God that we have access to at any time. Now, let's get back to the manna.

From this we can see the connection with the *"rhema"* or spoken Word of God with the manna. If you keep reading chapter six of the Gospel of John, Jesus identifies His body as the Bread. However you see it, the rhema Word of God, or the presence of Jesus in your life, the Bread brings a knowledge of God's presence within our spirit.

Aaron's Rod

The third item in the ark was the almond branch that blossomed and had fruit. If we look at the story surrounding this item we can easily conclude what it represents in our lives.

The leaders of eleven tribes of Israel were grumbling that the tribe of Levi was named to be the tribe through which God ministered to the people. As a result of doubting that Moses was hearing from God, the Father instructed Moses to have a leader from each tribe take an almond branch and inscribe their name on it. Then it was to be laid at the temple over night. In the morning the rod that had Aaron's name on it had budded and bore fruit. This was proof of God's call upon that man and his posterity.

Read: Numbers 16:39-17:13

It is clear from this passage that the call and destiny of Aaron and the tribe of Levi was represented by the almond branch which had sprouted, blossomed, and was bearing fruit. That is the same process that we go through in reaching our destiny. We sprout, then we blossom and then we bear fruit. One thing to keep in mind too is that the blossom comes and disappears before the fruit appears. On this rod however all three stages were visible at once representing the whole span of time allotted to us to accomplish God's will for our lives.

The almond branch represents the call and destiny that God has placed in you for His purpose. When you look at why the almond branch is significant, it will become clear that it represents God's purpose that was built or woven into your spirit man. In your spirit are the gifting, talent, and empowerment to become what God called and purposed you to become. God has placed into your spirit the almond branch of destiny. It is there waiting for you to pick it up!

Spiritual Cravings

There are certain natural cravings that the spirit of man has. When we understand these cravings we can better understand certain behaviors that we see in the world today. Our spirits crave the spiritual. That is, God designed our spirits to have a longing to be connected with Him.

> **Psalm 107:8-9** *Let them give thanks to the Lord for His lovingkindness, And for His wonders to the sons of men! For He has satisfied the thirsty soul, And the hungry soul He has filled with what is good.*

We know the Bible says that God is Spirit and they that worship Him must worship Him in spirit and truth. So what happens when people experience this longing but they have not heard the gospel message and surrendered to Jesus and have, as a result, been eternally separated from God?

There is a movement called the occult that has been born out of this need and desire for spiritual connection. The members of which understand that they have a longing and they search for their spiritual connections. They make connections in the spirit realm, but it is not with God. Even in our American culture, we see a tremendous move toward the spiritual that is evidenced in the monetary successes of psychics and astrologers. We also see a tremendous growth in memberships in witchcraft (Wicca) and Satan worship.

That begs the question, *"Why is there such a move toward these spiritual forces in this nation at this time, when in the past this was not so?"* The answer lies in the fact that as a nation, we have taken great strides in eliminating the knowledge of God from our society; therefore, it is only a natural occurrence that this society is now seeking spiritual identity in the realm of the occult.

When our spirits are in this darkened state, there is a void in our inner man that seeks to be filled. In the absence of filling this void with Jesus, we develop a coping mechanism called *"the sinful nature."* The sinful nature exerts its pressure and control upon the mind of man to satisfy needs that only the Spirit of God can fulfill.

When a person becomes born again and their spirit becomes enlightened by the kabod glory of God, the darkness of that spirit is removed and it comes to life because the Bread from heaven has taken residence on the throne that was created for Him alone to sit upon. Note that even though the sinful nature is removed from the spirit of man, it is still very much present in the flesh or body of man. Because of this, a war is started between the spirit of man and the sinful nature or body (flesh) of man.

Before we are born again, one of the greatest needs that we as humans have, is the need to feel worthwhile. In the absence of God's presence in our lives, the sinful nature seeks to fulfill this need for self-worth or value. The sinful nature copes with this need by creating a sense of self-worth through affirmation from other people, intelligence, talents, or personal appearances. The problem here is that our self-worth becomes reliant and predicated on outward environments.

If you place your self-worth on any of these conditions, then when you lose them, you will be faced with a sense of great loss and your self-worth is diminished. If you placed your self-worth on your physical appearances and you were in an accident or you aged and lost your appearance, you would lose your self-worth along with it. This is the sinful nature's coping mechanism to feel valued, loved, and accepted. You can fill the gap your spirit has to be valued, loved, and accepted by getting these things from God just as Adam and Eve had.

The flesh's coping mechanism is to put you on what I call the **ego scale**. Now at the high end of that scale, we have **egotism** and at the low end of that scale, we have **poor self-esteem**. Psychologists and psychiatrists try to get you to the middle of that scale to achieve a **balance** of self-worth in your being. Again, the problem with this is that our self-value is reliant upon outward environments. We have no control over loss of these outward elements to make us feel valued. *God intended this need to be met internally not externally.* Think for a moment if you will about people who do not have one of those four (affirmation, intelligence, talent, beauty) elements in their evaluation of themselves.

What happens to those who do not have much of these outward stimuli to reconfirm their worth as a person? It produces poor self-esteem. What happens when there are too much outward stimuli? It produces egotism. What happens to those who do not have a physical appearance that would cause them to value themselves? Those that don't have physical appearance become focused on intelligence, talent and/or people. Those that don't have people to affirm them either focus on intelligence or talent.

When we are born again and the Spirit of God comes to dwell within us, **we then get our affirmation from God who is now in touch with our spirit man.** This gap is eliminated upon the revelation that God loves me and there is no one higher Being than God, therefore His **greatness** is transferred into **great** love for me and I am taken off of the ego scale and put upon the foundation of grace. This foundation has no extremes, so there are no swings from feeling good to feeling bad about yourself. When we come to the revelation that Jesus gave Himself upon a cross for each one of us, then our self-worth is established or fixed and there is nothing that can change it, for God is unchangeable.

Identity

Your true identity is established through your spirit man. Who you are, is who your spirit is. As children, we form our identities through our fathers and mothers. As children, our name is from our parents; our moral teaching is from our parents; our sense of safety is from our parents, our physical appearance is from our parents, and our sense of provision is from our parents.

When we were children, we looked to our parents and we got a sense of comfort because we were seeing our own sense of existence in and through them. However, when we mature, we find that our paternal and maternal identity is not enough and we seek to find out who we really are. This is where the problem of rebellion often arises in teens when they come to this point in their lives where they have a strong need to find their spiritual identity, and they have not been connected with God.

Because God is the true Father of our spirits, not our earthly parents, our true identity is found in God, not in our physical roots. When we connect with God, we get a sense of spiritual identity, destiny and self-worth that will drive us toward the call that each of us were created to accomplish.

The Mind

The mind is not your brain. The mind is the seat of power in your life. It is part of what we call *"self."* This part makes decisions between choices and thus is the state of free-will in your life. The mind is like a screen upon which four sources of information are projecting their desires.

The Holy Spirit, your spirit, your flesh, and your enemy, project their thoughts upon the screen of your mind. It is therefore the job of your free-will (which is located in the mind) to choose which projector to listen to, and thereby react according to what it accepts. If the Bible exhorts us to not listen to the enemy, then we must assume that the enemy can indeed plant thoughts in our minds. We certainly know that God does from the Bible. We find that the mind is a part of the inner man as evidenced in:

> *Romans 7:22-23 For I joyfully concur with the law of God in the inner man, but I see a different law in the members of my body, waging war against the law of my mind and making me a prisoner of the law of sin which is in my members.*

We see here that the mind is part of the inner man, and is not a part of our physical bodies. The problem with the mind is that it is incapable of making good decisions on its own. On its own it is severely limited in the information upon which it makes decisions. With God's Spirit in him, man is then enlightened with information that will provide that necessary missing component in decision making. Why do you think the mind is unable to see the truth without enlightenment?

> *II Corinthians 4:4 in whose case the god of this world has **blinded the minds** of the unbelieving so*

that they might not see the light of the gospel of the glory of Christ, who is the image of God.

It is therefore a fact that those that are unbelieving are that way because the enemy is hiding the truth from them. We find then that the mind is also transformed by the receiving of Jesus in our lives as the spirit of man is. How do we, who believe in Christ, protect ourselves when listening to these four sources of information?

II Corinthians 10:3-5 For though we walk in the flesh, we do not war according to the flesh, for the weapons of our warfare are not of the flesh, but divinely powerful for the destruction of fortresses. We are destroying speculations and every lofty thing raised up against the knowledge of God, and we are taking every thought captive to the obedience of Christ,

Our weapon to fight this is TRUTH! With truth, we destroy every argument that wages war in our mind against the knowledge of God. Jesus is the embodiment of truth and having access to His mind means that we have access to truth, and by it we destroy the lies of the enemy that seek to captivate us.

Holy Place

We also find that the model of the temple shows us that the mind corresponds to the *"Holy Place."* It is the place where judgments are made. Here we find that there is a source of both natural light and manmade light in the inner court.

This shows us that the senses corresponding to natural light along with the reasoning ability. The man made light represents the Holy Spirit's enlightenment of man's study. Light in the Bible usually represents the truth.

Now when we look at the model of the temple, there is a veil between the Holy of Holies, which represents our spirits, and the Holy Place, which represents our minds. With this veil in place, the light of God's presence is unable to penetrate into the Holy Place which represents your mind.

Furniture

The first piece of furniture is the **altar of incense**. The second piece of furniture is the **table of showbread** upon which were twelve cakes of bread. The third piece of furniture is the **menorah** which is a lamp stand with seven lamps.

Menorah

The man made light refers to the Holy Spirit. Not that man made the Holy Spirit, but that God commanded man to make the menorah to represent the Spirit of God. We have man's effort coupled with the Holy Spirit in order to gain truth. The menorah was made to have one main stem in the middle and three stems that come out of the middle one on each side. This is a picture of the Holy Spirit and is revealed when we read the prophecies concerning the seven spirits of God. In the book of Revelation we find a progression of revelation concerning the seven Spirits of God. Let's take a look.

*Revelation 1:4 John to the seven churches that are in Asia: Grace to you and peace, from Him who is and who was and who is to come, and from the **seven Spirits** who are before His throne,*

The first revelation shows us the position of the seven Spirits. They are before His throne. Note that the menorah is a picture of the seven Spirits and the Holy of Holies is a picture of the throne of God in heaven. The position of the menorah then is before the throne of God in the Holy Place.

*Revelation 3:1 "To the angel of the church in Sardis write: He who **has the seven Spirits of God** and the seven stars, says this: 'I know your deeds, that you have a name that you are alive, but you are dead.*

Whereas the first revelation revealed position, this revelation reveals possession. Jesus has the seven Spirits and the seven stars. According to Revelation 1:20 the seven stars represent the seven angels to the seven Churches.

*Revelation 4:5 Out from the throne come flashes of lightning and sounds and peals of thunder. And there were **seven lamps of fire** burning before the throne, which are the seven Spirits of God;*

The third revelation makes the connection to the seven lamps or menorah. This reveals the representation of the menorah found in the Holy Place.

*Revelation 5:6 And I saw between the throne (with the four living creatures) and the elders a Lamb standing, as if slain, having seven horns **and seven eyes, which are the seven Spirits of God**, sent out into all the earth.*

Here we find that the Lamb, Jesus is symbolized as having seven eyes which are the seven Spirits of God. This is a very important revelation. Does it mean that Jesus had seven literal eyes? No, it is symbolic of something. Let's see what that is.

> *Luke 11:34 "The eye is the lamp of your body; when your eye is clear, your whole body also is full of light; but when it is bad, your body also is full of darkness.*

If you finish reading this in its context you will find that the light Jesus is talking about is truth and the darkness is deception. So the seven Spirits of God represent the light or truth of God. Now let's identify each of these Spirits.

> *Isaiah 11:2 The Spirit of the Lord will rest on Him, The spirit of wisdom and understanding, The spirit of counsel and strength, The spirit of knowledge and the fear of the Lord.*

1. The Spirit Himself is the main stem and out of Him flows:
2. The Spirit of wisdom
3. The Spirit of understanding
4. The Spirit of counsel
5. The Spirit of strength
6. The Spirit of knowledge
7. The Spirit of the fear of the Lord

Look at the close relationship between these seven Spirits and truth. Consequently, the menorah represents God's ability in our minds to reveal truth, but there must be the application of man's effort as well represented by the natural light. If man does not apply himself to read the Word, to hear the Word, then he will not benefit from it.

Table of Showbread

The other piece of furniture in the Holy Place is the **table of showbread**. The Levites were to bake twelve cakes and arrange them in two rows of six. Note that six is the number of man. Bread represents God's Word. Because this bread was baked by man and not handed down from God out of heaven as the manna was, it represents the written or logos Word of God.

The reason for the twelve is that the Old Testament was written and protected by the twelve tribes of Israel. The New Testament was entrusted to the twelve apostles. Both the Old and New Testaments were a partnership between God and man. God inspired man, and man wrote. We have this same picture in the Holy Place that represents our minds. The natural light (man's effort) and the menorah (Holy Spirit's effort) will enlighten the mind with the written Word of God. (The twelve cakes of bread)

Altar of Incense

The last piece of furniture in the Holy Place is the altar of incense. What does this represent concerning our minds? The Word of God always has the answer to itself. All we need do is search and we shall find.

*Psalm 141:2 May my **prayer** be counted as **incense** before You; The lifting up of my hands as the evening offering.*

*Luke 1:10 And the whole multitude of the people were in **prayer** outside at the hour of the **incense** offering.*

*Revelation 5:8 When He had taken the book, the four living creatures and the twenty-four elders fell down before the Lamb, each one holding a harp and golden bowls full of **incense, which are the prayers of the saints.***

There you have it; the incense represents your prayers.

Before we leave our study of the mind, we need to talk about the veil. The veil is the thick curtain that separated the Holy Place from the Holy of Holies. It was necessary to protect man from the glory of God inside the Holy of Holies. If man were not sinful then there would be no need for the veil because we could enter into the presence of God without being slain by the glory and holiness of God.

What is the connection the veil has concerning our spirit and our mind? When a veil is present there is a disconnect between mind and spirit. We then find that the connection between mind and spirit is dependent upon the tearing away of that veil. We also find that the veil corresponds to the body or flesh of Jesus. When the flesh of Jesus was torn on the cross, so was the disconnection between the mind and spirit and the veil that was torn in the temple!

*Hebrews 10:20 by a new and living way which He inaugurated for us **through the veil,** that is, **His flesh,***

*Inaugurate: To induct into office by a formal
ceremony. 2. To cause to begin, especially officially
or formally [9]*

Hebrews 6:19-20 *This hope we have as an anchor
of the soul, a hope both sure and steadfast and one
which **enters within the veil**, where Jesus has
entered as a forerunner for us, having become a
high priest forever according to the order of
Melchizedek.*

The Christian has great hope that has gone within the veil into our spirits, because Jesus has also gone within our veil into our spirits and has become the High Priest of our lives forever. By the tearing of this veil, the light of God in the Holy of Holies is able to penetrate the mind. This enables us to be able to have a third source of truth in our minds, which enables us to have the mind of Christ!

I Corinthians 2:16 *For who has known the mind of
the Lord, that he will instruct Him? **But we have the
mind of Christ**.*

This verse states that we have the mind of Christ. It is precisely because Jesus has entered within the veil between our minds and spirits and taken up residence in our spirits. His flesh represents the veil because He becomes the protecting force between sinful man and a holy God. His righteousness and death

---

9 Excerpted from American Heritage Talking Dictionary Copyright © 1997

The Learning Company, Inc. All Rights Reserved.

cleanse us from sin by His body (the veil) and made it possible to access to the God of heaven. Therefore, His mind is available to our mind. This act of God is not forced upon us so that is why we also see the call to *"renew our minds."* We are hid with Christ in God.

> **Romans 12:2** *And do not be conformed to this world, but be transformed **by the renewing of your mind,** so that you may prove what the will of God is, that which is good and acceptable and perfect.*

We notice here that the renewing of our minds is not automatic. It must be noted that having the mind of Christ does not produce the renewing of the mind. Renewing of the mind takes place through your effort by learning of Jesus. Paul exhorted us to *"let this mind be in you that was also in Christ Jesus."*

This is why this is the area of warfare in our lives as we seek to do the will of God. When the mind has a decision to make, it has resources that will help it in making the correct decision. One of these resources is the mind of Christ. To have the mind of Christ applied is simply seeing things through His eyes.

That which is hidden becomes revealed to the mind when we allow the mind of God to reach through that veil and tear it from top to bottom. This will allow the kabod glory of God to shine upon the mind of man and cause us to see that which is hidden and, as a consequence, we display the glory of God in our lives.

> **II Corinthians 4:6-7** *For God, who said, **"Light shall shine out of darkness,"** is the One who **has shone in our hearts to give the Light of the knowledge of the glory of God in the face of Christ.** But we have this treasure in earthen vessels, so that the*

surpassing greatness of the power will be of God and not from ourselves;

WOW! The light of God's knowledge shining from our spirits to our minds through the veil that has been torn for us that we might reveal the wisdom and power of God to the world. What a powerful statement of who you and I are after we have received Jesus as our Savior. We have a tremendous treasure within!

Cravings

Since the nature of the mind is emotional, the cravings of the mind are emotional. The mind craves love and acceptance; it craves peace and joy. But some of the ways that the mind seeks to fulfill those needs are not in accordance with God's Laws. For instance, someone may get a feeling of joy from stealing or cheating. Therefore, we must address the mind and how to bring it into a place of true peace through meeting our emotional needs in Godly ways. The sins of the mind are listed in Romans.

Romans 1:28-32 And just as they did not see fit to acknowledge God any longer, God gave them over to a depraved mind, to do those things which are not proper, being filled with all unrighteousness, wickedness, greed, evil; full of envy, murder, strife, deceit, malice; they are gossips, slanderers, haters of God, insolent, arrogant, boastful, inventors of evil, disobedient to parents, without understanding, untrustworthy, unloving, unmerciful; and although they know the ordinance of God, that those who practice such things are worthy of death, they not

*only do the same, but also give hearty approval to
those who practice them.*

We can defeat these by allowing the mind of Christ to be in us to operate through us. We can be different people, but it takes an act of your will to give up the right to direct your own life. When we give Jesus the right to direct our lives and we consider ourselves dead, then God will begin to tear down that veil in our lives and begin to reveal His hidden wisdom to you.

Body

Now the body is the visible and tangible part of you. It is the same as the *"flesh"* as talked about in the Bible. We have turned the word *"flesh"* into a natural tendency to sin. This is so because we realize that our desire to sin emanates from the appetites of the body.

Now remember that Adam's spirit went into darkness at the fall, this provided an environment where the desires of the body and the mind had no moral compass to rule them. Therefore, they began to meet basic needs in ways that are contrary to God's Law. If the body is hungry, stealing food from your neighbor is a way to meet that need.

Cravings

*Ephesians 2:1-3 And you were dead in your
trespasses and sins, in which you formerly walked
according to the course of this world, according to
the prince of the power of the air, of the spirit that*

is now working in the sons of disobedience. Among them we too all formerly lived in the lusts of our flesh, indulging the desires of the flesh and of the mind, and were by nature children of wrath, even as the rest.

Unlike our spirit, the body possesses a self-preservation nature because it is mortal. Our spirits do not possess this because they are **immortal**. Since the nature of the body is physical, its cravings are also physical.

__Galatians 5:19-21__ Now the deeds of the flesh are evident, which are: immorality, impurity, sensuality, idolatry, sorcery, enmities, strife, jealousy, outbursts of anger, disputes, dissensions, factions, envying, drunkenness, carousing, and things like these, of which I forewarn you, just as I have forewarned you, that those who practice such things will not inherit the kingdom of God.

Furniture

There are two things located in the outer court. They are the **altar of sacrifice** and the **bronze laver.**

Altar of Sacrifice

__Romans 12:1__ Therefore I urge you, brethren, by the mercies of God, to present your bodies a living and

holy sacrifice, acceptable to God, which is your
spiritual service of worship.

The body needs to be sacrificed on the altar so that our wills will be presented to God. In fact this is the first step in renewing your mind with the mind of Christ.

Laver

This laver was made from the mirrors that the women took from Egypt. With this in mind, read this passage:

Ephesians 5:26 *so that He might sanctify her, having cleansed her by the washing of water with the word,*

The laver represents the mirror of the Law of God that causes us to see ourselves as the sinful beings that we are. We cannot be cleansed of our sin until we know that we are sinners and the Law plays that function for us. By seeing yourself as God sees, you prepare yourself for receiving Christ.

Summation

We have found that each part of our being has a nature. That nature is responsible for the appetites of that part of us. We find that in each case there is a corruption of that nature when it is without Christ. The spirit of man seeks spiritual sensations and finds it in the occult. The mind of man seeks emotional sensations and seeks it in ungodly ways. The body of man seeks physical sensations and finds it in sexual immorality. The Bible rightly says that sin has pleasure for a season.

The problem is that sin will bring forth death. It destroys and tears down. Families are destroyed by it. Individuals are destroyed by it. Churches are destroyed by it. Cities are destroyed by it. Nations are destroyed by it. God's ways of meeting our needs are such that they produce a crop of fruit. This fruit is peace, joy, love, long suffering, patience, gentleness, kindness, goodness, and faithfulness.

When we accept the words of other people about who we are, **we become limited to their vision of us.** They can only see me right now. They see my weaknesses, my social standing, my physical stature, but they do not and cannot see my potential.

God sees me in my potential because He created me and planted His destiny in me. When I define myself through God's eyes, I am no longer inhibited in reaching my potential. I am not limited to the perceptions of others. I realize through the eyes of Jesus, that I can do anything—no, I can do all things. That is the terminology that Paul used. I can do all things through Christ who strengthens me.

Biblical Principles of Prosperity

Chapter Twelve

> PURPOSE: *This lesson is intended to give the reader the principles of prosperity that God designed for us to access the supernatural laws of the kingdom of God. We will also put to rest questions concerning tithing that are the most prominent.*

Part One: The Kingdom of God

In the Gospels we read that both John and Jesus first began to preach, *"Repent, for the kingdom of heaven is at hand."* To understand what they were saying one needs to dig a little bit to get the true meaning. Often it is the case that much is lost in meaning by not understanding the culture in which it was stated. With that in mind, we need to take a look at what is meant by *"kingdom."*

A kingdom is the domain of the king. That means that there is a border which defines the realm, influence and power of the king. What the king says becomes law within the sphere of that kingdom. Another way of saying *"kingdom of heaven is at hand"* is the *"governing principles of heaven are now here."* The word *"repent"* means to change your way of thinking. So, to restate what Jesus and John said, we would say, *"Change the way you think because the governing principles of heaven are now here."* That means we need to change the way we think about things by hearing what the King says and doing it.

Jesus also stated that He came to give us life and to give it more abundantly (John 10:10). An earthly king is known by how well the people of that kingdom live. All that we need to do to access this abundance is to do what the King says to do.

Concerning financial blessing, the King of heaven said, *"Give, and it shall be given back. Pressed down, shaken together, and running over shall men give unto your bosom"* (Luke 6:38). Therefore, if we follow this principle of God's kingdom, we will find our wealth in giving. Do you see why Jesus had to say to change the way you think? It may not make sense to our logic or the logic of this world, but if God established a thing, it is so.

I can hear it now. Someone is bound to say, *"Oh no that would amount to giving to get!"* What did Jesus say? Did He say give and it would be given back in a greater measure? Do you think He said this to motivate people to give and trust Him to give back more because that is what He promised? Now most giving is done based upon the benevolence of the giver, but I don't think we can discount the facts of what Jesus said either. In my mind what a testament to the glory of God that people would follow His instructions because He is faithful!

Sowing

Giving is likened to sowing. If you put seed in the ground, you get more seed than what you put in the ground. Do you know anyone who plants seed without the expectation of getting more back? Why then is it suddenly immoral to expect a return on your giving? How dare those greedy evil farmers expect more back then what they put into the ground. I hope you know that I am being facetious.

If we do not give away or plant our seed, we will not grow a harvest. This is why the Bible says that God gives seed to the sower. He does not give seed to the eater; He does not give seed to the keeper; He only gives seed to the sower. This means that we have to become sowers in order to increase our financial well-being. It is going to take a change in thinking to get you to become a sower.

> *Isaiah 9:6 ~ KJV ~ For unto us a child is born, unto us a son is given: and the **government shall be upon his shoulder**: and his name shall be called Wonderful, Counsellor, The mighty God, The everlasting Father, The Prince of Peace.*

> *Matthew 11:29-30 Take my yoke upon you, and learn of me; for I am meek and lowly in heart: and ye shall find rest unto your souls. For my yoke is easy, and my burden is light.*

Keep in mind that a yoke fits upon the shoulders of an ox. Therefore, the governing principles of heaven are upon His shoulders. Notice what Jesus is saying. He is telling us to take that yoke of government upon ourselves and to learn of Him. Learning of Him and doing His will are how we take the governing principles of heaven upon ourselves. Jesus also tells us that His yoke is easy and His burden is light.

> *Matthew 6:31-33 ~ KJV ~ Therefore take no thought, saying, What shall we eat? or, What shall we drink? or, Wherewithal shall we be clothed?*

(For after all these things do the Gentiles seek:) for your heavenly Father knoweth that ye have need of all these things. But seek ye first the kingdom of God, and his righteousness; and all these things shall be added unto you.

Biblical Principles

There are normal pursuits that we as humans have. We pursue food, clothing, drink, shelter, and the finances to acquire them. **It is not wrong to seek these things, but there are wrong ways to pursue them.** If we would just listen to what Jesus said and put as a priority the learning of the governing principles of heaven, all those things would be added.

Matthew 16:19 ~ KJV ~ And I will give unto thee the keys of the kingdom of heaven: and whatsoever thou shalt bind on earth shall be bound in heaven: and whatsoever thou shalt loose on earth shall be loosed in heaven.

First, we must remember that these are keys **OF** the kingdom not keys to the kingdom. This means that the keys came from and belong to the kingdom of heaven. What are these keys?

Luke 11:52 ~ KJV ~ Woe unto you, lawyers! for ye have taken away the key of knowledge: ye entered not in yourselves, and them that were entering in ye hindered.

It is, therefore, the knowledge of God that gives us access to the working and promises of the kingdom of God and the benefits that operate by God's divine power and upon God's divine nature. This supports the idea that the keys of the kingdom of heaven are the governing principles of God.

Is Tithing a Valid Principle?

Perhaps this is one of the most misunderstood subjects in the Bible. Most Christians have heard that we are commanded to give a tenth of our income to the Church. The supporting Scripture most often used is found in the last book of the Old Testament. What we need to do then is take a close look at tithing because if tithing is something that we are commanded to do, then we need to do it according to God's command. That is our purpose here; we need to understand the command of tithing and follow that command to the letter if it is a New Testament principle.

> *Deuteronomy 12:32* Whatever I command you, you shall be careful to do; you shall not add to nor take away from it.

We need to take great care **NOT** to change what God has said. That means that we should not remove something because it disagrees with something we believe, nor should we add anything that is not there. In addition, we should not hide from people things we know are in the Word but that disagree with something we are teaching. The reason that I make this an important part of this lesson is that what we hear about tithing from the pulpit often looks far removed from what we see in the Bible.

God is the One Who established the principle of tithing, so we need to look carefully at what He said and see how that applies to us in a post-Old Testament period. First, I want to lay out the tithing principle as it has been presented to us, then we will look at what the Bible has to say. This should give us enough information with which to make an informed decision.

What They Say

One Scripture that I hear often is this:

Malachi 3:8 ~ NKJV ~ "Will a man rob God? Yet you have robbed Me! But you say, 'In what way have we robbed You?' In tithes and offerings.

After quoting this verse, it is usually followed by:

Malachi 3:10 ~ NKJV ~ Bring all the tithes into the storehouse, That there may be food in My house, And try Me now in this," Says the Lord of hosts, "If I will not open for you the windows of heaven And pour out for you such blessing That there will not be room enough to receive it.

Comparing the storehouse with the church-house, this verse is used to direct the tithe giver as to where the tithe should be placed. If someone makes the statement that we are not under the Law anymore, they usually counter by going to Genesis to reference the story of Abraham. Abraham gave a tenth of the spoils that he got from a battle that he had just fought. The appeal to this story is made to show that tithing was an established principle before God gave the Law of tithing several years later. This story is a good place to begin because it is the very first place that tithing is mentioned. Let's take a look.

What the Bible Says

It is necessary to set this story up so that you can link it without confusion. Some kings banded together and began to take over other kings. They came to Sodom and Gomorrah and took them captive. They took all of their food supplies and people from Sodom and Gomorrah. Then a fugitive came to Abraham and told him what had happened. The reason this information is important to Abraham is that Lot, Abraham's nephew, is among those taken captive. Abraham gathers his trained men, a mere three hundred and eighteen men, and pursues those kings and their armies. Abraham and his men defeat them and get all of the food supplies and the people back. Now let's join the story.

> *Genesis 14:17-20 Then after his return from the defeat of Chedorlaomer and the kings who were with him, the king of Sodom went out to meet him at the valley of Shaveh (that is, the King's Valley). And Melchizedek king of Salem brought out bread and wine; now he was a priest of God Most High. And he blessed him and said, "Blessed be Abram of God Most High, Possessor of heaven and earth; And blessed be God Most High, Who has delivered your enemies into your hand." And he gave him a tenth of all.*

Abraham meets Melchizedek, the king of Salem and gives him a tenth of the spoils. There are a number of things that need to be pointed out here.

- This is the first time recorded that Abraham paid a tithe.
- There is no record that Abraham ever paid a tithe before that time nor again after it.

- It should be noted that this is also the first time the word *"tithe"* is mentioned.
- This is also the first time the word *"priest"* is mentioned.

The significance of these points cannot go unnoticed. There is a wealth of truth here that needs to be mined. I have a couple of questions for those who use this account to claim that tithing is a principle established before the Law was given and therefore should be followed by us with or without the Law.

1. If this is a principle to be followed, why is this the first time Abraham paid it?
2. If this is a principle to be followed, why doesn't Abraham continue the practice?

The answer to these questions can bring us to a greater understanding of the principle of tithing. To continue, we need to go to the next time tithing is mentioned.

> ***Genesis 28:11-22*** *And he came to a certain place and spent the night there, because the sun had set; and he took one of the stones of the place and put it under his head, and lay down in that place. And he had a dream, and behold, a ladder was set on the earth with its top reaching to heaven; and behold, the angels of God were ascending and descending on it. And behold, the Lord stood above it and said, "I am the Lord, the God of your father Abraham and the God of Isaac; the land on which you lie, I will give it to you and to your descendants. "Your descendants shall also be like the dust of the earth, and you shall spread out to the west and to the east and to the north and to the south; and in you and in your descendants shall all the families of the earth be blessed. "And behold, I am with you,*

and will keep you wherever you go, and will bring
you back to this land; for I will not leave you until I
have done what I have promised you." Then Jacob
awoke from his sleep and said, "Surely the Lord is in
this place, and I did not know it." And he was afraid
and said, "How awesome is this place! This is none
*other than **the house of God**, and this is the gate of*
heaven." So Jacob rose early in the morning, and
took the stone that he had put under his head and
set it up as a pillar, and poured oil on its top. And
he called the name of that place Bethel; however,
previously the name of the city had been Luz. Then
*Jacob **made a vow**, saying, "If God will be with me*
and will keep me on this journey that I take, and
will give me food to eat and garments to wear, and
I return to my father's house in safety, then the
Lord will be my God. "And this stone, which I have
*set up as a pillar, will be **God's house**; and of all*
that Thou dost give me I will surely give a tenth to
Thee."

This is the second mention of a tithe, and it, too, is before the Law of tithing is established. Jacob is running for his life after taking part in a deception against his brother, Esau. He stops upon this hill and lays his head upon a rock. He dreams a dream about a ladder extending to heaven. Upon this ladder are the angels ascending and descending. At the top of this ladder the Lord is standing. God speaks to Jacob and reiterates His promise to Abraham. When Jacob wakes up he sets up an altar. What is interesting is that the altar is set up to resemble the dream.

The rock upon which his head was laid during the dream is used in the altar. Notice that Jacob stands the rock up on end. This represents the ladder. Then he pours oil upon the top of the rock. Remember that it is the Lord Who stood at the top of the ladder, thus the oil represents the anointing of God that flows down the ladder to the earth. This anointing is being carried by the angels of God. Jacob then names the place *"Bethel,"* which is a compound Hebrew word. *"Beth"* means house and *"el"* means God. "Bethlehem" means house of bread. *"Bethel"* means house of God.

What is the significance of these things? For now, you need to remember that Jacob saw this place as the house of God. You will later see the importance of this. Let us continue now to the next occurrence.

> ***Deuteronomy 12:5-6*** *"But you shall seek the Lord at the place which the Lord your God shall choose from all your tribes, to establish His name there for **His dwelling**, and there you shall come. "And **there you shall bring** your burnt offerings, your sacrifices, **your tithes**, the contribution of your hand, your votive offerings, your freewill offerings, and the first-born of your herd and of your flock.*

Remember that Jacob made a vow to God concerning the tithe. First, Jacob established that wherever God dwelled, there he would give a tenth. Later in life, after he wrestled with the angel and refused to let him go until he blessed him, Jacob has his name changed. The angel said that Jacob would no longer be called Jacob, but Israel. Jacob is known as the father of the nation of Israel. **The vow he made would be valid not only for him but for his posterity, which would be anyone of the nation of Israel.**

We have established that Israel made a vow to pay a tenth of all he had any place God dwelled. God then established this vow and gave directions concerning it. **God tells the Israelites to seek the Lord at the place which God establishes as His dwelling place and to bring the tithe there.** Now let's take a look at what God says to do with the tithe.

> ***Deuteronomy 12:6-7*** *"There you shall bring your burnt offerings, your sacrifices, your tithes, the contribution of your hand, your votive offerings, your freewill offerings, and the firstborn of your herd and of your flock. "There also you and your households shall eat before the Lord your God, and rejoice in all your undertakings in which the Lord your God has blessed you.*

> ***Deuteronomy 12:11-12*** *then it shall come about that the place in which the Lord your God shall choose for His name to dwell, there you shall bring all that I command you: your burnt offerings and your sacrifices, your tithes and the contribution of your hand, and all your choice votive offerings which you will vow to the Lord. **"And you shall rejoice before the Lord your God, you and your sons and daughters, your male and female servants, and the Levite who is within your gates, since he has no portion or inheritance with you.***

Here God restates what He said in verse 7 and 8, but notice He makes mention of the Levites *"within your gates."* The Levites are those of the tribe of Levi. This tribe was set aside to be **priests.** They were not allowed to have an inheritance as the other tribes were, thus the other eleven tribes were to use the tithe to take care of the Levites. What if the distance to the house of God was too great to travel? What were they to do with the tithe if they were unable to get to the dwelling place of the Lord?

Deuteronomy 14:24-26 "And if the distance is so great for you that you are not able to bring the tithe, since the place where the Lord your God chooses to set His name is too far away from you when the Lord your God blesses you, then you shall exchange it for money, and bind the money in your hand and go to the place which the Lord your God chooses. "And you may spend the money for whatever your heart desires, for oxen, or sheep, or wine, or strong drink, or whatever your heart desires; and there you shall eat in the presence of the Lord your God and rejoice, you and your household.

Spend it on whatever your heart desires? I don't think I have heard that preached. Yes, that is what it says. Remember we are not to take away from nor add to the commandments of the Lord.

*Deuteronomy 14:27-29 Also you shall not neglect the Levite who is in your town, for he has no portion or inheritance among you. "At the end of every **third** year you shall bring out all the tithe of your produce in that year, and shall **deposit** it in your town. "And the Levite, because he has no portion or inheritance among you, and the alien, the orphan and the widow who are in your town, shall come and eat and be satisfied, in order that the Lord your God may bless you in all the work of your hand which you do.*

Now we get more details concerning the tithe. Remember that Jacob is the one who made the vow. The vow then falls upon all those of his household, which would be the whole of the nation of Israel. God has lessened the vow by declaring that the vow is to be paid, but in a way in which the Israelite would get the benefit of the vow. The first two tithes were to be used to have a feast and rejoice before the Lord. The third tithe, however, was to go to the Levites, that priestly tribe who was responsible to teach the Law and to service the temple, **God's house.**

I would like to address something here. I have often had the question, *"What makes you think that Jacob's vow passed to his posterity?"* That is a good and valid question. First, look at the wording of the vow. Jacob put a condition on it. If God would do His part, then Jacob would pay the vow. This suggests to me that as long as God is doing his part, the vow is still valid. Also, if Hebrews tells us that Levi paid a tithe to Melchizedek while he was still in his father's loins, then I don't think it a stretch that that vow was extended perpetually.

"What is a priest?" If we ask this question, we can conclude some things that agree with Jacob's original vow and Abraham's original tithe.

> *Exodus 28:43 "And they shall be on Aaron and on his sons when they enter the **tent of meeting**, or when they approach the altar to **minister** in the holy place, so that they do not incur guilt and die. It shall be a statute forever to him and to his descendants after him.*

Priests are servants in God's house. **They minister to God where He dwells.** Again, we see the connection with Jacob's vow and Abraham's tithe. Abraham gave to a priest, who is a servant to

God in His dwelling place. The tithe, then, is connected to God's dwelling place.

Revisit Malachi

Now let's revisit that piece of Scripture in Malachi that is so often used to get people to give a tithe to the Church.

Malachi 3:8 ~ NKJV ~ "Will a man rob God? Yet you have robbed Me! But you say, 'In what way have we robbed You?' In tithes and offerings.

*Malachi 3:10 ~ NKJV ~ Bring all the tithes into the storehouse, That there may be food in **My house**, And try Me now in this," Says the Lord of hosts, "If I will not open for you the windows of heaven And pour out for you such blessing That there will not be room enough to receive it.*

The first question we must ask is, *"Whom is God talking to?"* It is the Israelites, the descendents of Jacob who made the vow of the tenth unto the dwelling place of God. The answer to the question, *"Who is it that robbed God?"* is Israel! You should notice that it is God Who says to bring the tithe into the storehouse so that there may be food in MY HOUSE. That is the fulfillment of the vow of Jacob, the father of the nation of Israel.

Is Tithing a Command That the Christian Should Follow?

The following list represents the reasons that I give for the belief that Christians are **not** bound by the command of tithing.

- We are not descendants of Jacob.
- Jacob is the one who made the vow of tithing to God's house or dwelling.
- If the tithe is for God's dwelling, God no longer dwells in a building but in people.
- Christians are the temple of the Holy Spirit.
- The New Testament does not compel Gentiles to pay tithes.
- The Apostle Paul does not appeal to the Law of tithing when rebuking the Corinthian Church for not giving.

The tithe had to go to the priest, who was the minister of God's house; the New Testament declares that we are all kings and priests. Jesus did not command us to tithe, but He did command us to give. He also said that if you give sparingly, you will reap sparingly, and if you give bountifully, you will reap bountifully. Notice He did not put a certain percentage on what you give.

If We Are Not Bound by Tithing How Are We to Give?

We are to give out of **obedience to the Holy Spirit.** Just because we are not bound by the 10% rule, doesn't mean that we are to neglect giving. In fact, Apostle Paul rebukes the churches who would not give by telling them it was their duty to give. What I want you to see is that if every Christian would be obedient to the Holy Spirit, then the work of God would be financed. It is your duty to pray and ask the Holy Spirit how much you are to give.

It has been my experience and also the reason why pastors will not reveal this truth, that once people find out they are not bound by the 10% rule, they quit giving. **They start thinking that the Holy Spirit is telling someone else to give so they don't hav**

to. I am sure the Holy Spirit did not tell everyone to stop giving. If we prepare ourselves to give and ask the Holy Spirit what He wants us to give, then we become responsible for giving the gift. If we do not give at this point we walk into disobedience and the discipline of God will come into our lives.

What does it look like to reap a harvest of stinginess? Would it not be lack of some kind in our own lives? I reveal this information because I promised God that I would align myself to His Word no matter what. If we would just obey the Holy Spirit we would find that He sustains our needs. Let us be ready to be obedient to His instructions and He will be ready to bless us.

What Are the Biblical Instructions Concerning Giving?

*II Corinthians 9:6-15 Now this I say, he who **sows sparingly** will also **reap sparingly**, and he who **sows bountifully** will **also reap bountifully**. Each one must do just as he has purposed in his heart, **not grudgingly or under compulsion**, for God loves a cheerful giver. And God is able to make all grace abound to you, so that always having all sufficiency in everything, you may have an abundance for every good deed; as it is written, "HE SCATTERED ABROAD, HE GAVE TO THE POOR, HIS RIGHTEOUSNESS ENDURES FOREVER."*

Now He who supplies seed to the sower and bread for food will supply and multiply your seed for sowing and increase the harvest of your righteousness; you will be enriched in everything for all liberality, which through us is producing thanksgiving to God. For the ministry of this service is not only fully supplying the needs of the saints, but is also overflowing through many thanksgivings to God. Because of the proof given by this ministry, they will glorify God for your obedience to your confession of the gospel of Christ and for the liberality of your contribution to them and to all, while they also, by prayer on your behalf, yearn for you because of the surpassing grace of God in you. Thanks be to God for His indescribable gift!

The formula for giving is based in what you want in return. For instance, if a farmer wants to produce 7000 bushels of corn, he realizes that he has to sow a set number of bushels of seed. There will be multiplication on the seed. But if the farmer never put the seed in the ground, he would not get a harvest. This is the seed principle of giving. Now the farmer sows his seed in hope believing that he will receive a harvest. If farmers did not believe in the harvest, they would not sow the seed. Many believers do not believe in the harvest that comes from God and as a result, they don't sow the seed.

Luke 6:38 "Give, and it will be given to you. They will pour into your lap a good measure—pressed down, shaken together, and running over. For by your standard of measure it will be measured to you in return."

Your harvest is guaranteed by the Lord of the harvest. He is not only the Lord of the harvest of souls but He is the Lord of the harvest of your giving. He determines what you get back and it is always a multiplication of what you gave. It does not mean that God will give you money for money. God knows your greatest needs and He will give into those needs. Nevertheless, you will know that you have received a harvest. God does not nor can He lie. God looks upon your sowing and your need. He will answer you accordingly.

God also looks upon what is given and values it different than you or I would. Someone could put one dollar in the offering and give more than the person who put one thousand dollars in the offering. This is a principle of giving I like to call *"appraised value giving."*

Mark 12:41-44 And He sat down opposite the treasury, and began observing how the people were putting money into the treasury; and many rich people were putting in large sums. A poor widow came and put in two small copper coins, which amount to a cent. Calling His disciples to Him, He said to them, "Truly I say to you, this poor widow put in more than all the contributors to the treasury; for they all put in out of their surplus, but she, out of her poverty, put in all she owned, all she had to live on."

Here Jesus reveals the principle of appraised value giving to us. This poor woman had given more than all of the previous rich givers combined! That is great news for us who do not have much to give. If you do not have much to give, you do not need to feel ashamed for God does not see like man sees. God will value your gift, no matter how small, above those that have much to give. The reason God gave for this is that the woman was not giving of her surplus, but she was giving of her very need to survive.

Part Three: To Whom Do We Give?

This is another frequently asked question concerning giving. There are some guidelines that the Bible gives us, so let us now take a look at those.

> *I Corinthians 9:1-14 Am I not free? Am I not an apostle? Have I not seen Jesus our Lord? Are you not my work in the Lord? If to others I am not an apostle, at least I am to you; for you are the seal of my apostleship in the Lord. My defense to those who examine me is this:* **Do we not have a right to eat and drink? Do we not have a right to take along a believing wife, even as the rest of the apostles and the brothers of the Lord and Cephas? Or do only Barnabas and I not have a right to refrain from working?** *Who at any time serves as a soldier at his own expense? Who plants a vineyard and does not eat the fruit of it? Or who tends a flock and does not use the milk of the flock? I am not speaking these things according to human judgment, am I? Or does not the Law also say these things? For it is written in the Law of Moses, "You shall not muzzle the ox while he is threshing." God is not concerned about oxen, is He? Or is He speaking altogether for our sake? Yes, for our sake it was written, because the plowman ought to plow in hope, and the thresher to thresh in hope of sharing the crops.* **If we sowed spiritual things in you, is it too much if we reap material things from you?** *If others share the right over you, do we not*

more? Nevertheless, we did not use this right, but we endure all things so that we will cause no hindrance to the gospel of Christ. Do you not know that those who perform sacred services eat the food of the temple, and those who attend regularly to the altar have their share from the altar? So also the Lord directed those who proclaim the gospel to get their living from the gospel.

Paul is rebuking the Corinthian Church for not supporting him. He appeals to them by showing that other churches take care of their leaders, so he challenges them for not taking care of him. This culminates in Paul telling the Corinthians, *"Don't we have a right not to have to work to support ourselves?"* Finally, he ends with the statement that those who proclaim the gospel have a right to get their living from the gospel. This identifies those to whom you are supposed to give.

Galatians 6:6 The one who is taught the word is to share all good things with the one who teaches him.

Again, Paul is reiterating to the Galatians that which he also communicated to the Corinthians. It is important to note to whom Paul is speaking. The Church that did give to Paul was the Philippian Church. It is interesting to note some of the things that Paul says to the Philippian Church that he did not communicate to the others.

Philippians 4:18-19 But I have received everything in full and have an abundance; I am amply supplied, having received from Epaphroditus what you have sent, a fragrant aroma, an acceptable sacrifice, well-pleasing to God. And my God will

supply all your needs according to His riches in
glory in Christ Jesus.

Paul did not say this to any other church. It was conveyed only to the church that gave and supported his ministry. Paul did not say this because he was just speaking a blessing to the ones that gave to him. He was communicating a biblical principle to them.

I also want you to notice the conspicuous absence of something. If tithing were a principle that the gentile Church was to follow, wouldn't Paul have appealed to the Law of tithing to encourage the Corinthian Church to give?

Instead, he appeals to the Law that the ox is not to be muzzled while he threshes. The principle behind this saying is that the ox has the right to eat of the fruit of its labor, therefore, Paul also has a right to expect to be able to eat of the fruit of his labor in that church. No mention of the tithe is a powerful argument that tithing is not for the Gentiles.

We are also responsible to give to the poor. Remember the Scripture where Jesus said, *"I was hungry and you fed me, I was thirsty and you gave me drink, I was sick and you visited me."* Then those to whom this was being said asked, *"When did we see you hungry or thirsty or sick?"* and Jesus replied, *"You did it unto the least of these my brethren you did it unto me."*

> **Luke 3:11** *And he would answer and say to them, "The man who has two tunics is to share with him who has none; and he who has food is to do likewise."*

What Jesus is saying here is to give if you have the means. Jesus did not say that if you see someone without a coat and you have a coat, give him one. No, Jesus says that if you have a surplus, that means is you have another coat, then you are to give.

If God brings someone across your path that has a need and you have the means to meet that need, then you are to meet it.

Watering Your Seed

Just as there are different levels of harvest in the physical world, we find the same in the spiritual. Remember the parable of the sower? The good ground produced thirty, sixty, and one hundred fold. That parable has a spiritual application; so we can deduce that there are different levels of harvest in the spiritual world. What we can learn from this is that many things are based upon the seed principle.

If we understand seed principle than we need to make sure that we are not eating our seed. Our seed represents the power to be able to produce more for eating. The key to effective giving is understanding this so that you are always in a position of harvest. If you sow seed only once in a while, you will only harvest once in a while.

II Corinthians 9:10 Now He who supplies seed to the sower and bread for food will supply and multiply your seed for sowing and increase the harvest of your righteousness;

How does sowing increase the harvest of your righteousness? It is because of your giving. When you give to ministries that are equipping you for ministry, you are taking part in that ministry. That means that your righteousness is increasing because of the work of ministry that is being accomplished. When you give to the poor, that too is a righteous deed and God promises that when you give to the poor you are lending to God and He will repay you.

In I Kings 17:10-16 there is the story of the woman who was about to bake her last loaf of bread. This last bit of bread would then be consumed by her and her son after which she expected that they would both die of starvation. The prophet comes to her and tells her to bake him a cake too. By portioning out a seed from her oil and flour, she sustained herself, her son, and the prophet for the rest of the famine.

The question that arises is, *"What if she had refused to plant that seed and ate it instead?"* The answer is obvious. She and her son would have died of starvation. How many people put themselves in poverty because they do not follow the seed principle of giving? I suppose that poor woman thought that that little bit of oil and flour did not amount to much of an offering, yet God valued it differently than she had.

There have been many times in my life that I had given up on a harvest. There were times that I had given up on giving because of the condition of poverty. I began to measure the truthfulness of God's Word on my expectations of harvest. In other words, when I was giving regularly and then fell on hard times, I became disgruntled at the promises of God. As a result, I quit sowing seed. When I quit sowing seed, I quit reaping a harvest.

The moral of this story is don't give up on the harvest. God is faithful and will not leave you without. He promises that if we just follow some guidelines we will position ourselves to be cared for by Him.

Psalm 126:5-6 Those who sow in tears shall reap with joyful shouting. He who goes to and fro weeping, carrying his bag of seed, Shall indeed come again with a shout of joy, bringing his sheaves with him.

We may be in sorrow and poverty when we sow, but we will have a harvest. God will not be in debt to any man. If you give to Him, He will return it with multiplication. That is a fact of the Word of God. It is because I did not believe it that I fell into poverty. Father taught me my lessons in giving through many tears.

Seed needs certain elements in order to grow and produce a harvest. Of course it needs good ground. Good ground is ground that has been prepared to receive the seed. It literally is being set aside for the purpose of producing a harvest. One of the many questions that saints have is, *"How do I know a ministry is good ground?"* That answer is found in obedience.

First, if we ignore the clear instructions in the Bible, we should not expect that we will receive a harvest. As I have shown earlier in this lesson, we are to give to those who teach us. Those who are putting all of their effort into discipling you (sowing into you) should be the one who reaps from you. Those that receive discipleship and then only give to other churches including TV ministries are in disobedience to the Word and they will not reap a harvest. Take care of your minister first, then if God directs, give according to His directions.

Leviticus 11:37-38 'If a part of their carcass falls on any seed for sowing which is to be sown, it is clean. 'Though if water is put on the seed and a part of their carcass falls on it, it is unclean to you.

Seed does not come alive until water touches it. This is why seed that had not been watered was not unclean by the dead body of an animal. Only after being watered has it come alive. Much like you may have come alive after being washed by the water of the Word of God. How do we water our seed when we give?

Isaiah 55:10-11 "For as the rain and the snow come down from heaven, And do not return there without watering the earth And making it bear and sprout, And furnishing seed to the sower and bread to the eater; So will My word be which goes forth from My mouth; It will not return to Me empty, Without accomplishing what I desire, And without succeeding in the matter for which I sent it.

When we apply the Word of God to our giving, we are watering our seed! It has to produce a crop because God's Word is productive. You see when I was giving early in my Christian life, it was not mixed with faith. I really did not believe that God would return it and as a consequence, I suffered poverty. I gave, but it was grudgingly. I had no hope of a harvest. It was much like a farmer who does not believe in the power of that seed to produce and as a result does not sow it. Or, he gives it away to someone else not realizing its value.

I Corinthians 15:36-38 You fool! That which you sow does not come to life unless it dies; and that which you sow, you do not sow the body which is to be, but a bare grain, perhaps of wheat or of something else. But God gives it a body just as He wished, and to each of the seeds a body of its own.

Don't always look for your harvest in one area. The thing planted does not always look like the thing that is produced. When we develop a habit of sowing we will always be producing a harvest. We will not always see what God has given us. How would we know that He protected us from a disease, or a calamity? God is faithful and you can trust that He rewards those who seek Him with diligence.

We must always remember that God is the Lord of the harvest. You may think He is withholding from you what you have sown, but this is not so. God will repay, His timing, His disbursements are just, right, true, and exactly what you need. Glorify God in your giving by being obedient, and you will begin the journey toward being a cheerful giver!

About the Author

Bishop Mark Shaw and his wife Kathryn, are co-founders and directors of *Five Fold Ministries Training Academy (FFMTA)* and *Collegium Bible Institute* where the next generation of ministers is being equipped for God's service around the world. Bishop Shaw is the author of *"Is God Calling You to Ministry?"* and the senior editor of *A Voice in the Wilderness* newsletter, which is published quarterly. He is also founder of Collegium Books, which is a publishing and distribution firm that seeks to offer educational materials for the equipping of the saints for the work of God. Shaw has been in ministry for thirty-two years. He was vice-director of Five Fold Ministries for twelve years and has been director for the last nine years. He also presides as pastor over *Adonai Worship Center* in Pine Island, Minnesota.

Shaw teaches on the structure and government of the Church with emphasis on divine order. He brings clarity to the Scripture by revealing a Hebraic understanding and emphasizes the causes and conditions upon which we develop our faith. His desire is to return true discipleship back to the Church so that true leaders are being forged with truth and integrity. He has a vision for the Church that is cutting edge and Spirit mandated.

In 2008 Shaw founded the Five Fold Ministries on-line E-learning center. The E-learning center is designed to distribute world class learning to students through internet technology that brings the school into the living room. The purpose is to develop leaders nationally and internationally that are willing to arrange the Church and its leaders in such a way that validates the Church as a voice in a secular society.

Called to the office of ministry, Kathryn Colton Shaw has a heart and a voice to teach those that are hungry to walk in the ways of the Lord, and awaken them to do what God has called them to do. It is Kathryn's desire to bring healing to the whole person in order that they may be released to accomplish the destiny for which they were created. Kathryn has a gift for networking and hosting seminars and educational programs. She is also gifted in administration and is a valuable asset in giving direction to the Church. Pastor Kathryn is the co-founder of *FFMTA* and *Collegium Bible Institute* where she serves as Academic Dean/Counselor and continues to develop curriculum to impact the next generation for Christ. The Shaws reside in Minnesota and they have six children and ten grandchildren that live in California and North Carolina.

Collegium Bible Institute

The International Equipping School of the Five Fold Ministry

Collegium Bible Institute registers new students for the local campus every March. For more information on our ordination program at the local campus, write us at PO Box 6885, Rochester, MN 55903 or call us at 888-808-5455. Our website is: www.collegiumbibleinstitute.com

If you are interested in the Online E-Learning Center visit us at: www.5fold.org

The Lord commanded His disciples to go into all the world and make disciples of all nations, teaching them to observe all that He said. The question then is have you been discipled yet?

Bringing the Church Back into alignment with God

Church Government

Divine Order Produces Divine Presence

How is it that we expect God to listen to us when we are unwilling to listen to Him?

Mark David Shaw

"Let All Things be Done Decently and in Order"
I Corinthians 14:40

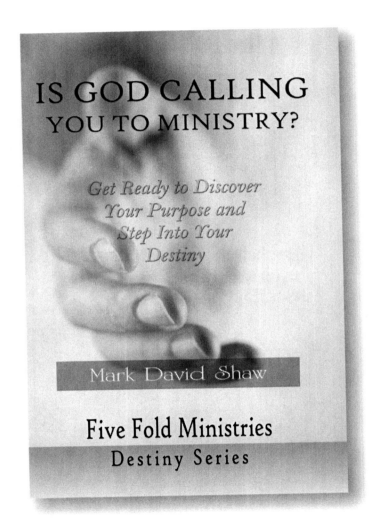

2985824

Made in the USA